# EXAM✓CRAM

# 70-291

# Implementing, Managing, and Maintaining a Windows Server 2003 Network Infrastructure

**Diana Huggins**

**que°**

**CERTIFICATION**

Que Certification • 800 East 96th Street • Indianapolis, Indiana 46240

# MCSA/MCSE 70-291 Exam Cram: Implementing, Managing, and Maintaining a Windows Server 2003 Network Infrastructure

International Standard Book Number: 0-7897-3618-7

Library of Congress Catalog Card Number: 2006925983

Printed in the United States of America

First Printing: June 2006

09  08  07  06      4  3  2  1

## Trademarks

## Warning and Disclaimer

Que offers excellent discounts on this book when ordered in quantity for bulk purchases or special sales. For more information, please contact

**U.S. Corporate and Government Sales**
**1-800-382-3419**
**corpsales@pearsontechgroup.com**

For sales outside of the U.S., please contact

**International Sales**
**1-317-581-3793**
**international@pearsontechgroup.com**

**Publisher**
Paul Boger

**Executive Editor**
Jeff Riley

**Acquisitions Editors**
Todd Green
Betsy Brown

**Development Editors**
Mark Reddin
Todd Green

**Managing Editor**
Patrick Kanouse

**Project Editor**
Seth Kerney

**Copy Editor**
Kate Givens

**Indexer**
Rebecca Salerno

**Proofreader**
Linda Seifert

**Technical Editors**
James Michael
Stewart
Marc Savage

**Team Coordinator**
Cindy Teeters

**Multimedia Developer**
Dan Scherf

**Interior Designer**
Gary Adair

**Cover Designer**
Anne Jones

**Page Layout**
ICC

# Contents at a Glance

# Table of Contents

Chapter 4:
Maintaining Network Security ........................................... 129

# About the Author

**Diana Huggins** is currently an independent contractor providing both technical writing and consulting services. Before this, she worked as a senior systems consultant. Some of the projects she worked on include a security review of Microsoft's official Curriculum, content development for private companies, and network infrastructure design and implementation projects.

Diana's main focus over the past few years has been on writing certification study guides, including *Windows 2000 Directory Services Design (Exam Cram 70-219)* as well as *Installing, Configuring, Managing, Monitoring, and Troubleshooting DNS in a Windows 2000 Network Infrastructure (Exam Cram 70-216)*. To complement her efforts, she also spends a portion of her time consulting for small to medium-size companies in a variety of areas and continues to work as an independent technical trainer.

Diana currently has her Microsoft Certified Systems Engineer (MCSE) and Microsoft Certified Trainer (MCT) certifications, along with several other certifications from different vendors, including A+, I-NET+, and Server+. Although her focus is on the information technology industry, she also holds a bachelor's degree in education. Diana runs her own company, DKB Consulting Services. The main focus of the company is on developing certification training courseware and practice exams, as well as content delivery.

*This book is dedicated with all my love to my son, Brandon.*

—*Diana Huggins*

# Acknowledgments

First and foremost, I'd like to once again thank my son for being so patient and understanding when things get a little hectic. And, of course, my dad, who probably doesn't know how much he is appreciated.

Once again, thanks to Jeff Riley for giving me the opportunity to work on this book and to the staff at Que Publishing for all your hard work. Finally, to all those people in my life who support me and encourage me when I'm struggling to get things done and that one person who always manages to drag me away from work when I do need to get things done. Thanks to you all!

# We Want to Hear from You!

As the reader of this book, you are our most important critic and commentator. We value your opinion and want to know what we're doing right, what we could do better, what areas you'd like to see us publish in, and any other words of wisdom you're willing to pass our way.

As an executive editor for Que, I welcome your comments. You can email or write me directly to let me know what you did or didn't like about this book—as well as what we can do to make our books better.

Please note that I cannot help you with technical problems related to the *topic* of this book. We do have a User Services group, however, where I will forward specific technical questions related to the book.

When you write, please be sure to include this book's title and author, as well as your name, email address, and phone number. I will carefully review your comments and share them with the author and editors who worked on the book.

Email:   feedback@quepublishing.com

Mail:    Jeff Riley
         Executive Editor
         Que
         800 East 96th Street
         Indianapolis, IN 46240 USA

For more information about this book or another Que title, visit our website at www.quepublishing.com. Type the ISBN (excluding hyphens) or the title of a book in the Search field to find the page you're looking for. For information about the Exam Cram series, visit www.examcram.com.

# Introduction

Welcome to the *MCSA/MCSE 70-291 Exam Cram*! Whether this is your first or your fifteenth *Exam Cram* series book, you'll find information here that will help ensure your success as you pursue knowledge, experience, and certification. This introduction explains Microsoft's certification programs in general and talks about how the *Exam Cram* series can help you prepare for Microsoft's Certified Systems Engineer (MCSE) and Microsoft's Certified Systems Administrator (MCSA) exams. Chapter 1, "Microsoft Certification Exams," discusses the basics of Microsoft certification exams, including a description of the testing environment and a discussion of test-taking strategies. Chapters 2–6 are designed to remind you of everything you'll need to know to take—and pass—the 70-291 Microsoft MCSE/MCSA certification exam. The two sample tests at the end of the book should give you a reasonably accurate assessment of your knowledge—and, yes, we've provided the answers (and their explanations) to the tests. Read the book and understand the material, and you'll stand a very good chance of passing the test.

*Exam Cram* books help you understand and appreciate the subjects and materials you need to pass Microsoft certification exams. *Exam Cram* books are aimed strictly at test preparation and review. They do not teach you everything you need to know about a topic. Instead, I present and dissect the questions and problems I've found that you're likely to encounter on a test. I've worked to bring together as much information as possible about Microsoft certification exams.

Nevertheless, to completely prepare yourself for any Microsoft test, I recommend that you begin by taking the Self-Assessment that is included in this book, immediately following this introduction. The Self-Assessment tool will help you evaluate your knowledge base against the requirements for a Microsoft Certified Systems Administrator (MCSA) or Microsoft Certified Systems Engineer (MCSE) certification under both ideal and real circumstances.

Based on what you learn from the Self-Assessment, you might decide to begin your studies with some classroom training, some practice with Windows Server 2003, or some background reading. On the other hand, you might decide to pick up and read one of the many study guides available from Microsoft or third-party vendors on certain topics. We also recommend that you supplement your study program with visits to www.examcram.com to receive additional practice questions, get advice, and track the MCSE and MCSA program.

I also strongly recommend that you install, configure, and spend some time working with Windows Server 2003 and the various services that you'll be tested on. Nothing beats hands-on experience and familiarity when it comes to understanding the questions you're likely to encounter on a certification test. Book learning is essential, but without a doubt, hands-on experience is the best teacher of all! Many of the chapters include step-by-step instructions on how to perform various tasks in Windows Server 2003 to assist you in getting familiar with the product.

# Taking a Certification Exam

After you've prepared for your exam, you need to register with a testing center. Each computer-based MCP exam costs $125; if you don't pass, you can retest for an additional $125 for each additional try. In the United States and Canada, tests are administered by Prometric and by VUE. Here's how you can contact them:

▶ *Prometric*—You can sign up for a test through the company's website at www.prometric.com. Within the United States and Canada, you can register by phone at 1-800-755-3926. If you live outside this region, you should check the Prometric website for the appropriate phone number.

▶ *VUE*—You can sign up for a test or get the phone numbers for local testing centers through the Web at www.vue.com/ms.

To sign up for a test, you must possess a valid credit card or contact either Prometric or VUE for mailing instructions to send a check (in the United States). Only when payment is verified or your check has cleared can you actually register for the test.

To schedule an exam, you need to call the number or visit either of the web pages at least one day in advance. To cancel or reschedule an exam, you must call before 7 p.m. Pacific Standard Time the day before the scheduled test time (or you might be charged, even if you don't show up to take the test). When you want to schedule a test, you should have the following information ready:

▶ Your name, organization, and mailing address.

▶ Your Microsoft test ID. (Inside the United States, this usually means your Social Security number; citizens of other nations should call ahead to find out what type of identification number is required to register for a test.)

▶ The name and number of the exam you want to take.

▶ A method of payment. (As mentioned previously, a credit card is the most convenient method, but alternate means can be arranged in advance, if necessary.)

After you sign up for a test, you are told when and where the test is scheduled. You should try to arrive at least 15 minutes early. You must supply two forms of identification—one of which must be a photo ID—and sign a nondisclosure agreement to be admitted into the testing room.

All Microsoft exams are completely closed book. In fact, you are not permitted to take anything with you into the testing area, but you are given a blank sheet of paper and a pen (or, in some cases, an erasable plastic sheet and an erasable pen). We suggest that you immediately write down on that sheet of paper all the information you've memorized for the test. You are given some time to compose yourself, record this information, and take a sample orientation exam before you begin the real thing. I suggest that you take the orientation test before taking your first exam, but because all the certification exams are more or less identical in layout, behavior, and controls, you probably don't need to do this more than once.

When you complete a Microsoft certification exam, the software tells you immediately whether you've passed or failed. If you need to retake an exam, you have to schedule a new test with Prometric or VUE and pay another $125.

> **NOTE**
>
> The first time you fail a test, you can retake the test as soon as the next day. However, if you fail a second time, you must wait 14 days before retaking that test. The 14-day waiting period remains in effect for all retakes after the second failure.

# Tracking MCP Status

As soon as you pass any Microsoft exam, you attain MCP status. Microsoft generates transcripts that indicate which exams you have passed. You can view a copy of your transcript at any time by going to the MCP secured site and selecting Transcript Tool. This tool enables you to print a copy of your current transcript and confirm your certification status.

After you pass the necessary set of exams, you are certified. Official certification is normally granted after three to six weeks, so you shouldn't expect to get your credentials overnight. The package for official certification that arrives includes a Welcome Kit that contains a number of elements (see Microsoft's website for other benefits of specific certifications):

▶ A certificate that is suitable for framing, along with a wallet card and lapel pin.

▶ A license to use the applicable logo, which means you can use the logo in advertisements, promotions, and documents, and on letterheads, business cards, and so on. Along with the license comes a logo sheet, which includes camera-ready artwork. (Note that before you use any of the artwork, you must sign and return a licensing agreement that indicates you'll abide by its terms and conditions.)

▶ A subscription to *Redmond Magazine*, which provides ongoing data about testing and certification activities, requirements, and changes to the program.

Many people believe that the benefits of MCP certification go well beyond the perks that Microsoft provides to newly anointed members of this elite group. We're seeing more job listings that request or require applicants to have MCP, MCSA, and other certifications, and many individuals who complete Microsoft certification programs can qualify for increases in pay or responsibility. As an official recognition of hard work and broad knowledge, one of the MCP credentials is a badge of honor in many IT organizations.

# How to Prepare for an Exam

Preparing for any MCSE- or MCSA-related test (including Exam 70-291) requires that you obtain and study materials designed to provide comprehensive information about the product and its capabilities that will appear on the specific exam for which you are preparing. The following list of materials can help you study and prepare:

▶ The Windows Server 2003 product CD. One of the best resources you can use when preparing for an exam is the help files included with the operating system. They usually cover different aspects of all the technologies included with the operating system.

▶ The exam-preparation materials, practice tests, and self-assessment exams on the Microsoft Training & Services page, at www.microsoft .com/traincert. The Exam Resources link offers examples of the new question types found on the MCSA and MCSE exams. You should find the materials, download them, and use them!

▶ The exam-preparation advice, practice tests, questions of the day, and discussion groups on the www.examcram.com e-learning and certification destination website.

In addition, you might find any or all of the following materials useful in your quest for Windows Server 2003 expertise:

▶ *Microsoft training kits*—Microsoft Press offers a training kit that specifically targets Exam 70-291. For more information, visit www.microsoft .com/mspress/books/5433.asp. This training kit contains information that you will find useful in preparing for the test.

▶ *Microsoft TechNet*—This monthly publication provides information on the latest technologies and topics, some of which pertain to the exam topics covered in Exam 70-291.

▶ *Study guides*—Several publishers, including Que Publishing, offer certification titles. Que Publishing offers the following:

  ▶ *The Exam Cram series*—These books give you information about the material you need to know to pass the tests.

  ▶ *The Exam Prep series*—These books provide a greater level of detail than the *Exam Cram* books and are designed to teach you everything you need to know about the subject covered by an exam. Each book includes exclusive access to MeasureUp practice exams in a variety of testing formats.

  Together, these two series make a perfect pair.

▶ *Classroom training*—Microsoft Certified Partners for Learning (CPLS), online partners, and third-party training companies all offer classroom training on Windows Server 2003. These companies aim to help you prepare to pass Exam 70-291 (or other exams). Although such training runs upward of $350 per day in class, most of the individuals lucky enough to partake find this training to be quite worthwhile.

▶ *Other publications*—There's no shortage of materials available about Windows Server 2003. The "Need to Know More?" resource sections at the end of each chapter in this book give you an idea of where we think you should look for further discussion.

This set of recommended materials represents an unparalleled collection of sources and resources for Windows Server 2003 and related topics. I hope you'll find that this book belongs in this company.

# What This Book Will Not Do

This book will *not* teach you everything you need to know about computers, or even about a given topic. Nor is this book an introduction to computer technology. If you're new to network administration or networking in general and are looking for an initial preparation guide, check out www.examcram.com, where you will find a whole section dedicated to the MCSE/MCSA certifications. This book reviews what you need to know before you take the test, with the fundamental purpose dedicated to reviewing the information needed on the Microsoft 70-291 certification exam.

This book uses a variety of teaching and memorization techniques to analyze the exam-related topics and to provide you with ways to input, index, and retrieve everything you'll need to know to pass the test. Once again, it is *not* an introduction to networking and network administration, nor does it cover introductory topics as they pertain to Windows Server 2003.

# What This Book Is Designed to Do

This book is designed to be read as a pointer to the areas of knowledge you will be tested on. In other words, you might want to read the book one time, just to get an insight into how comprehensive your knowledge of computers is. The book is also designed to be read shortly before you go for the actual test and to give you a distillation of the entire field of implementing, managing, and maintaining a Windows Server 2003 network infrastructure in as few pages as possible. We think you can use this book to get a sense of the underlying context of any topic in the chapters—or to skim for Exam Alerts, bulleted points, summaries, and topic headings.

The material covered in this book is based on Microsoft's own listing of exam objectives. These are the topics that Microsoft intends to test you on during the exam. The book also covers a number of other topics that you are likely to encounter both on the exam and on the job.

Exam 70-291 makes a basic assumption that you already have a strong background of experience with Windows Server 2003 and its related technologies and terminology. I've tried to demystify the jargon, acronyms, terms, and concepts. Also, wherever I think you're likely to zip past an important concept, I've defined the assumptions and premises behind that concept.

# About This Book

The topics in this book have been structured around the objectives outlined by Microsoft for Exam 70-291. This ensures that you are familiar with the topics that you'll encounter on the exam.

Some of the topics covered later in the book might require an understanding of topics covered in earlier chapters. Therefore, it's recommended that you read the book from start to finish for your initial reading. After you've read the book, you can brush up on a certain area by using the index or the table of contents to go straight to the topics and questions that you want to reexamine. I've tried to use the headings and subheadings to provide outline information about each given topic. After you've been certified, I think you'll find this book useful as a tightly focused reference and an essential foundation of Windows Server 2003 reference material.

# Chapter Formats

Each *Exam Cram* chapter follows a regular structure, along with graphical cues about especially important or useful material. The structure of a typical chapter is as follows:

- ▶ *Opening hotlists*—Each chapter begins with lists of the terms you'll need to understand and the concepts you'll need to master before you can be fully conversant with the chapter's subject matter. I follow the hotlists with a few introductory paragraphs, setting the stage for the rest of the chapter.

- ▶ *Topical coverage*—After the opening hotlists, each chapter covers the topics related to the chapter's subject.

- ▶ *Alerts*—Throughout the topical coverage section, I highlight material most likely to appear on the exam by using a special Exam Alert layout that looks like this:

**EXAM ALERT**

This is what an Exam Alert looks like. An Exam Alert stresses concepts, terms, software, or activities that will most likely appear in one or more certification exam questions. For that reason, I think any information found offset in Exam Alert format is worthy of unusual attentiveness on your part.

Even if material isn't flagged as an Exam Alert, *all* the content in this book is associated in some way with test-related material. What appears in the chapter content is critical knowledge.

▶ *Notes*—This book is an overall examination of computers. As such, I'll dip into many aspects of Windows Server 2003. Where a body of knowledge is deeper than the scope of the book, I use notes to indicate areas of concern or specialty training.

**NOTE**

Cramming for an exam will get you through a test, but it won't make you a competent IT professional. Although you can memorize just the facts you need to become certified, your daily work in the field will rapidly put you in water over your head if you don't know the underlying principles of application development.

▶ *Tips*—I provide tips that will help you to build a better foundation of knowledge or to focus your attention on an important concept that will reappear later in the book. Tips provide a helpful way to remind you of the context surrounding a particular area of a topic under discussion.

**TIP**

You should also read Chapter 1 for helpful strategies used in taking a test. The introduction to Practice Exam #1 in Chapter 7 contains additional tips on how to figure out the correct response to a question and what to do if you draw a complete blank.

▶ *Practice questions*—This section presents a short list of test questions related to the specific chapter topic. Each question has a following explanation of both correct and incorrect answers. The practice questions highlight the areas we found to be most important on the exam.

▶ *"Need to Know More?"*—Each chapter ends with a listing of additional resources offering more details about the chapter topics.

The bulk of the book follows this chapter structure, but there are a few other elements that we would like to point out:

▶ *Practice exams*—The practice exams, which appear in Chapters 7 and 9 (with answer keys in Chapters 8 and 10), are very close approximations of the types of questions you are likely to see on the current Exam 70-291.

- ▶ *Glossary*—This is an extensive glossary of important terms used in this book.

- ▶ *The Cram Sheet*—This appears as a tear-away sheet, inside the front cover of this *Exam Cram* book. It is a valuable tool that represents a collection of the most difficult-to-remember facts and numbers we think you should memorize before taking the test. Remember, you can dump this information out of your head onto a piece of paper as soon as you enter the testing room. These are usually facts that we've found require brute-force memorization. You need to remember this information only long enough to write it down when you walk into the test room. Be advised that you will be asked to surrender all personal belongings before you enter the exam room itself.

You might want to look at the Cram Sheet in your car or in the lobby of the testing center just before you walk into the testing room. The Cram Sheet is divided under headings, so you can review the appropriate parts just before each test.

## Contacting the Author

I've tried to create a real-world tool that you can use to prepare for and pass the 70-291 MCSE/MCSA certification exam. I'm interested in any feedback you would care to share about the book, especially if you have ideas about how I can improve it for future test takers. I'll consider everything you say carefully and will respond to all reasonable suggestions and comments. You can reach me via email at dhuggins@skyweb.ca.

Let me know if you found this book to be helpful in your preparation efforts. I'd also like to know how you felt about your chances of passing the exam *before* you read the book and then *after* you read the book. Of course, I'd love to hear that you passed the exam, so even if you just want to share your triumph, I'd be happy to hear from you.

Thanks for choosing me as your personal trainer, and enjoy the book. I would wish you luck on the exam, but I know that if you read through all the chapters and work with the product, you won't need luck—you'll pass the test on the strength of real knowledge!

# Self-Assessment

I included a Self-Assessment in this *Exam Cram* book to help you evaluate your readiness to tackle Microsoft certifications. This should also help you understand what you need to know to master the topic of this book—namely, Exam 70-291, "Implementing, Managing, and Maintaining a Windows Server 2003 Network Infrastructure." But before you tackle this Self-Assessment, let's address concerns you might face when pursuing an MCSE (Microsoft Certified Systems Engineer) or MCSA (Microsoft Certified Systems Administrator) certification for the Windows Server 2003 and what an ideal MCSE candidate might look like.

> **TIP**
>
> Your exclusive access to MeasureUp practice tests (see inside back cover) includes a free assessment!

## MCSEs in the Real World

In this section, I describe an ideal MCSE candidate, knowing full well that only a few real candidates will meet this ideal. In fact, my description of that ideal candidate might seem downright scary. But take heart: Although the requirements to obtain an MCSE might seem formidable, they are by no means impossible to meet. However, be keenly aware that it does take time, involves some expense, and requires real effort to get through the process.

More than 200,000 MCSEs are already certified, so it's obviously an attainable goal. You can get all the real-world motivation you need from knowing that many others have gone before; you will be able to follow in their footsteps. If you're willing to tackle the process seriously and do what it takes to obtain the necessary experience and knowledge, you can take—and pass—all the certification tests involved in obtaining an MCSE. In fact, we've designed *Exam Cram* to make it as easy on you as possible to prepare for these exams. But prepare you must!

The same, of course, is true for other Microsoft certifications, some of which include these:

   ▶ *MCSA (Microsoft Certified Systems Administrator)*—This is the certification that Microsoft has provided for Microsoft professionals who will administer networks rather than design them. This certification includes three core exams and a single elective.

▶ *MCSD (Microsoft Certified Solutions Developer)*—This is aimed at software developers and requires one specific exam, two more exams on client and distributed topics, plus a fourth elective exam drawn from a different but limited pool of options.

▶ *MCAD (Microsoft Certified Application Developer)*—This is aimed at software developers functioning at a departmental level with one to two years of applications-development experience. The MCAD certification requires two specific exams, plus a third elective exam drawn from a limited pool of options. The 70-306 exam is a core exam for the MCAD credential.

▶ *MCDBA (Microsoft Certified Database Administrator)*—This is aimed at database administrators and developers who work with Microsoft SQL Server. The MCDBA certification requires three core exams and one elective exam.

# The Ideal MCSE Candidate

Just to give you some idea of what an ideal MCSE candidate is like, here are some relevant statistics about the background and experience that such an individual might have. Don't worry if you don't meet these qualifications or don't come that close—this is a far-from-ideal world, and where you fall short is simply where you'll have more work to do.

▶ Academic or professional training in network theory, concepts, and operations. This includes everything from networking media and transmission techniques through network operating systems, services, and applications.

▶ Three-plus years of professional networking experience, including experience with Ethernet, token ring, modems, and other networking media. This must include installation, configuration, upgrade, and troubleshooting experience.

▶ Two-plus years in a networked environment that includes hands-on experience with Windows Server 2003, Windows XP, Windows 2000 Server, Windows 2000 Professional, Windows NT Server, Windows NT Workstation, and Windows 95 or Windows 98. A solid understanding of each system's architecture, installation, configuration, maintenance, and troubleshooting is also essential.

▶ Knowledge of the various methods for installing Windows Server 2003, including manual and unattended installations.

▶ A thorough understanding of key networking protocols, addressing, and name resolution, including TCP/IP, IPX/SPX, and NetBEUI.

▶ A thorough understanding of NetBIOS naming, browsing, and file and print services.

▶ Familiarity with key Windows Server 2003 TCP/IP–based services, including HTTP (web servers), DHCP, WINS, and DNS, plus familiarity with one or more of the following: Internet Information Server (IIS), Index Server, and ISA Server.

▶ An understanding of how to implement different connectivity models, such as remote access, IP routing, Internet Connection Sharing (ICS), Network Address Translation (NAT), and virtual private networks (VPNs).

▶ An understanding of how to implement security for key network data in a Windows Server 2003 environment.

▶ Working knowledge of NetWare 3.x and 4.x, including IPX/SPX frame formats; NetWare file, print, and directory services; and both Novell and Microsoft client software. Working knowledge of Microsoft's Client Service for NetWare (CSNW), Gateway Service for NetWare (GSNW), the NetWare Migration Tool (NWCONV), and the NetWare Client for Windows (NT, 95, and 98) is essential.

Fundamentally, this boils down to a Bachelor's degree in computer science, plus three years of experience working in a position involving network design, installation, configuration, and maintenance. We believe that well under half of all certification candidates meet these requirements and that, in fact, most meet less than half of these requirements—at least, when they begin the certification process. But because all 200,000 people who already have been certified have survived this ordeal, you can survive it, too—especially if you heed what our Self-Assessment can tell you about what you already know and what you need to learn.

# Put Yourself to the Test

The following series of questions and observations is designed to help you figure out how much work you must do to pursue Microsoft certification and what kinds of resources you should consult on your quest. Be absolutely honest in your answers; otherwise, you'll end up wasting money on exams you're not yet ready to take. There is no right or wrong answer, only steps along the path to certification. Only you can decide where you really belong in the broad spectrum of aspiring candidates.

Two things should be clear from the outset, however:

▶ Even a modest background in computer science and programming will be helpful.

▶ Hands-on experience with Microsoft products and technologies is an essential ingredient to Microsoft certification success.

# Educational Background

Following are questions related to your education:

1. Have you ever taken any computer-related classes? [Yes or No]

   If Yes, proceed to Question 2; if No, proceed to Question 4.

2. Have you taken any classes on computer operating systems? [Yes or No]

   If Yes, you will probably be able to handle Microsoft's architecture and system component discussions. If you're rusty, brush up on basic operating system concepts and general computer security topics.

   If No, consider some reading in this area. We strongly recommend a good operating systems book, such as *Absolute Beginner's Guide to Microsoft Windows XP, 2nd Edition*, by Shelley O'Hara (Que, 2005), *Special Edition Using Microsoft Windows XP Professional, 3rd Edition*, by Robert Cowart and Brian Knittel (Que, 2005), or *Microsoft Windows Server 2003 Unleashed, R2 Edition*, by Rand Morimoto et al. (Sams, 2006). If these don't appeal to you, check out reviews for other, similar titles at your favorite online bookstore.

3. Have you taken any networking concepts or technology classes? [Yes or No]

   If Yes, you will probably be able to handle Microsoft's networking terminology, concepts, and technologies (brace yourself for frequent departures from normal usage). If you're rusty, brush up on basic networking concepts and terminology, especially networking media, transmission types, the OSI Reference Model, and networking technologies such as Ethernet, token ring, FDDI, and WAN links. Skip to the next section, "Hands-On Experience."

   If No, you might want to read one or two books in this topic area. The two best books that we know of are *Computer Networks, 4th Edition*, by Andrew S. Tanenbaum (Prentice-Hall, 2002, ISBN 0-13-066102-3) and *Computer Networks and Internets, 3rd Edition*, by Douglas E. Comer (Prentice-Hall, 2001, ISBN 0-130-91449-5).

4. Have you read operating system or network publications? [Yes or No]

If No, consult the recommended reading for both topics. A strong background will help you prepare for the Microsoft exams better than just about anything else.

# Hands-on Experience

The most important key to success on all of the Microsoft tests is hands-on experience, especially with Windows Server 2003, plus the many add-on services and BackOffice components around which so many of the Microsoft certification exams revolve. If we leave you with only one realization after taking this Self-Assessment, it should be that there's no substitute for time spent installing, configuring, and using the various Microsoft products upon which you'll be tested repeatedly and in depth.

5. Have you installed, configured, and worked with Windows Server 2003? [Yes or No]

If Yes, make sure you are familiar with not only installing and configuring the operating system, but also using the different services included. When studying for Exam 70-291, you should pay close attention to the TCP/IP interfaces, utilities, and services. Some of the other services that you need to be very familiar with are DNS, DHCP, WINS, RRAS, and Certificate Services. The exam requires in-depth knowledge and a fair amount of experience with each one.

> **TIP**
>
> You can download objectives, practice exams, and other data about Microsoft exams from the Training and Certification page at www.microsoft.com/train_cert/. Use the Find an Exam link to obtain specific exam information.

If you haven't worked with Windows Server 2003, TCP/IP, and IIS (or whatever product you choose for your final elective), you must obtain one or two machines and a copy of Windows Server 2003. Then learn the operating system. Do the same for TCP/IP and whatever other software components you'll be tested on.

In fact, we recommend that you obtain two computers, each with a network interface, and set up a two-node network on which to practice. With decent Windows Server 2003–capable computers selling for about $500 to $600 apiece these days, this shouldn't be too much of a financial hardship. You might have to scrounge to come up with the necessary software, but if you scour the Microsoft website, you can usually find low-cost options to obtain evaluation copies of most of the software that you'll need.

**TIP**

For any and all of these Microsoft exams, the Resource Kits for the topics involved are a good study resource. You can purchase softcover Resource Kits from Microsoft Press (search for them at http://mspress.microsoft.com/), but they also appear on the TechNet CDs (www.microsoft.com/technet). We believe that Resource Kits are among the best preparation tools available, along with the Exam Cram series of books.

6. For any specific Microsoft product that is not itself an operating system (for example, FrontPage, SQL Server, and so on), have you installed, configured, used, and upgraded this software? [Yes or No]

If the answer is Yes, skip to the "Testing Your Exam-Readiness" section. If it's No, you must get some experience. Read on for suggestions on how to do this.

Experience is a must with any Microsoft product exam, whether it is something as simple as FrontPage 2003 or as challenging as Exchange Server 2003 or SQL Server 2005. For trial copies of other software, search Microsoft's website using the name of the product as your search term. Also search for bundles such as BackOffice or Small Business Server.

**TIP**

If you have the funds or your employer will pay your way, consider taking a class at a Microsoft Certified Partners for Learning Solutions (CPLS) or at an Authorized Academic Training Partner (AATP). In addition to classroom exposure to the topic of your choice, you get a copy of the software that is the focus of your course, along with a trial version of whatever operating system it needs, with the training materials for that class.

Before you even think about taking any Microsoft exam, make sure you've spent enough time with the related software to understand how it can be installed and configured (depending on the exam, this could be an operating system or specific services and applications), how to maintain such an installation, and how to troubleshoot that software when things go wrong. This will help you in the exam and in real life!

# Testing Your Exam-Readiness

Whether you attend a formal class on a specific topic to get ready for an exam or use written materials to study on your own, some preparation for the Microsoft certification exams is essential. At $125 a try, pass or fail, you want to do everything you can to pass on your first try. That's where studying comes in.

We have included two practice exams in this book (Chapters 7 and 9), so if you don't score that well on the first, you can study more and then tackle the second.

> **TIP**
>
> Your exclusive access to MeasureUp practice tests (see inside back cover) includes a free assessment!

For any given subject, consider taking a class if you've tackled self-study materials, taken the test, and failed anyway. The opportunity to interact with an instructor and fellow students can make all the difference in the world, if you can afford that privilege. For information about Microsoft classes, visit the Training and Certification page at http://directory.microsoft.com/mprd/Search.aspx?SearchGroup=TrainingRadio&languageDropDown=173 for Microsoft Certified Partners for Learning Solutions.

If you can't afford to take a class, visit the Training page at www.microsoft.com/traincert/training/find/default.asp anyway—it also includes pointers to free practice exams and to Microsoft Certified Professional Approved Study Guides and other self-study tools. Even if you can't afford to spend much at all, you should still invest in some low-cost practice exams from commercial vendors.

7. Have you taken a practice exam on your chosen test subject? [Yes or No]

   If Yes and you scored 70% or better, you're probably ready to tackle the real thing. If your score isn't above that threshold, keep at it until you break that barrier.

   If No, obtain all the free and low-budget practice tests you can find, and get to work. Keep at it until you can break the passing threshold comfortably.

> **TIP**
>
> When it comes to assessing your test readiness, there is no better way than to take a good-quality practice exam and pass with a score of 70% or better. When I'm preparing myself, I shoot for 80% or more, just to leave room for the fact that you might encounter a question or two on the exam that makes little sense due to its wording.

# Assessing Readiness for Exam 70-291

In addition to following the general exam-readiness information in the previous section, you can do several things to prepare for Exam 70-291. I suggest that you join an active Microsoft mailing list, obtain a Microsoft TechNet subscription, and regularly visit the Windows Server 2003 website for new information (see www.microsoft.com/windowsserver2003/default.mspx).

Microsoft exam mavens also recommend checking the Microsoft Knowledge Base (integrated into the TechNet CD-ROM, or on the Microsoft website at http://support.microsoft.com/default.aspx) for "meaningful technical support issues" that relate to your exam's topics. Although I'm not sure exactly what the quoted phrase means, I have noticed some overlap between technical support questions on particular products and troubleshooting questions on the exams for those products.

# What's Next?

After you've assessed your readiness, undertaken the right background studies, obtained the hands-on experience that will help you understand the products and technologies at work, and reviewed the many sources of information to help you prepare for a test, you'll be ready to take a round of practice tests. When your scores come back positive enough to get you through the exam, you're ready to go after the real thing. If you follow our assessment regime, you'll not only know what you need to study, but you'll also know when you're ready to make a test date at Prometric (www.prometric.com) or VUE (www.vue.com). Good luck!

CHAPTER ONE

# Microsoft Certification Exams

---

## Terms you'll need to understand:

✓ Case study

✓ Multiple-choice question format

✓ Build-list-and-reorder question format

✓ Create-a-tree question format

✓ Drag-and-connect question format

✓ Select-and-place question format

✓ Hot area question format

✓ Active screen question format

✓ Fixed-length test

✓ Simulation

✓ Adaptive test

✓ Short-form test

---

## Techniques you'll need to master:

✓ Assessing your exam-readiness

✓ Answering Microsoft's various question types

✓ Altering your test strategy depending on the exam format

✓ Practicing to make perfect

✓ Making the best use of the testing software

✓ Budgeting your time

✓ Guessing as a last resort

Exam taking is not something that most people look forward to, no matter how well-prepared they might be. In most cases, familiarity helps offset test anxiety. In plain English, this means you probably won't be as nervous when you take your fourth or fifth Microsoft certification exam as you'll be when you take your first one.

Whether it's your first exam or your tenth, understanding the details of taking the new exams (how much time to spend on questions, the environment you'll be in, and so on) and the new exam software will help you concentrate on the material rather than on the setting. Likewise, mastering a few basic exam-taking skills should help you recognize—and perhaps even outfox—some of the tricks and snares you're bound to find in some exam questions.

Besides explaining the exam environment and software, this chapter describes some proven exam-taking strategies that you should be able to use to your advantage. Taking the time to read through the information and recommendations presented in this chapter will bring you one step closer to achieving success on a Microsoft exam.

# Assessing Exam-Readiness

We strongly recommend that you read through and take the self-assessment included with this book (it appears just before this chapter). This will help you compare your knowledge base to the requirements for obtaining the Microsoft Certified Systems Engineer (MCSE) certification, and it will help you identify parts of your background or experience that might be in need of improvement, enhancement, or further learning. If you get the right set of basics under your belt, obtaining Microsoft certification will be that much easier.

After you've gone through the self-assessment, you can remedy those topical areas where your background or experience might not measure up to those of an ideal certification candidate. But you can also tackle subject matter for individual tests at the same time, so you can continue making progress while you're catching up in some areas.

After you've worked through an *Exam Cram* series book, read the supplementary materials, and taken the practice test, you'll have a pretty clear idea of when you should be ready to take the real exam. Although we strongly recommend that you keep practicing until your scores top the 75% mark, 80% would be a good goal, to give yourself some margin for error in a real exam situation (where stress will play more of a role than when you practice). After you hit that point, you should be ready to challenge the exam. But if you get through the practice exam in this book without attaining that score, you should keep taking practice tests and studying the materials until you get there. You'll find more pointers on how to study and prepare in the self-assessment. At this point, let's talk about the exam itself.

# What to Expect at the Testing Center

When you arrive at the testing center where you scheduled your exam, you need to sign in with an exam coordinator. He or she will ask you to show two forms of identification, one of which must be a photo ID. After you sign in and when your time slot arrives, you will be asked to deposit any books, bags, or other items you brought with you. Then you will be escorted into a closed room.

All exams are completely closed book. In fact, you are not permitted to take anything with you into the testing area, but you are furnished with a blank sheet of paper and a pen or, in some cases, an erasable plastic sheet and an erasable pen. Before the exam, be sure to carefully review this book's Cram Sheet, located in the very front of the book. You should memorize as much of the important material as you can so that you can write that information on the blank sheet as soon as you are seated in front of the computer. You can refer to that piece of paper anytime you like during the test, but you have to surrender the sheet when you leave the room. You are given some time to compose yourself, to record important information, and answer a few survey questions.

Typically, the testing room is furnished with anywhere from one to six computers, and each workstation is separated from the others by dividers designed to keep you from seeing what's happening on someone else's computer. Most testing rooms feature a wall with a large picture window. This permits the exam coordinator to monitor the room, to prevent exam takers from talking to one another and to observe anything out of the ordinary that might go on. The exam coordinator will have preloaded the appropriate Microsoft certification exam—for this book, that's Exam 70-291, "Implementing, Managing, and Maintaining a Windows Server 2003 Network Infrastructure"—and you are permitted to start as soon as you're seated in front of the computer.

All Microsoft certification exams allow a certain maximum amount of testing time (this time is indicated on the exam by an onscreen timer clock, so you can check the time remaining whenever you like). All Microsoft certification exams are computer generated. In addition to multiple-choice questions, most exams contain select–and-place (drag-and-drop), create-a-tree (categorization and prioritization), drag-and-connect, and build-list-and-reorder (list prioritization) types of questions. Although this might sound quite simple, the questions are constructed not only to check your mastery of basic facts and figures about a Windows Server 2003 network infrastructure, but also to require you to evaluate one or more sets of circumstances or requirements. Often you are asked to give more than one answer to a question. Likewise, you might be asked to select the best or most effective solution to a problem from a range of choices, all of which are technically correct. Taking the exam is quite an adventure, and it involves real thinking. This book shows you what to expect and how to deal with the potential problems, puzzles, and predicaments.

# Exam Layout and Design

The format of Microsoft's Windows Server 2003 and Windows 2000 MCSA (Microsoft Certified Systems Administrator) and MCSE series of exams is different from that of its previous exams covering Windows NT 4.0. For the design exams, each exam consists entirely of a series of case studies, and the questions can be any of six types (see the sections entitled Traditional Exam Question Formats and New Exam Question Formats). Some of the MCSE design exams include the following:

- ▶ 70-219, "Designing a Microsoft Windows 2000 Directory Services Infrastructure"

- ▶ 70-220, "Designing Security for a Microsoft Windows 2000 Network"

- ▶ 70-221, "Designing a Microsoft Windows 2000 Network Infrastructure"

- ▶ 70-226, "Designing Highly Available Web Solutions with Microsoft Windows 2000 Server Technologies"

- ▶ 70-229, "Designing and Implementing Databases with Microsoft SQL Server 2000 Enterprise Edition"

- ▶ 70-297, "Designing a Microsoft Windows Server 2003 Active Directory and Network Infrastructure"

- ▶ 70-298, "Designing Security for a Microsoft Windows Server 2003 Network"

For design exams, each case study or *testlet* presents a detailed problem that you must read and analyze. Figure 1.1 shows an example of what a case study looks like. You must select the different tabs in the case study to view the entire case.

Following each case study is a set of questions related to the case study; these questions can be one of six types (which are discussed in the following sections). Careful attention to details provided in the case study is the key to success. You should be prepared to frequently toggle between the case study and the questions as you work. Some of the case studies include diagrams, which are called *exhibits*, which you'll need to examine closely to understand how to answer the questions.

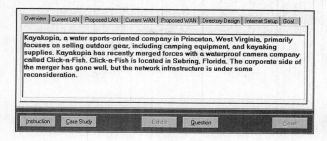

**FIGURE 1.1** The format for case study questions.

After you complete a case study, you can review all the questions and your answers. However, after you move on to the next case study, you might not be able to return to the previous case study to make any changes.

For the MCSA and MCSE core exams and the upgrade exams, the same six types of questions might appear, but you are not likely to encounter complex multi-question case studies. The MCSA/MCSE core exams and upgrade exams for the Windows 2000 track and the Windows Server 2003 track include the following:

- ▶ 70-210, "Installing, Configuring, and Administering Microsoft Windows 2000 Professional"

- ▶ 70-270, "Installing, Configuring, and Administering Microsoft Windows XP Professional"

- ▶ 70-215, "Installing, Configuring, and Administering Microsoft Windows 2000 Server"

- ▶ 70-216, "Implementing and Administering a Microsoft Windows 2000 Network Infrastructure"

- ▶ 70-217, "Implementing and Administering a Microsoft Windows 2000 Directory Services Infrastructure"

- ▶ 70-218, "Managing a Microsoft Windows 2000 Network Environment"

- ▶ 70-290, "Managing and Maintaining a Microsoft Windows Server 2003 Environment"

- ▶ 70-291, "Implementing, Managing, and Maintaining a Microsoft Windows Server 2003 Network Infrastructure"

- ▶ 70-292, "Managing and Maintaining a Microsoft Windows Server 2003 Environment for an MCSA Certified on Windows 2000"

- ▶ 70-293, "Planning and Maintaining a Microsoft Windows Server 2003 Network Infrastructure"

- ▶ 70-294, "Planning, Implementing, and Maintaining a Microsoft Windows Server 2003 Active Directory Infrastructure"

- ▶ 70-296, "Planning, Implementing, and Maintaining a Microsoft Windows Server 2003 Environment for an MCSE Certified on Windows 2000"

# Traditional Exam Question Formats

Historically, six types of question formats have appeared on Microsoft certification exams. These types of questions continue to appear on current Microsoft tests, and they are discussed in the following sections:

- ▶ Multiple-choice, single-answer

- ▶ Multiple-choice, multiple-answer

- ▶ Build-list-and-reorder (list prioritization)

- ▶ Create-a-tree

- ▶ Drag-and-connect

- ▶ Select-and-place (drag-and-drop)

**EXAM ALERT**

You can expect to encounter all the question formats listed previously on the 70-291 exam.

## The Single-Answer and Multiple-Answer Multiple-Choice Question Formats

Some exam questions require you to select a single answer, whereas others ask you to select multiple correct answers. The following multiple-choice question requires you to select a single correct answer. Following the question is a brief summary of each potential answer and why it is either right or wrong.

### Question 1

You have three domains connected to an empty root domain under one contiguous domain name: tutu.com. This organization is formed into a forest arrangement, with a secondary domain called frog.com. How many schema masters exist for this arrangement?

- ○ **A.** 1
- ○ **B.** 2

○ **C.** 3

○ **D.** 4

Answer A is correct because only one schema master is necessary for a forest arrangement. The other answers (answers B, C, and D) are misleading because they try to make you believe that schema masters might be in each domain or perhaps that you should have one for each contiguous namespace domain.

This sample question format corresponds closely to the Microsoft certification exam format. The only difference is that on the exam, the questions are not followed by answers and their explanations. To select an answer, you position the cursor over the radio button next to the answer you want to select. Then you click the mouse button to select the answer.

Let's examine a question in which one or more answers are possible. This type of question provides check boxes rather than option buttons for marking all appropriate selections.

---

## Question 2

What can you use to seize FSMO roles? (Select all the correct answers.)

○ **A.** The ntdsutil.exe utility

○ **B.** The Replication Monitor

○ **C.** The secedit.exe utility

○ **D.** Active Directory domains and trusts

Answers A and B are correct. You can seize roles from a server that is still running through the Replication Monitor, or, in the case of a server failure, you can seize roles with the ntdsutil.exe utility. The secedit.exe utility is used to force group policies into play; therefore, answer C is incorrect. Active Directory domains and trusts are a combination of truth and fiction; therefore, answer D is incorrect.

For this particular question, two answers are required. For question 2, you must mark the check boxes next to answers A and B to obtain credit for a correct answer. Notice that choosing the right answers also means knowing why the other answers are wrong!

## The Build-List-and-Reorder Question Format

Questions in the build-list-and-reorder format present two lists of items—one on the left and one on the right. To answer the question, you must move items from the list on the right to the list on the left. The final list must then be reordered into a specific order.

These questions generally sound like this: "From the following list of choices, pick the choices that answer the question. Arrange the list in a certain order." To give you practice with this type of question, some questions of this type are included in this book. Question 3 shows an example of how they appear in this book; for an example of how they appear on the test, see Figure 1.2.

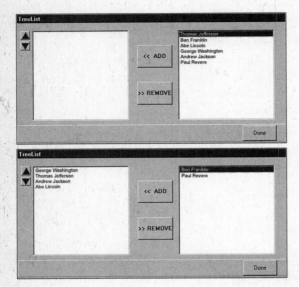

**FIGURE 1.2**  The format for build-list-and-reorder questions.

## Question 3

From the following list of famous people, choose those who have been elected president of the United States. Arrange the list in the order in which the presidents served.

Thomas Jefferson

Ben Franklin

Abe Lincoln

George Washington

Andrew Jackson

Paul Revere

The correct answer is

George Washington

Thomas Jefferson

Andrew Jackson

Abe Lincoln

On an actual exam, the entire list of famous people would initially appear in the list on the right. You would move the four correct answers to the list on the left and then reorder the list on the left. Notice that the answer to question 3 does not include all items from the initial list. However, that might not always be the case.

To move an item from the right list to the left list on the exam, you first select the item by clicking it, and then you click the Add button (left arrow). After you move an item from one list to the other, you can move the item back by first selecting the item and then clicking the appropriate button (either the Add button or the Remove button). After items have been moved to the left list, you can move an item by selecting the item and clicking the up or down buttons.

## The Create-a-Tree Question Format

Questions in the create-a-tree format also present two lists—one on the left side of the screen and one on the right side of the screen. The list on the right consists of individual items, and the list on the left consists of nodes in a tree. To answer the question, you must move items from the list on the right to the appropriate node in the tree.

These questions can best be characterized as simply a matching exercise. Items from the list on the right are placed under the appropriate category in the list on the left. Question 4 shows an example of how they appear in this book; for a sample of how they appear on the test, see Figure 1.3.

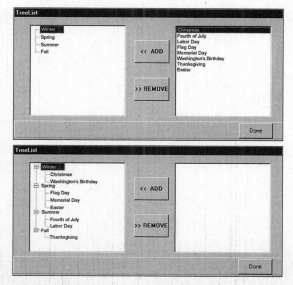

**FIGURE 1.3** The create-a-tree question format.

## Question 4

The calendar year is divided into four seasons:

Winter

Spring

Summer

Fall

Identify the season during which each of the following holidays occurs:

Christmas

Fourth of July

Labor Day

Flag Day

Memorial Day

Washington's Birthday

Thanksgiving

Easter

The correct answer is

▶ Winter

Christmas

Washington's Birthday

▶ Spring

Flag Day

Memorial Day

Easter

▶ Summer

Fourth of July

Labor Day

▶ Fall

Thanksgiving

In this case, all the items in the list are used. However, that might not always be the case.

To move an item from the right list to its appropriate location in the tree, you must first select the appropriate tree node by clicking it. Then you select the item to be moved and click the Add button. If one or more items have been added to a tree node, the node is displayed with a + icon to the left of the node name. You can click this icon to expand the node and view the item(s) that has been added. If any item has been added to the wrong tree node, you can remove it by selecting it and clicking the Remove button.

## The Drag-and-Connect Question Format

Questions in the drag-and-connect format present a group of objects and a list of connections. To answer the question, you must move the appropriate connections between the objects.

This type of question is best described using graphics. Question 5 shows an example.

### Question 5

The following objects represent the different states of water:

| Ice | Water Vapor | Water | Steam |
|-----|-------------|-------|-------|

Use items from the following list to connect the objects so that they are scientifically correct:

Sublimates to form

Freezes to form

Evaporates to form

Boils to form

Condenses to form

Melts to form

The correct answer is

For this type of question, it's not necessary to use every object, and each connection can be used multiple times.

## The Select-and-Place Question Format

Questions in the select-and-place (drag-and-drop) format present a diagram with blank boxes and a list of labels that need to be dragged to correctly fill in the blank boxes. To answer such a question, you must move the labels to their appropriate positions on the diagram.

This type of question is best described using graphics. Question 6 shows an example.

### Question 6

Place the items in their proper order, by number, on the following flowchart. Some items might be used more than once, and some items might not be used at all:

The correct answer is

**FIGURE 1.4** A sample select-and-place question.

# New Exam Question Formats

Microsoft is introducing several new question types in addition to the more traditional types of questions that are still widely used on all Microsoft exams. These new, innovative question types were highly researched and tested by Microsoft before they were chosen to be included in many of the newer exams for the MCSA/MCSE on Windows 2000 track and the MCSA/MCSE on Windows Server 2003 track. These new question types are as follows:

- ▶ Hot area questions
- ▶ Active screen questions
- ▶ New drag-and-drop type questions
- ▶ Simulation questions

## Hot Area Question Types

Hot area questions ask you to indicate the correct answer by selecting one or more elements within a graphic. For example, you might be asked to select multiple objects within a list, as shown in Figure 1.5.

**FIGURE 1.5** Selecting objects within a list box to answer a hot area question.

## Active Screen Question Types

Active screen questions ask you to configure a dialog box by modifying one or more elements. These types of questions offer a realistic interface in which you must properly configure various settings, just as you would within the actual software product. For example, you might be asked to select the proper option within a drop-down list box, as shown in Figure 1.6.

## New Drag-and-Drop Question Types

New drag-and-drop questions ask you to drag source elements to their appropriate corresponding targets within a work area. These types of questions test your knowledge of specific concepts and their definitions or descriptions. For example, you might be asked to match a description of a computer program to the actual software application, as shown in Figure 1.7.

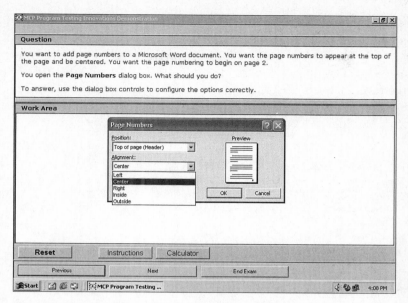

**FIGURE 1.6** Configuring an option from a dialog box's drop-down list box to answer an active screen question.

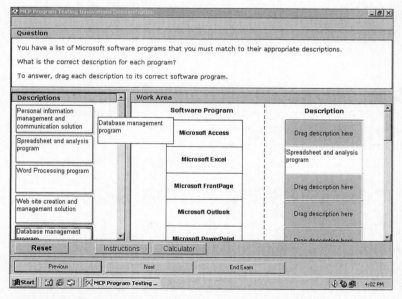

**FIGURE 1.7** Using drag-and-drop to match the correct application description to each software program listed.

## Simulation Question Types

Simulation questions ask you to indicate the correct answer by performing specific tasks, such as configuring and installing network adapters or drivers, configuring and controlling access to files, or troubleshooting hardware devices. Many of the tasks that systems administrators and systems engineers perform can be presented more accurately in simulations than in most traditional exam question types (see Figure 1.8).

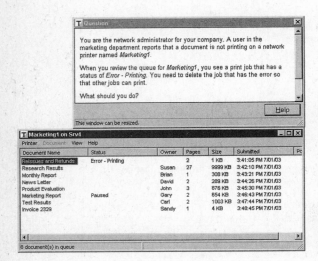

**FIGURE 1.8** Answering a simulation question about how to troubleshoot a network printing problem.

---

**TIP**

When in doubt, don't change your first instinct! If you're not sure of the possible answers, always go with your first instinct.

---

# Microsoft's Testing Formats

Currently, Microsoft uses four different testing formats:

▶ Case study

▶ Fixed-length

▶ Adaptive

▶ Short-form

As mentioned earlier, the case study approach is used with Microsoft's design exams. These exams consist of a set of case studies that you must analyze so that you can answer questions related to the case studies. Such exams include one or more case studies (tabbed topic areas), each of which is followed by 4 to 10 questions. The question types for design exams and for the four core exams are multiple-choice, build-list-and-reorder, create-a-tree, drag-and-connect, and select-and-place. Depending on the test topic, some exams are totally case based, whereas others are not.

Other Microsoft exams employ advanced testing capabilities that might not be immediately apparent. Although the questions that appear are primarily multiple-choice, the logic that drives them is more complex than that in older Microsoft tests, which use a fixed sequence of questions, called a *fixed-length test*. Some questions employ a sophisticated user interface, which Microsoft calls a *simulation*, to test your knowledge of the software and systems under consideration in a more or less "live" environment that behaves just like the real thing. You should review the Microsoft Training and Certification web pages at http://www.microsoft.com/learning/default.mspx for more information.

For some exams, Microsoft has turned to a well-known technique called *adaptive testing* to establish a test taker's level of knowledge and product competence. Adaptive exams look the same as fixed-length exams, but they discover the level of difficulty at which an individual test taker can correctly answer questions. Test takers with differing levels of knowledge or ability therefore see different sets of questions; individuals with high levels of knowledge or ability are presented with a smaller set of more difficult questions, whereas individuals with lower levels of knowledge are presented with a larger set of easier questions. Two individuals might answer the same percentage of questions correctly, but the test taker with a higher knowledge or ability level will score higher because his or her questions are worth more. Also, the lower-level test taker will probably answer more questions than his or her more knowledgeable colleague. This explains why adaptive tests use ranges of values to define the number of questions and the amount of time it takes to complete the test.

Adaptive tests work by evaluating the test taker's most recent answer. A correct answer leads to a more difficult question, and the test software's estimate of the test taker's knowledge and ability level is raised. An incorrect answer leads to a less difficult question, and the test software's estimate of the test taker's knowledge and ability level is lowered. This process continues until the test targets the test taker's true ability level. The exam ends when the test taker's level of accuracy meets a statistically acceptable value (in other words, when his or her performance demonstrates an acceptable level of knowledge and ability) or when the maximum number of items has been presented (in which case the test taker is almost certain to fail).

Microsoft has also introduced a short-form test for its most popular tests. This test delivers 25 to 30 questions to its takers, giving them exactly 60 minutes to complete the exam. This type of exam is similar to a fixed-length test, in that it allows readers to jump ahead or return to earlier questions and to cycle through the questions until the test is done. Microsoft does not use adaptive logic in short-form tests, but it claims that statistical analysis of the question pool is such that the 25 to 30 questions delivered during a short-form exam conclusively measure a test taker's knowledge of the subject matter in much the same way as an adaptive test. You can think of the short-form test as a kind of greatest-hits version of an adaptive exam on the same topic—that is, the most important questions are covered.

**NOTE**

Microsoft certification exams might use either the adaptive-question format or the more traditional fixed-length question format. Historically, Microsoft tests have been primarily fixed-length format, but the company seems to be moving in the direction of publishing more adaptive-question format exams.

Because you won't know which form the Microsoft exam will be, you should be prepared for an adaptive exam instead of a fixed-length or a short-form exam. The penalties for answering incorrectly are built in to the test itself on an adaptive exam, whereas the layout remains the same for a fixed-length or short-form test, no matter how many questions you answer incorrectly.

**TIP**

The biggest difference between adaptive tests and fixed-length or short-form tests is that you can mark and revisit questions on fixed-length and short-form tests after you've read them. On an adaptive test, you must answer the question when it is presented, and you cannot go back to that question later.

# Strategies for Different Testing Formats

Before you choose a test-taking strategy, you must determine what type of test it is—case study, fixed-length, short-form, or adaptive:

▶ *Case study* tests consist of a tabbed window that allows you to navigate easily through the sections of the case.

▶ *Fixed-length* tests consist of 50 to 70 questions, with a check box for each question. You can return to these questions if you want.

▶ *Short-form* tests have 25 to 30 questions, with a check box for each question. You can return to these questions if you want.

▶ *Adaptive* tests are identified in the introductory material of the test. Questions have no check boxes and can be visited (and answered) only once. You do not have the option of reviewing any questions after you have answered them all.

---

**TIP**

You'll be able to tell for sure whether you are taking an adaptive, fixed-length, or short-form test by the first question. Fixed-length and short-form tests include a check box that allows you to mark the question for later review. Adaptive test questions include no such check box and can be visited (and answered) only once.

---

# Case Study Exam Strategy

Most test takers find that the case study type of test used for the design exams (including exams 70-219, 70-220, 70-221, and 70-226, among others) is the most difficult to master. When it comes to studying for a case study test, your best bet is to approach each case study as a standalone test. The biggest challenge you're likely to encounter with this type of test is that you might feel that you won't have enough time to get through all the cases that are presented.

---

**TIP**

Each case study provides a lot of material that you need to read and study before you can effectively answer the questions that follow. The trick to taking a case study exam is to first scan the case study to get the highlights. You should make sure that you read the overview section of the case so that you understand the context of the problem at hand. Then you should quickly move on to scanning the questions.

As you are scanning the questions, you should make mental notes to yourself so that you'll remember which sections of the case study you should focus on. Some case studies might provide a fair amount of extra information that you don't really need to answer the questions. The goal with this scanning approach is to avoid having to study and analyze material that is not completely relevant.

---

When studying a case, read the tabbed information carefully. It is important to answer each and every question. You will be able to toggle back and forth from case to questions, and from question to question within a case testlet. However, after you leave the case and move on, you might not be able to return to it. We suggest that you take notes while reading useful information to help you when you tackle the test questions. It's hard to go wrong with this strategy when taking any kind of Microsoft certification test.

# The Fixed-Length and Short-Form Exam Strategies

A well-known principle when taking fixed-length or short-form exams is first to read through the entire exam from start to finish. Answer only those questions that you feel absolutely sure you know. On subsequent passes, you can dive into more complex questions more deeply, knowing how many such questions you have left and the amount of time remaining.

> **TIP**
>
> There's at least one potential benefit to reading the exam completely before answering the trickier questions: Sometimes information supplied in later questions sheds more light on earlier questions. At other times, information you read in later questions might jog your memory about facts, figures, or behavior and help you answer earlier questions. Either way, you'll come out ahead if you answer only those questions on the first pass that you're absolutely confident about.

Fortunately, the Microsoft exam software for fixed-length and short-form tests makes the multiple-visit approach easy to implement. At the top-left corner of each question is a check box that permits you to mark that question for a later visit.

Here are some question-handling strategies that apply to fixed-length and short-form tests. Use them if you have the chance:

- ▶ When returning to a question after your initial read-through, read every word again; otherwise, your mind can miss important details. Sometimes revisiting a question after turning your attention elsewhere lets you see something you missed, but the strong tendency is to see what you've seen before. Try to avoid that tendency at all costs.

- ▶ If you return to a question more than twice, try to articulate to yourself what you don't understand about the question, why answers don't appear to make sense, or what appears to be missing. If you chew on the subject a while, your subconscious might provide the missing details, or you might notice a trick that points to the right answer.

As you work your way through the exam, another counter that Microsoft provides will come in handy—the number of questions completed and questions outstanding. For fixed-length and short-form tests, it's wise to budget your time by making sure that you've completed one quarter of the questions one quarter of the way through the exam period, and three quarters of the questions three quarters of the way through.

If you're not finished when only five minutes remain, use that time to guess your way through any remaining questions. Remember, guessing is potentially more valuable than not answering. Blank answers are always wrong, but a guess can turn out to be right. If you don't have a clue about any of the remaining questions, pick answers at random or choose all A's, B's, and so on. Questions left unanswered are counted as answered incorrectly, so a guess is better than nothing at all.

---

**TIP**

At the very end of your exam period, you're better off guessing than leaving questions unanswered.

---

# The Adaptive Exam Strategy

If there's one principle that applies to taking an adaptive test, it could be summed up as "Get it right the first time." You cannot elect to skip a question and move on to the next one when taking an adaptive test because the testing software uses your answer to the current question to select the question it presents next. You also cannot return to a question after you've moved on because the software gives you only one chance to answer the question. However, you can take notes, and sometimes information supplied in earlier questions sheds more light on later questions.

Also, when you answer a question correctly, you are presented with a more difficult question next, to help the software gauge your level of skill and ability. When you answer a question incorrectly, you are presented with a less difficult question, and the software lowers its current estimate of your skill and ability. This continues until the program settles into a reasonably accurate estimate of what you know and can do; it takes, on average, somewhere between 15 and 30 questions to complete the test.

The good news is that if you know your stuff, you are likely to finish most adaptive tests in 30 minutes or so. The bad news is that you must really, really know your stuff to do your best on an adaptive test. That's because some questions are so convoluted, complex, or hard to follow that you're bound to miss one or two, at a minimum, even if you do know your stuff. So the more you know, the better you'll do on an adaptive test, even accounting for the occasionally weird or unfathomable questions that appear on these exams.

**TIP**

Because you can't always tell in advance whether a test is a fixed-length, short-form, or adaptive exam, you should prepare for the exam as if it were adaptive. That way, you will be prepared to pass no matter what kind of test you take. But if you do take a fixed-length or short-form test, you need to remember the tips from the preceding sections. These tips should help you perform even better on a fixed-length or short-form exam than on an adaptive test. When studying for the 70-291 exam, be prepared to encounter any of these three test formats.

If you encounter a question on an adaptive test that you can't answer, you must guess an answer immediately. Because of how the software works, however, you might suffer for your guess on the next question if you guess right because you get a more difficult question next!

# Question-Handling Strategies

For questions that have only one right answer, usually two or three of the answers will be obviously incorrect, and two of the answers will be plausible. Unless the answer leaps out at you (if it does, reread the question to look for a trick—sometimes those are the ones you're most likely to get wrong), begin the process of answering by eliminating those answers that are most obviously wrong.

At least one answer out of the possible choices for a question can usually be eliminated immediately because it matches one of these conditions:

▶ The answer does not apply to the situation.

▶ The answer describes a nonexistent issue, an invalid option, or an imaginary state.

After you eliminate all answers that are obviously wrong, you can apply your retained knowledge to eliminate further answers. You should look for items that sound correct but refer to actions, commands, or features that are not present or not available in the situation that the question describes.

If you're still faced with a blind guess among two or more potentially correct answers, reread the question. Try to picture how each of the possible remaining answers would alter the situation. Be especially sensitive to terminology; sometimes the choice of words (*remove* instead of *disable*) can make the difference between a right answer and a wrong one.

You should guess at an answer only after you've exhausted your ability to eliminate answers and are still unclear about which of the remaining possibilities is correct. An unanswered question offers you no points, but guessing gives you at least some chance of getting a question right; just don't be too hasty when making a blind guess.

> **NOTE**
>
> If you're taking a fixed-length or a short-form test, you can wait until the last round of reviewing marked questions (just as you're about to run out of time or unanswered questions) before you start making guesses. You will usually have the same option within each case study testlet (but once you leave a testlet, you might not be allowed to return to it). If you're taking an adaptive test, you'll have to guess to move on to the next question if you can't figure out an answer some other way. Either way, guessing should be your technique of last resort!

Numerous questions assume that the default behavior of a particular utility is in effect. If you know the defaults and understand what they mean, this knowledge will help you cut through many of the trickier questions. Simple final actions can be critical as well. If a utility must be restarted before proposed changes take effect, a correct answer might require this step as well.

# Mastering the Inner Game

In the final analysis, knowledge breeds confidence, and confidence breeds success. If you study the materials in this book carefully and review all the practice questions at the end of each chapter, you should become aware of the areas in which you need additional learning and study.

After you've worked your way through the book, take the practice exam in the back of the book. Taking this test provides a reality check and helps you identify areas to study further. Make sure you follow up and review materials related to the questions you miss on the practice exam before scheduling a real exam. Don't schedule your exam appointment until after you've thoroughly studied the material and feel comfortable with the whole scope of the practice exam. You should score 80% or better on the practice exam before proceeding to the real thing (otherwise, obtain some additional practice tests so that you can keep trying until you hit this magic number).

> **TIP**
>
> If you take a practice exam and don't get at least 70% to 80% of the questions correct, keep practicing. Microsoft provides links to practice exam providers and also self-assessment exams at http://www.microsoft.com/learning/mcpexams/prepare/default.asp.

Armed with the information in this book and with the determination to augment your knowledge, you should be able to pass the certification exam. However, you need to work at it, or you'll spend the exam fee more than once before you finally pass. If you prepare seriously, you should do well.

The next section covers other sources that you can use to prepare for Microsoft certification exams.

# Additional Resources

A good source of information about Microsoft Certification Exams comes from Microsoft itself. Because its products and technologies—and the exams that go with them—change frequently, the best place to go for exam-related information is online. Additional information can always be found by reviewing the online Resource Kit associated with the operating system in question, as well as the online Knowledge Base and TechNET websites. These are invaluable resources for both exam preparation and real-world problem solving.

If you haven't already visited the Microsoft Training and Certification website, you should do so right now. Microsoft's Training and Certification home page resides at http://www.microsoft.com/learning/default.mspx (see Figure 1.9).

**FIGURE 1.9**   The Microsoft Learning home page.

# Coping with Change on the Web

Sooner or later, all the information we've shared with you about the Microsoft Certified Professional pages and the other web-based resources mentioned throughout the rest of this book will go stale or be replaced by newer information. In some cases, the URLs you find here might lead you to their replacements; in other cases, the URLs will go nowhere, leaving you with the dreaded "404 File not found" error message. When that happens, don't give up.

There's always a way to find what you want on the Web if you're willing to invest some time and energy. Most large or complex websites—and Microsoft's qualifies on both counts—offer search engines. On all of Microsoft's web pages, a Search button appears at the top edge of the page. As long as you can access Microsoft's site (it should stay at www.microsoft.com for a long time), you can use the Search button to find what you need.

The more focused you can make a search request, the more likely it is that the results will include information you can use. For example, you can search for this string to produce a lot of data about the subject in general:

```
"training and certification"
```

However, if you're looking for the preparation guide for Exam 70-291, "Implementing, Managing, and Maintaining a Windows Server 2003 Network Infrastructure," you'll be more likely to get there quickly if you use a search string similar to the following:

```
"Exam 70-291" AND "preparation guide"
```

Likewise, if you want to find the Training and Certification downloads, you should try a search string such as this:

```
"training and certification" AND "download page"
```

Finally, you should feel free to use general search tools—such as www.google.com, www.altavista.com, and www.excite.com—to look for related information. Although Microsoft offers great information about its certification exams online, there are plenty of third-party sources of information and assistance that need not follow Microsoft's party line. Therefore, if you can't find something where the book says it lives, you should intensify your search.

CHAPTER TWO

# Managing IP Addressing

---

## Terms you'll need to understand:

✓ Dynamic Host Configuration Protocol (DHCP)
✓ Transmission Control Protocol/Internet Protocol (TCP/IP)
✓ Scope
✓ DHCP database
✓ Lease
✓ DHCP clients

---

## Techniques you'll need to master:

✓ Configuring TCP/IP on a server computer
✓ Managing a DHCP server
✓ Managing DHCP clients
✓ Managing the DHCP database
✓ Configuring and managing DHCP scope options
✓ Troubleshooting TCP/IP

One of the requirements of Active Directory is the *Transmission Control Protocol/Internet Protocol (TCP/IP)* suite. For computers on a TCP/IP network to communicate, each computer must be assigned a unique IP address. In some cases, it might make sense to configure each workstation with a static IP address or to use automatic private IP addressing. However, statically configuring IP addresses can add a lot of administrative overhead. Not only can it become time-consuming, but it also increases the possibility of a workstation being configured with incorrect parameters. Imagine having to visit 10,000 workstations and type in 10,000 IP addresses without making a single error. The *Dynamic Host Configuration Protocol (DHCP)* service can be implemented to centralize the administration and assignment of IP addresses. DHCP automates and centralizes many of the tasks associated with IP addressing.

This chapter discusses how to configure TCP/IP on a server computer and how to implement a DHCP server, including the installation process, the authorization of the server, and the configuration of DHCP scopes. This chapter also looks at some of the management tasks associated with running DHCP.

# Overview of the OSI Model

TCP/IP, like most protocols, is a suite of protocols rather than being a single monolithic protocol. The Open Systems Interconnection (OSI) model describes how suites of protocols work together and it establishes an industry standard for network communication. The OSI model is a conceptual theory that describes how protocols should work. TCP/IP does not exactly map to the OSI model on a one-to-one basis, but it maps closely enough to offer insights into how the protocol functions in general.

The OSI model is made up of seven layers, with each layer performing a different function to enable network communication. Each of the protocols within the TCP/IP protocol suite operate at one of the OSI layers.

The seven layers of the OSI model include the following:

> ▶ *Application*—Layer 7 is the top layer of the OSI model. This layer defines how network applications gain access to the network.
>
> Applications and software do not actually reside inside of the Application layer; instead layer 7 serves as an API or interface between client/server software and the network protocol.
>
> ▶ *Presentation*—Layer 6 outlines how data is formatted, presented, and converted. Protocols working at this layer are responsible for encrypting and converting data.

- *Session*—Layer 5 defines communication sessions between two TCP/IP hosts. Protocols operating at this layer establish, maintain, and terminate communication sessions.

- *Transport*—Layer 4 provides flow control and error-checking to ensure packet delivery.

- *Network*—Layer 3 is responsible for addressing and routing packets.

- *Data Link*—Layer 2 provides error-free delivery of frames between two hosts over the network.

- *Physical*—Layer 1 defines the physical characteristics of the network.

Note: The physical elements of the network actually reside in the physical layer. This includes the NIC and the appropriate communication medium, whether copper cabling, fiber optic cabling, radio transmitter/receiver (for wireless), IR transmitter/receiver, and so on.

As data moves down the OSI model, each layer adds its own information. This process is known as *encapsulation*. On the receiving end, the information is stripped off as the data flows up the layers. This process is known as *de-encapsulation*.

## The Department of Defense (DoD) Model

TCP/IP maps to another conceptual model known as the Department of Defense (DoD) model or DARPA (Defense Advanced Research Projects Agency) model. It also describes how two hosts running TCP/IP communicate on a network. This model consists of four layers, each of which can be mapped to one or more of the seven layers of the OSI model. The TCP/IP/DOD/DARPA model more effectively and accurately describes the functions of the TCP/IP protocol.

As already mentioned, TCP/IP is made up a suite of protocols. These protocols are organized into four layers. The four layers of the DoD model include the following:

- *Application*—This layer defines how applications gain access to the network. Protocols operating at this layer include HTTP, FTP, SMTP, DNS, POP3, and SNMP.

- *Transport*—This layer defines communication sessions between two TCP/IP hosts. The two protocols working at this level are TCP and UDP.

- *Internet*—This layer is responsible for addressing and routing. Protocols at this level include IP, ARP, ICMP, and IGMP.

- *Network*—This layer is responsible for sending and receiving information over the physical network.

# Connection-Based and Connectionless Protocols

Some protocols are connection-based while others are connectionless. The orientation of a protocol will define the relationship between two hosts when transmitting data.

A protocol that is connection-based will require a formal relationship to be established between the transmission end-points before data is transferred. A connectionless protocol, on the other hand, requires no formal relationship to be established.

The *Transmission Control Protocol (TCP)* is a connection-based protocol, meaning before data can be sent between two hosts, a session must first be established. TCP offers reliable delivery of data through sequencing, error checking, and flow control.

TCP establishes a session through a process known as a three-way handshake. After a session is established, information can be reliably sent. Each datagram that is sent is assigned a sequence number. The sequence numbers ensure that the destination computer can reassemble the data in the proper order as it is received. The destination computer will send acknowledgments for segments that are received. If the source computer does not receive an acknowledgement within a certain amount of time, the segment will be retransmitted, thus ensuring delivery of information.

> **NOTE**
>
> FTP and Telnet are examples of programs that use TCP to transfer data between two TCP/IP hosts.

Unlike TCP, UDP is a connectionless protocol. This means that UDP does not establish a session before sending data nor does it provide for reliable delivery. When information is sent, acknowledgements are not returned so it is just assumed that it has been received. UDP is more often used in one-to-many situations where information is sent using a broadcast or for multicasting (TCP is used for one-to-one communication). If reliable delivery and sequencing of datagrams is required, it is the responsibility of the application or a higher level protocol to provide these services. For example, UDP is often used by videoconferencing and streaming media applications because they require fast delivery of data. The Session Information Protocol (SIP) used for streaming media relies on UDP but also uses its own retransmission mechanisms because UDP does not offer reliable delivery of data.

# IP Addressing

Each host on an IP network requires a unique IP address and a subnet mask. If a host must communicate with other hosts outside if the local network, the IP address of the default gateway must also be specified.

The IP address is a 32-bit number, represented in dotted-decimal notation format that identifies each host. An IP address consists of two parts: the network ID and the host ID. The network ID specifies the particular network or subnet that the host is on. The host ID uniquely identifies a host on a specific network or subnet. For example, with the IP address of 12.10.125.2 and a Class A subnet mask of 255.0.0.0, the network ID is 12 and the host ID is 10.125.2.

## IP Address Classes

IP addresses are organized into different address classes that define the number of bits out of the 32 that are used to identify the network and which are used to identify hosts on a network (see Table 2.1). By examining the address classes you can also determine the number of networks and the number of hosts.

**TABLE 2.1   IP Address Classes**

| Address Class | Range | Number of Network IDs | Number of Host IDs |
|---|---|---|---|
| Class A | 1–126 | 126 | 16,777,214 |
| Class B | 128–191 | 16,834 | 65,534 |
| Class C | 192–223 | 2,097,152 | 254 |

There is also a Class D and a Class E. Class D is reserved for multicasting and Class E is reserved for testing purposes. You can determine the class of an IP address by mapping the first decimal value to one of the ranges outlined in Table 2.1. For example, 198.221.10.254 would be a class C address. Class ranges are defined by the contents of the first few digits of the IP address when in binary format. A Class A address starts with 1, Class B with 10, and Class C with 110.

## Private IP Address Ranges

Three ranges of IP addresses have been reserved via RFC 1918, meaning they are not valid for use on the Internet. Any public network node encountering a Private IP Address as the source or destination address in a packet will automatically drop the packet. However, you can use these private address ranges on your private network. One of the disadvantages to this is that a proxy server or NAT server is needed for Internet access because the private IP address must be mapped to or translated into a public address. In terms of advantages, private IP addressing is more cost-effective, can accommodate growth on your network, and can increase security.

If you do decide to implement a private IP address range, you can use IP addresses from any of the following classes:

Class A 10.0.0.0–10.255.255.255

Class B 172.16.0.0–172.31.255.255

Class C 192.16.8.0.0–192.168.255.255

One of the decisions you will be faced with when designing a TCP/IP network is whether you want to use a private IP address range or public IP addresses. There are disadvantages and advantages to both of them. In making your decisions, keep in mind that any computers having a direct connection to the Internet will require at least one public IP address. A *public IP address* is an address leased from an ISP that allows or enables direct Internet communication. But for those computers with no direct Internet connection, you have the option of using public or private addresses.

## Converting an IP Address to Binary Format

IP addresses, which consist of four octets, can be converted from decimal format to binary format. When in binary format, each set of 8 bits is known as an octet. When you convert each octet to a number, the value can range from 0 to 255. When these decimal equivalents are written side-by-side separated by a period, this is known as *dotted-decimal notation*.

The values assigned to each of the placeholders in a single octet are as follows:

| 1 | 1 | 1 | 1 | 1 | 1 | 1 | 1 |
|-----|-----|-----|-----|-----|-----|-----|-----|
| 128 | 64 | 32 | 16 | 8 | 4 | 2 | 1 |

Let's take a look at an example. An IP address of 131.107.2.10 can be converted to the following binary number:

10000011 01101011 00000010 00000001

Conversely, a binary number of 11000000 11110000 00101000 11110010 can be converted to the following decimal number:

11000000 11110000 00101000 11110010

192.240.40.242

# Subnet Masks

When assigning IP addresses, each host requires a subnet mask to determine which part of an IP address is used as the network ID and which is used as the host ID.

The default subnet masks for the three IP address classes are

- Class A: 255.0.0.0
- Class B: 255.255.0.0
- Class C: 255.255.255.0

For example, the default subnet mask for a Class C address is 255.255.255.0, which means the first three octets identify the network and the last octet identifies the host.

The subnet mask is also used to determine whether the destination host is on the local subnet or a remote subnet. The subnet mask of the local host is compared against the IP address of the destination host and through a process known as "Anding" it is determined whether the destination IP address is the local or a remote network.

Basically the number of 1s in the binary address of the subnet mask are masked against the binary form of the IP address to determine whether the address is on the local network or a remote network.

When the bits of the subnet mask are compared against the bits in the IP address, the ANDing process converts the combinations of 1 and 0, 0 and 1, or 0 and 0 into a value of 0, and converts the combination of 1 and 1 into a value of 1.

Let's look at an example of how this process works. The source host has an IP address of 192.168.0.10 and subnet mask of 255.255.255.0. The destination host has an IP address of 192.168.20.2.

| | |
|---|---|
| IP address | 11000000 10101000 00000000 00001010 (192.168.0.10) |
| Subnet mask | 11111111 11111111 11111111 00000000 (255.255.255.0) |
| **AND Results** | 11000000 10101000 00000000 00000000 |
| IP address | 11000000 10101000 00010010 00000010 (192.168.20.20) |
| Subnet mask | 11111111 11111111 11111111 00000000 (255.255.255.0) |
| **AND Results** | 11000000 10101000 00010010 00000000 |

As you can see from this example, the source IP address is ANDed against the subnet mask. The destination address is ANDed against the subnet mask assigned to the source host. If the results are not the same, the destination host is on a different network or subnet. Conversely, if the results are the same, it is determined that the destination host is on the local network.

# Subnetting an IP Address

Subnetting is a popular exam topic across many different Microsoft certification exams. It allows you to divide a network into smaller logical networks. Subnetting offers many benefits that include the following:

▸ Reduce the size of the routing tables.

▸ Reduce network traffic. Broadcast traffic can be isolated within a single logical network.

▸ Provide a way to secure network traffic by isolating it from the rest of the network.

Subnetting works by taking some of the bits that would normally be used for host IDs to identify logical networks. The number of logical networks you require will determine the number of bits you take away from the host IDs.

The first step in subnetting is to determine the number of logical networks you need and the maximum number of hosts that each logical network will support. After you have determined this you can then establish the subnet mask.

The following steps outline the general process to follow:

1. Identify the number of logical networks you will require. For example, you might require six logical networks, but you'll want to factor in future growth as well.

2. Convert this number to binary format. Using the previous example, you would convert the number 6 to binary format to obtain a value of 00000110.

3. Count the number of bits required to support the number of networks. Referring back to step 2, 3 bits (00000**110**) are required to support six subnets.

4. Convert the number of bits to high order (left to right). If the required number of bits is 3, the high order binary value will be **111**00000.

5. Convert the binary number back to a decimal. 11100000 would be 224. If you have a class C address the subnet mask would then become 255.255.255.224.

Let's take a look at an example of subnetting a Class B address. The network ID is 131.107.0.0 and the default subnet mask is 255.255.0.0. You require 10 logical networks. To start off the process, convert the number 10 to binary format.

Convert to Binary 00001010

Convert to High Order **1111**0000

Convert to a Decimal 240

Based on this example, the new subnet mask will be 255.255.240.0.

When choosing a subnet mask, you also need to be able to determine the number of hosts and subnets that a given subnet mask will support. For example, the subnet mask of 255.255.255.224 would allow for eight subnets.

You can determine the number of hosts a subnet mask will support by using the following formula:

$2^x$ where $x$ is the number of host bits used for the subnet ID

The subnet ID of 224 requires 3 bits. Using this formula, $2^3$ equals 8 subnets.

The formula used to determine the number of hosts per subnet is $(2^x) - 2$. For this calculation, $x$ equals the number of bits remaining for the host ID. Because 3 bits are being used for the subnet ID, this leaves 5 bits remaining (remember each octet consists of 8 bits). Because $(2^5) - 2$ equals 30, each subnet can have a maximum of 30 hosts. The two host IDs are removed from the calculation because

▶ The first host ID is the same as the network ID and it cannot be used as a host ID.

▶ The last host ID is the broadcast address for that subnet and it cannot be used as a host ID.

If you can remember these formulas, you will be able to determine the number of subnets and hosts that a specific subnet mask will support.

**EXAM ALERT**

Be prepared to perform subnetting calculations on the exam. For example, you might be required to choose the correct subnet mask based on specific subnetting requirements. Make sure you also have the formulas down for determining the number of hosts and subnets a given subnet mask supports.

# Configuring TCP/IP on a Server Computer

IP addresses can be dynamic or static. With static IP addressing, a computer (or other device) is configured to always use the same IP address. With dynamic addressing, the IP address can change periodically and is managed by a centralized network service.

In some cases it is necessary to use static IP addresses. This is often the case with servers on the network. Some of the components that you might install on a server require that the server be configured with a static IP address. For example, during the installation of Active Directory or the domain name system (DNS), a message appears informing you that the server should be configured with a static IP address.

## DHCP IP Address Assignments

If you plan to use DHCP to assign IP addresses to clients, you can leave the default client configuration for TCP/IP as-is. During the installation of Windows Server 2003, the default configuration is to obtain an IP address automatically (that is, pull addresses from a DHCP server). This is also the case with Windows 2000 and Windows XP clients.

---

**NOTE**

Automatic private IP addressing (APIPA) is a feature mainly found in Microsoft operating systems and is not normally used as a method of purposefully assigning IP addresses. It is limited in use because it does not automatically configure additional parameters such as a default gateway or DNS servers. It is designed to be used in single-subnet networks (networks that are not routed). It is also useful if a DHCP server is unavailable. *DHCP clients* can assign themselves an IP address in the range of 169.254.0.1 to 169.254.255.254 with a default Class B subnet mask of 255.255.0.0. APIPA enables clients to still communicate with other computers on the same network segment until an IP address can be obtained from a DHCP server, allowing the machine to fully participate on the network. Usually, if you notice your system has been assigned a 169.254.*x.y* IP address, you can assume that the DHCP client/server communication did not function as expected.

---

## Static IP Addressing

To statically configure IP address parameters, you need to edit the properties of TCP/IP for the network connection.

To statically configure TCP/IP, follow these steps:

1. From the Windows Server 2003 desktop, right-click My Network Places and select Properties from the menu.

2. From the Network Connections window, right-click the network connection for which you want to configure a static IP address, and click Properties.

3. Select Internet Protocol (TCP/IP) and click the Properties button.

4. Select the option Use the Following IP Address (see Figure 2.1). Enter a unique IP address, the subnet mask, the IP address of the default gateway, and the IP address of the primary and secondary DNS servers. Click OK.

**FIGURE 2.1** You can statically configure IP address parameters from the General tab of the TCP/IP Properties dialog box.

# Configuring Advanced Settings

Aside from basic address configuration, you can configure a number of advanced settings for TCP/IP. Clicking the Advanced button shown in Figure 2.1 opens the Advanced TCP/IP Settings window (see Figure 2.2).

From the IP Settings tab shown in Figure 2.2, you can configure additional IP addresses and gateways for the network connection. Additional IP addresses for the interface might need to be configured if the computer is connected to a single network subnet and requires multiple IP addresses to communicate on the network, or if the computer needs to communicate with multiple subnets. Similarly, you can configure multiple default gateways to be used by the connection.

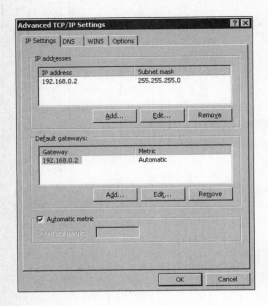

**FIGURE 2.2** You can configure additional TCP/IP settings via the Advanced TCP/IP Settings dialog box.

The metric is used to assign a numeric value for the gateway that is used in routing. The default setting of Automatic Metric assigns a metric value to the gateway based on interface speed. Deselecting the Automatic Metric option enables you to manually configure this value. The gateway with the lowest value is favored.

Selecting the DNS tab shown in Figure 2.3 enables you to configure advanced DNS settings for the network connection if multiple DNS servers are in use on your network. Additional DNS servers can be configured, along with the order in which they are used for name resolution.

You can also select from the following three options to configure name resolution:

▶ *Append Primary and Connection-Specific DNS Suffixes*—This option specifies that name resolution for unqualified names is limited to the primary DNS suffix as well as connection-specific suffixes.

▶ *Append Parent Suffix of the Primary DNS Suffix*—This option specifies whether the parent suffix of the primary DNS suffix is used for name resolution.

▶ *Append These DNS Suffixes*—When this option is selected, the primary and connection-specific suffixes are not used for unqualified name resolution. Instead, unqualified name resolution is limited to the domain suffixes listed in the Append These DNS Suffixes list.

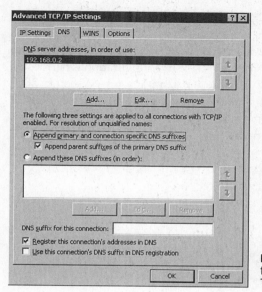

From the bottom of the DNS tab, you can configure the DNS suffix for the connection as well as specify whether the IP address and the connection's DNS suffix should be automatically registered with a DNS server.

**NOTE**

The HOSTS file is manually created and is used to map Internet Protocol (IP) addresses to host names. When a new host is added, the HOSTS file must be updated to reflect the new IP address and host name. The HOSTS file is used when a DNS server is not available.

Using the WINS tab shown in Figure 2.4, you can configure the IP addresses of the WINS servers on the network and specify the order in which they will be used for NetBIOS name resolution. You also can enable LMHOSTS for name resolution.

**NOTE**

DNS is the primary namespace used in a Windows Server 2003 environment. NetBIOS is also supported for backward-compatibility. Windows Internet Name Service (WINS) is used to centralize the process of registering and resolving NetBIOS names to IP addresses. The LMHOSTS file is a static method of resolving NetBIOS names to IP addresses in the same way that the HOSTS file is a static method of resolving domain names into IP addresses. An LMHOSTS file is a text file that maps NetBIOS names to IP addresses; it must be manually configured and updated.

The three options at the bottom of the dialog box enable you to configure additional NetBIOS settings. The first option, Default, should be selected if the NetBIOS settings are assigned through a DHCP server. The remaining two options allow you to enable or disable NetBIOS if IP configuration is performed manually. For example, if the network does not have any pre–Windows 2000 clients and all names are registered with a DNS server, NetBIOS over TCP/IP can be disabled. On the other hand, this option should be enabled if there are legacy clients or services on the network.

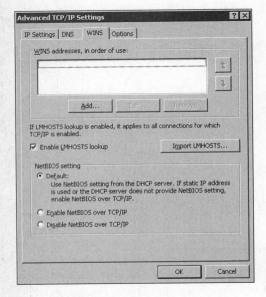

**FIGURE 2.4** You can configure WINS settings from the WINS tab of the Advanced TCP/IP Settings dialog box.

**FIGURE 2.5** You can configure TCP/IP filtering by clicking the Properties button on the Options tab of the Advanced TCP/IP Settings dialog box and adjusting settings on the TCP/IP Filtering dialog box.

The Options tab allows you to enable TCP/IP filtering to control the type of TCP/IP traffic that reaches your computer. Clicking the Properties button on the Options tab opens the TCP/IP filtering window (see Figure 2.5), where you can enable filtering to specify the type of traffic that is permitted based on Transmission Control Protocol (TCP) and User Datagram Protocol (UDP) ports (*ports* are the endpoints for the logical connections), as well as specific IPs.

# Managing DHCP

Every workstation (actually, every device with a network interface card) on an IP network requires a unique IP address and a corresponding subnet mask. The previous section outlined how to manually configure an IP address on Windows Server 2003. The process is very similar for other clients, such as Windows 2000 and Windows XP. Manual assignment is one method for assigning IP addresses, although it might not be suitable for many network environments.

Continuing the earlier illustration of how difficult it could be to manually assign IP addresses, remember the large network with 10,000 users from the introduction. Although it is possible to visit each workstation and manually configure IP addresses, the work does not stop there. Any changes that must be made to IP parameters, such as the addition of a DNS server, will again require you to revisit a number of workstations, if not all of them, to reconfigure the parameters. The more efficient solution is to implement a DHCP server to centralize administration and automate IP address assignment.

To implement this solution on Windows Server 2003 (or another platform such as Windows 2000 Server), the DHCP service must be running and configured. The service can be installed on a domain controller, a member server, or a server that is a member of a workgroup.

Before a DHCP server can be fully functional on a network, the following steps must be completed:

1. The server that will be assigned the role of DHCP server must be configured with a static IP address.

2. The DHCP server component must be installed.

3. The DHCP server must be configured with a range of IP addresses (also known as a *scope*) to be *leased* to DHCP clients. Each DHCP server requires at least one scope, and the scope must be activated.

4. The DHCP server must be authorized within Active Directory.

After all of these steps have been performed, your DHCP server will be capable of leasing IP addresses to DHCP clients. The process of leasing an IP address occurs in the following four phases:

> **TIP**
>
> Acronyms are always a great way to remember information. An easy way to remember the four phases of the IP address lease process is DORA: discover, offer, request, acknowledge.

1. *Discovery*—The DHCP client broadcasts a DHCP discover message on the network containing its MAC address and NetBIOS name. If no DHCP servers respond to the request, the client continues to broadcast up to four times at 2, 4, 8, and 16 seconds. If a response is not received during this time, the client continues to broadcast every five minutes.

2. *Offer*—Each DHCP server on the network that receives the request responds with a DHCP offer message. An offered IP address is included in the message.

3. *Request*—If multiple DHCP servers respond, the client selects the first offer it receives and broadcasts a DHCP request for the IP address. The message is broadcast on the network because the client has not yet been assigned an IP address; it has only been offered one.

4. *Acknowledge*—The DHCP server responds with a DHCPACK (acknowledgment) granting the client's request to use the IP address. The DHCPACK also contains information about any DHCP options that have been configured on the server (such as the IP address of the DNS server).

> **EXAM ALERT**
>
> Remember that if a DHCP server is unavailable or does not respond to any of the first four discovery queries, the DHCP client continues to broadcast the DHCP discover message every five minutes until a DHCP server responds. However, the client assigns itself an IP address in the range of 169.254.0.0 to 169.254.255.255 after the fourth failed discovery queries if APIPA is present. The client can communicate on the network, but only with other clients on the same subnet that also are using an IP address in this range. If clients are running Windows XP, you can use the Alternate Configuration tab from the Internet Protocol (TCP/IP) window to manually configure the automatically assigned IP address and other parameters that should be used if the DHCP server is unavailable.

# Installing DHCP

To automate the process of assigning IP addresses to network clients, the DHCP Server service must be installed on at least one server. The service can be installed in a number of ways. You can opt to install it during the installation of Windows Server 2003, or you can install it later using the Configure Your Server Wizard or through the Add or Remove Programs applet within the Control Panel.

To install DHCP using the Configure Your Server Wizard, perform the following steps:

1. Click Start and click Manage Your Server.

2. Within the Manage Your Server window, select Add or Remove a Role. This launches the Configure Your Server Wizard. Click Next after reviewing the list of preliminary steps that should be completed.

3. Select DHCP server from the list of server roles (see Figure 2.6). Click Next.

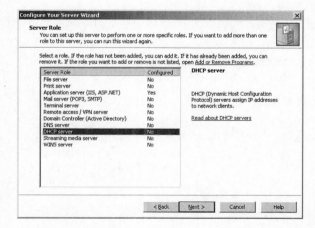

**FIGURE 2.6** You can select a server role through the Configure Your Server Wizard.

4. A summary of selections appears listing the tasks that will be performed. Click Next.

5. After the service has been installed, the New Scope Wizard launches automatically. At this point, you can click Next to configure a scope for the DHCP server or click Cancel. The scope can then be configured later through the DHCP console. The concepts of DHCP scopes are discussed in the following section. Click Finish.

**EXAM ALERT**

Before a DHCP server is fully functional on a network, it must be configured with at least one scope and must be activated. A scope is a range, or pool, of IP addresses that can be leased to DHCP clients by the server when requested. The DHCP server must also be authorized within Active Directory.

To install DHCP using the Add/Remove Programs applet, follow these steps:

1. Click Start, point to Control Panel, and click Add or Remove Programs.

2. Click Add/Remove Windows Components.

3. Click Networking Services in the Components list and click the Details button.

4. Select Dynamic Host Configuration Protocol from the list of Networking Services (see Figure 2.7). Click OK. Click Next to continue.

5. Click Finish.

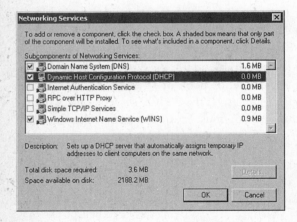

**FIGURE 2.7** You can install DHCP through the Add or Remove Programs applet in the Control Panel.

# Authorizing a DHCP Server

The authorization of DHCP servers was a feature introduced in Windows 2000 and is included with Windows Server 2003. Before a DHCP server that is a member of an Active Directory domain can lease IP addresses to clients on a network, it must be authorized to do so. This prevents a DHCP server with incorrect information from being introduced on the network. For example, a DHCP server with incorrect scope information can't lease providing DHCP clients with incorrect IP parameters. DHCP servers are authorized through the

DHCP management console; this process must be performed by a user who is a member of the Enterprise Admins group.

To authorize a DHCP in Active Directory, follow these steps:

1. Click Start, point to Administrative Tools, and select DHCP.

2. Within the DHCP management console, right-click the DHCP server and click Authorize. Any server not yet authorized appears with a red arrow beside it.

3. After the server has been successfully authorized within Active Directory, it appears with a green arrow beside it.

If a DHCP server needs to be removed from the network—for example, if it has been replaced by another one—you will want to "unauthorize" the server so that it no longer has the capability to lease IP addresses to clients. To do so, right-click the DHCP server within the DHCP console and select the Unauthorize option. Click Yes to confirm your actions. The DHCP server then is removed from Active Directory.

# Creating Scopes

For a DHCP server to provide clients with IP addresses, the server must be configured with a scope. A scope is a range, or pool, of IP addresses that can be leased to DHCP clients on a given subnet. (If the DHCP server services multiple subnets, each with DHCP clients, you must create multiple scopes.)

In addition to IP addresses, a scope can include optional parameters that can be assigned to DHCP clients, including the IP address of DNS servers, WINS servers, and routers. The optional parameters are discussed in the "Managing DHCP Scope Options" section later in this chapter.

Before creating scopes, you should keep the following guidelines in mind:

▶ All DHCP servers on the network require a scope to be active.

▶ Any IP addresses within the scope that should not be leased to DHCP clients must be excluded from the scope. This eliminates the possibility of duplicate IP addresses.

▶ A DHCP server can be configured with multiple scopes.

▶ DHCP servers do not share scope information, meaning that one DHCP server will not know the IP addresses being leased by another DHCP server. With this in mind, make sure the IP addresses in each scope do not overlap, again to eliminate the possibility of duplicate IP addresses.

**EXAM ALERT**

Chances are, you will run into scenarios that include multiple DHCP servers. You can provide redundancy on the network for DHCP servers without the possibility of duplicate IP addresses. To accomplish this, use the *80/20 rule*. That is, 80% of the IP addresses for the local subnet are added to a scope on the local DHCP server, and the remaining 20% of the IP addresses are added to a scope for the same subnet on another DHCP server. In other words, 80% of the IP addresses are from the local subnet, and 20% are from a remote subnet. Because both servers have IP addresses available for the same subnet, clients can always obtain an IP address if one of the servers becomes unavailable (until the scope runs out of available addresses).

After the DHCP component has been installed, you can create scopes from within the DHCP management console. A scope can also be configured when installing DHCP using the Configure Your Server Wizard, as you saw earlier in the chapter. Each scope created consists of the following information:

- A range of IP addresses that can be leased to clients.

- A subnet mask that determines the subnet for the IP address.

- A scope name that appears in the DHCP management console.

- The lease duration, which determines when a DHCP client must renew its IP address.

- Optional parameters, also known as scope options, that need to be assigned to clients, such as the IP address of the DNS server, default gateway, and WINS server.

- Client reservations. If a client requires the same IP address at all times, a client reservation can be configured to ensure that it always leases the same IP address. This is done by mapping an IP address from a scope to the MAC address of the client's NIC.

To create a new scope using the DHCP management console, perform the following steps:

1. Click Start, point to Administrative Tools, and click DHCP.

2. Within the DHCP management console, right-click your DHCP server and click the New Scope option. This launches the New Scope Wizard. Click Next to continue.

3. Type in a name and description for the scope that will make it easily identifiable within the management console. Click Next.

4. Enter the range of IP addresses for the scope (see Figure 2.8). Verify the length and subnet mask.

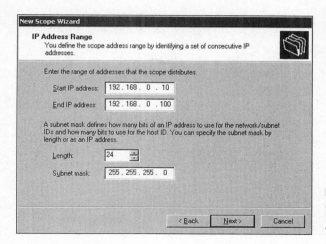

**FIGURE 2.8** The first step in configuring a scope is entering the range of IP addresses to use.

5. Configure any IP addresses that should be excluded from the scope (see Figure 2.9), and then click the Add button. Click Next.

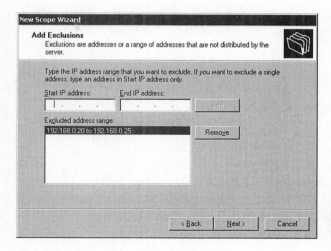

**FIGURE 2.9** You can exclude addresses from the scope via the Add Exclusions screen.

6. Next, configure the lease duration for the scope (see Figure 2.10). The lease duration determines the length of time a client can use an IP address before it must be renewed. The default value is eight days. Click Next.

7. At this point, you can configure additional parameters to assign to DHCP clients. Select No, I Will Configure These Options Later. Click Next. The scope options are discussed later in the chapter.

8. Click Finish.

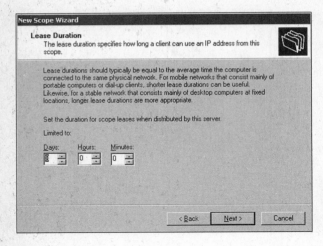

**FIGURE 2.10** You can configure the lease duration for a scope in days, hours, and minutes.

The new scope now appears under the DHCP server within the management console. Before the DHCP server can lease IP addresses from the scope, however, it must be activated. To do so, right-click the new scope and click Activate.

## Superscopes

Aside from a regular scope, you can create a second type of scope known as a *superscope*. In a multinetted environment (one that has multiple logical IP subnets defined on a single physical network), superscopes allow a DHCP server to assign leases to clients on multiple subnets.

For example, a physical network is divided into two subnets, Subnet A and Subnet B, connected by a router. Subnet B contains two multinets. A single DHCP server is located on Subnet A. The DHCP server contains a single scope with a range of IP addresses to lease to clients on Subnet A. To have the DHCP assign IP addresses to clients on Subnet B, you can create a superscope and add to it the IP address ranges for the multinets on Subnet B. The scope configuration on the DHCP server could be similar to the following:

**Subnet A:**

Scope 1: 192.168.1.2 to 192.168.1.254

**Subnet B:**

Superscope for Subnet B:

Scope 2: 192.168.2.2 to 192.168.2.254

Scope 3: 192.168.3.2 to 192.168.3.254

One of the biggest advantages of creating superscopes is to ease the administration in a multinetted environment. It can be difficult in terms of administration to identify which scopes go with which networks. Creating superscopes and grouping scopes in some logical manner can make them easier to administer. For example, you might group all the scopes from a single floor in a large office building into a superscope.

To create a new superscope within the DHCP management console, perform the following steps:

1. Right-click the DHCP server from within the DHCP management console and select the New Superscope option from the menu. This launches the New Superscope Wizard. Click Next.

2. Type in a descriptive name for the superscope (something that makes it easy to identify). This is the name that will appear within the DHCP management console. Click Next.

3. From the list of available scopes, select the ones to include in the superscope (see Figure 2.11). Keep in mind that you can add only active scopes. Click Next.

4. Click Finish.

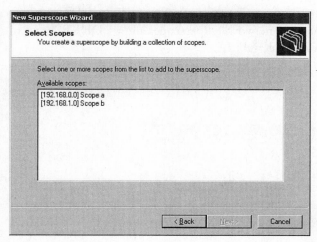

**FIGURE 2.11** You can create a superscope through the DHCP management console.

## Multicast Scopes

*Multicasting* is the process of sending a message to a group of recipients, as opposed to *unicasting*, in which a message is sent to a specific recipient.

Normally, DHCP is used to assign each DHCP client a single unique IP address from a range of IP addresses configured in a scope. Windows Server 2003 extends the functionality to enable you to create multicast scopes so that messages destined to a multicast IP address can be sent to all clients in a multicast group.

Multicast scopes are supported through a protocol known as the Multicast Address Dynamic Client Allocation Protocol (MADCAP). MADCAP controls how the DHCP servers dynamically assign IP addresses on a TCP/IP network.

The multicast server (in this case, the DHCP server) is configured with a group of Class D IP addresses (in the range of 224.0.0.0 to 239.255.255.255) that can be assigned to multicast clients. The server is also responsible for maintaining the group membership list and updating the list as members join and leave a group.

Before a client can obtain a multicast IP address, they must first be assigned a standard (unicast) IP address. This means the client will receive a normal network address as well as a multicast address.

To create a multicast scope, perform the following steps:

1. Within the DHCP management console, right-click the DHCP server and choose the New Multicast Scope option. This launches the New Multicast Scope Wizard. Click Next.

2. Type in a name and description for the scope. Click Next.

3. Specify a range of IP addresses and a TTL (see Figure 2.12). Click Next.

**FIGURE 2.12** You can configure a multicast scope by specifying a range of Class D IP addresses.

4. Type in any IP addresses that you want to exclude from the range. Click Next.

5. Specify a lease duration that defines how long a client can lease a multi-cast address from the scope. The default is 30 days. Click Next.

6. Click Yes to activate the scope. Click Next.

7. Click Finish.

# Configuring DHCP for DNS Integration

Pre–Windows 2000 operating systems use NetBIOS names to identify clients and servers on the network and the different services they are running. These names can be resolved to IP addresses using a WINS server or an LMHOSTS file. Because the WINS database is dynamic, meaning that clients dynamically register their NetBIOS name and IP addresses, integrating DHCP and WINS on a network is simple. The DNS database is static on a Windows NT network, so implementing DHCP and DNS requires the use of a WINS Server.

Windows 2000 and Windows Server 2003 primarily use DNS. DNS is required to locate clients, servers, and services on the network. Traditionally, administrators had to manually enter host records into the DNS database. To overcome this and allow DHCP and DNS to be integrated on a network without the use of a WINS, Windows 2000, Windows XP, and Windows Server 2003 workstations configured as DHCP clients can be automatically registered in the DNS database. These clients can automatically update their own A records (the records mapping their hostnames to their IP addresses), and the DHCP server updates the PTR records (the records that map the IP address to the hostname for reverse lookups). You can change the default behavior by configuring the properties of the DHCP server (as you will see later in the chapter).

## DHCP Clients

The workstation platform determines how the client interacts with the DHCP and DNS servers. Clients running Windows 2000 and later can send update requests directly to a DNS server to update their own pointer and address records, or the client can request that the DHCP server make the update on its behalf.

Clients running platforms earlier than Windows 2000 do not support dynamic DNS updates and cannot interact directly with a DNS server. In this case, when a pre–Windows 2000 client or a non-Microsoft client receives an IP address from a DHCP server, the DHCP server can be configured to perform the DNS updates on behalf of these clients.

**EXAM ALERT**

> Be sure you know which clients support dynamic DNS and how to configure DHCP for those clients that cannot update their own records. Remember that, by default, Windows 2000 and Windows XP clients register their own A records, and the DHCP server registers their PTR records.

## Configuring DHCP/DNS Integration

To configure DHCP for DNS integration, right-click the DHCP server within the management console and choose Properties. If you select the DNS tab, you'll see a window similar to the one shown in Figure 2.13.

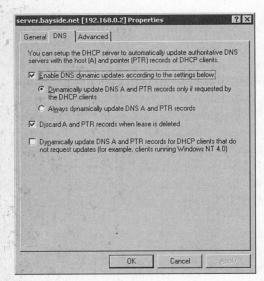

**FIGURE 2.13** You configure DHCP integration with DNS via the DHCP management console.

Here are the settings that can be configured for DHCP integration with DNS:

▶ *Enable DNS Dynamic Updates According to the Settings Below*—This option is selected by default. Deselecting this option means that the DHCP server will not perform any dynamic updates.

▶ *Dynamically Update DNS A and PTR Records Only If Requested by the DHCP Clients*—This option is selected by default. Selecting this option means that the DHCP server will perform the updates if requested to do so by the client.

▶ *Always Dynamically Update DNS A and PTR Records*—Selecting this option means that the DHCP server always updates DNS A and PTR records on behalf of DHCP clients.

▶ *Discard A and PTR Records When the Lease Is Deleted*—This option specifies whether the DHCP server should discard the records when a DHCP client lease expires.

▶ *Dynamically Update DNS A and PTR Records for DHCP Clients That Do Not Request Updates (for example, clients running Windows NT 4.0)*—Select this option if there are clients on the network that do not support dynamic updates, such as clients running Windows NT 4.0. In such cases, the DHCP server performs the updates on behalf of the client.

If you select the Advanced tab, you have the option of configuring the dynamic update registration credentials that can be used by the DHCP server when updating the DNS records. One of the reasons for doing this is to protect against unsecure updates to the DNS database. After you've created a dedicated user account, you can select the Credentials button and type in the username and password. These are the credentials that the DHCP server uses when registering names on behalf of DHCP clients.

Dynamic update credentials must be configured in the following situations:

▶ If the DHCP service is running on a domain controller. Because the DHCP server inherits the power of the domain controller, it has the capability to delete and update any records within the DNS database. By configuring dynamic update credentials, you can limit the power of the DHCP server.

▶ If the DHCP server has been configured to perform dynamic updates on behalf of DHCP clients.

▶ If the zone for which the DHCP server will be performing updates is configured only for secure updates.

# Managing DHCP Clients and Leases

Each DHCP scope is configured with a lease duration. This specifies how long a DHCP client can use an IP address before it must be renewed by a DHCP server. By default, this value is set to eight days. However, you might want to change this depending on the number of IP addresses available as compared to the number of DHCP clients.

The lease duration can be customized to meet the requirements of your network. If the number of IP addresses exceeds the number of DHCP clients on the network, you can configure a longer lease duration. However, if the number of IP addresses available in the scope is comparable to the number of DHCP-enabled clients, you should configure a shorter lease duration. Also, if your network consists of a number of mobile users who move between subnets, consider creating a shorter lease time. By shortening the lease duration, you might also see a slight increase in network traffic because IP addresses are being renewed at a more frequent interval.

As you saw earlier in the chapter, the lease duration for a scope can be configured when the scope is created. You can also change the lease duration at any time afterward through the DHCP management console. Simply right-click the scope, click Properties, and edit the lease duration (see Figure 2.14).

**FIGURE 2.14** You can reconfigure the lease duration for an active scope via its Properties page.

The renewal process between a DHCP client and a DHCP server begins after 50% of the configured lease duration expires. At this time, the client attempts to contact the original DHCP server that issued the lease. A DHCPRequest message is broadcast by the client requesting to renew the IP address with which it's currently configured. If the DHCP server is available, it responds with a DHCPACK, granting the client's request to renew the IP address.

If the client does not receive a response from the original DHCP server by the time 87.5% of the lease duration has expired, then it seeks out any available DHCP server with a broadcast request. If any DHCP server is available, the request for renewal is usually granted. If not, the client continues to use the IP address until the lease duration expires. When it does, the IP address lease process described earlier in the chapter must be repeated.

### Viewing Lease Information

As a DHCP server leases an IP address to DHCP clients, the management console provides administrators with an easy way of viewing lease information. The Active Leases container listed under the DHCP server lists all the IP addresses currently leased to clients. From here, you can also delete or cancel a lease, forcing a client to acquire a new IP address. To do so, right-click any of the active leases within the Active Leases container and click Delete.

### Verifying, Renewing, and Releasing IP Addresses

The IPCONFIG command-line utility can be used to verify IP parameters as well as release and renew an IP address that has been assigned by a DHCP server.

The `IPCONFIG /ALL` command can be used to view detailed information about the IP parameters of a TCP/IP host. It returns information such as the IP address assigned to the client, the subnet mask, the optional parameters (including the IP address of any DNS servers), and the DHCP server from which the client is leasing the IP address.

Although a client eventually releases and renews the IP address that it has been assigned from a DHCP server on its own, this can be done manually as well. Using the `IPCONFIG /RELEASE` command followed by the `IPCONFIG /RENEW` command manually releases and renews a DHCP client lease.

# Managing a DHCP Database

The *DHCP database* stores information about client leases. There is no limit to the number of entries that a single database can hold. Little management is associated with maintaining the database. For example, Windows Server 2003 automatically compacts the database to reclaim unused space, although it can also be performed manually by an administrator. The following sections look at some of the management tasks that an administrator might need or want to perform manually.

## Backing Up and Restoring a DHCP Database

Backups are an integral part of most administrators' jobs. If you are using DHCP on a network, the DHCP database should also be included in the backup routine, in case the database becomes corrupt or fails.

The DHCP database is automatically backed up every 60 minutes by default. You can also perform manual backups using the Backup option within the DHCP management console or by using the Windows Backup program (NTBackup.exe).

> **TIP**
>
> The default interval at which the database is automatically backed up can be changed by editing the value of the BackupInterval entry found under the HKEY_LOCAL_ MACHINE\SYSTEM\CurrentControlSet\Services\DHCPServer\Parameters Registry key.

During an automatic or manual backup of the DHCP database, the following information is backed up:

► Client reservations

► Any configured scopes, including superscopes and multicast scopes

► DHCP options

► IP address leases

► Any Registry information pertaining to the configuration of DHCP

To back up the DHCP database using the management console, perform the following steps:

1. Click Start, point to Administrative Tools, and click DHCP.

2. Select the DHCP server that you want to back up. From the Action menu, click Backup.

3. Browse to the folder where the backed-up files should be placed (see Figure 2.15). The default location is systemroot\system32\DHCP\ Backup. Click OK.

> **NOTE**
>
> When you back up the DHCP database using the Backup option within the management console, you must back up to a local drive. To back up to a nonlocal drive, you must use the Windows Backup program.

**FIGURE 2.15** You can choose a location for the DHCP backup files via the management console.

If the DHCP database needs to be restored, you can do so through the management console using the Restore option. To do so, select the appropriate server within the DHCP console and choose Restore from the Action menu. Browse to the location containing the database backup. After you click OK, a message appears informing you that the service must be stopped and restarted for the operation to complete. Click Yes to restore the database.

## Moving the DHCP Database

You can move the DHCP database from one DHCP server to another using the Backup and Restore options within the DHCP management console. To move the database, begin by performing a backup using the process outlined in the previous section. When the backup is complete, stop the DHCP service using the Services applet in the Control Panel. This ensures that the DHCP server does not continue to lease IP addresses to clients after the second server starts leasing the same addresses. The folder containing the backup of the database can then be copied to the destination DHCP server. You can use the Restore option to restore the database on the new DHCP server.

**NOTE**

To back up and restore the DHCP database, you must be a member of the DHCP Administrators group, the Backup Operators group, or the Administrators group. To move the database, you must belong to the appropriate groups on both servers.

# Managing DHCP Scope Options

After a scope has been created, you can configure several DHCP options. The options can be configured at one of the following four levels:

- ▶ Server
- ▶ Scope
- ▶ Class
- ▶ Client

Options configured at the server level are applied to all DHCP clients, regardless of the subnet on which they reside. Any options that should be applied to all DHCP clients should be configured at this level. For example, to configure all clients on the network to use the same DNS server, you can configure the option at the server level. Keep in mind that when you are configuring scope options, any options configured at the scope or client levels override those configured at the server level. To configure server-level options, right-click the Server Options container listed under the DHCP server and select Set Predefined Options from the menu.

If you want to configure DHCP options so that they apply only to DHCP clients on a specific subnet, configure the options at the scope level. For example, the IP address of the default gateway for a subnet should be configured at the scope level. Configuring scope-level options can be done by right-clicking the Scope Options container and selecting Configure Options from the menu.

Finally, if you want to apply DHCP options to only a specific DHCP client, you can configure the options at the client level. You can configure options at this level only for clients that have a client reservation, meaning that they are DHCP clients but always lease the same IP address. Any option that you configure at this level overrides any configured at the server and scope levels. To configure a client-level option, right-click the client reservation and select Configure Options.

Windows Server 2003 also allows DHCP options to be applied to groups of users or workstations with similar needs. User-class options can be used to assign options to DHCP clients that have common needs for similar DHCP configurations. For example, a user class can be used to configure options for mobile users. Vendor-class options can be used to assign DHCP options on the basis of vendor information. For example, specific options can be assigned to clients running a specific version of Windows.

**EXAM ALERT**

Be sure you are familiar with the order in which scope options are applied. The order is: server, scope, class, and then client.

Now that you're familiar with how DHCP options can be applied, let's take a look at the different DHCP options that can be assigned to clients.

As previously mentioned, a DHCP server can assign parameters other than just an IP address and subnet mask to a DHCP client. A number of different options can be configured, some of which are shown in Figure 2.16. To access the Server Options dialog box, highlight Server Options in the left pane of the DHCP management console and select Configure Options from the Action menu.

**FIGURE 2.16** Additional DHCP options that can be assigned to DHCP clients.

The following list provides a description of the commonly used DHCP options:

▶ *006 DNS Servers*—Specifies the IP address of the DNS servers available to clients on the network.

▶ *015 DNS Domain Name*—Specifies the DNS domain name used for client resolutions.

▶ *003 Router*—Specifies the IP address of the router or default gateway.

▶ *044 WINS/NBNS Servers*—Specifies the IP address of the WINS servers on the network available to clients.

- *046 WINS/NBT Node Type*—Specifies the name resolution type. The available options include 1 = B-node (broadcast), 2 = P-node (peer), 4 = M-node (mixed), and 8 = H-node (hybrid).

- *240 Classless Static Routes*—Specifies a list of static routes, including the destination network IP address, the subnet mask, and the router that is responsible for forwarding messages to that network.

Most of the options outlined in the preceding list can also be configured locally on the client. By doing so, any options configured on the DHCP server will be overwritten by those configured locally. If you are using DHCP, however, it would not make sense to configure the options locally as well, especially in terms of administrative overhead.

# Managing Reservations and Reserved Clients

In some instances, a workstation on the network requires a permanent IP address, but you still want that workstation to be a DHCP client. With a client reservation, the workstation can still be DHCP-enabled, but the DHCP server always assigns the client the same IP address. In terms of administration, the client network configuration settings remain the same, IP addressing remains centralized, and the clients can still be assigned optional parameters through the DHCP server.

> **NOTE**
>
> If multiple DHCP servers are configured with a range of IP addresses that cover the range of the reserved addresses, the client reservation must be duplicated on all DHCP servers. If not, the client might end up receiving an incorrect IP address (one other than the preferred address that has been reserved for the client on the first DHCP server).

Creating a client reservation is a relatively simple process. Within the DHCP management console, right-click the Reservations container listed under your DHCP server and click the New Reservation option. In the New Reservation dialog box, type in a descriptive name, the IP address to be reserved, and the MAC address of the client that will be assigned the IP address. Then click the Add button and the Close button. The reservation appears in the Reservations container in the DHCP management console.

Each client reservation that is created has a set of properties that can be used to change or configure the reservation. Any client reservations that have been configured appear under the Reservations container. To edit a client reservation, right-click the reservation and select Properties. From the properties window, you can use the General tab to change the information that was provided when the reservation was first configured. The only value that cannot be changed is the IP address. You can configure dynamic updates for the DHCP client via the DNS tab.

# Troubleshooting TCP/IP Addressing

TCP/IP is one of the protocols that requires a certain amount of configuration either on individual clients or centrally on a server. Many issues can arise related to such problems as incorrect IP parameters on a client or a nonresponsive DHCP server. To successfully implement TCP/IP and DHCP on a network, it's important to have a general understanding of some of the common issues that can arise, as well as how to troubleshoot them. The following section discusses some of the more common problems that might be encountered on a TCP/IP network.

## Diagnosing and Resolving Issues Related to Automatic Private IP Addressing

Automatic private IP addressing was introduced in Windows 98. It is enabled by default and is supported by the following clients:

- Windows 98
- Windows Me
- Windows 2000 (all platforms)
- Windows XP
- Windows Server 2003

Clients that support this feature can assign themselves an IP address in the following situations:

- When a DHCP client cannot contact a DHCP server or there is no DHCP server on the network
- When a DHCP client's attempt to renew its IP address leased from a DHCP server fails

In both cases, the client assigns itself an IP address in the range of 169.254.0.1 to 169.254.255.254. You can use the IPCONFIG command-line utility to verify that APIPA is enabled and that an IP address within the specific range has been assigned. Remember that APIPA is enabled by default. However, this feature can be disabled through the Registry. The APIPA settings on XP clients can also be manually adjusted in the network properties to match the addresses used on the local subnet. If you decide to do this, you need to make sure that the address used on the APIPA Settings dialog box is excluded from the DHCP scope, to avoid IP address conflicts.

If your network consists of multiple subnets, clients using APIPA can communicate only with hosts on their local subnet. APIPA does not include optional parameters. Clients assign themselves only an IP address and a subnet mask. Without the IP address of the default gateway and DNS server, communication outside of the local subnet will fail.

# Diagnosing and Resolving Issues Related to Incorrect TCP/IP Configuration

A number of command-line utilities can be used to test and diagnose incorrect TCP/IP configurations. To do so, click Start, All Programs, Accessories, Command Prompt, and type ipconfig (using the /all parameter brings up more detailed configuration information).

The following list outlines some of the common parameters that can be used with the ipconfig command:

- ▶ /all—Displays detailed IP configuration information
- ▶ /release—Releases the IP address for the specified adapter
- ▶ /renew—Renews the IP address for the specified adapter
- ▶ /flushDNS—Purges the entries in the DNS cache
- ▶ /registerDNS—Refreshes all leased IP addresses and reregisters DNS names
- ▶ /displayDNS—Displays the contents of the DNS cache

The PING command-line utility is useful in verifying connectivity with another TCP/IP host. Connectivity on the network is verified by sending Internet Control Message Protocol (ICMP) echo requests and replies. When the PING command is issued, the source computer sends echo request messages to another TCP/IP host. If reachable, the remote host then responds with four echo replies.

> **NOTE**
>
> Windows defaults to sending only four ECHO REQ packets, whereas other operating systems, such as Linux, will continuously send ECHO REQ packets until the command is terminated. You can configure Windows to send pings continuously by editing the Registry or by including a -t when issuing the PING command.

The PING command is also issued at the command prompt along with the TCP/IP address or domain name of the other TCP/IP host, as follows:

```
C:> PING 124.120.105.110
C:> PING www.bayside.net
```

> **TIP**
>
> To determine whether TCP/IP is initialized on the local computer, issue the PING command and specify the loopback address of 127.0.0.1.

The general steps for troubleshooting TCP/IP using the PING command are as follows:

1. PING the loopback address of 127.0.0.1 to ensure that TCP/IP is initialized on the local computer.

2. If successful, PING the IP address assigned to the local computer.

3. Next PING the IP address of the default gateway. If this fails, verify that the IP address of the default gateway is correct and that the gateway is operational.

4. Next PING the IP address of a host on a remote network. If this is unsuccessful, verify that the remote host is operational, verify the IP address of the remote host, and verify that all routers and gateways between the local computer and remote computer are operational.

> **TIP**
>
> A quick way of verifying TCP/IP connectivity is to complete step 4 from the preceding list. If you can successfully PING the IP address of a remote host, steps 1 through 3 will be successful. However, if step 4 fails, you'll need to work through steps 1 through 3 to discover at what point the problem exists.

Two other utilities that can be used for TCP/IP troubleshooting are tracert and pathping. The tracert command determines the route that is taken to a specific destination. You might want to use the tracert command if you are not able to successfully PING the IP address of a remote host. The results of the tracert command indicate whether there is a problem with a router or gateway between the local computer and the remote destination. The pathping command is basically a combination of the PING and tracert commands. When the command is issued, packets are sent to each router between the local computer and a remote computer. The results determine which routers and gateways could be causing problems on the network.

**NOTE**

On non-Windows systems, the tracert command is actually traceroute. They do not use the 8.3 naming convention truncated tracert that most Windows (that is, DOS-based operating systems) command line utilities are limited to.

# Diagnosing and Resolving Issues Related to DHCP Authorization

As mentioned earlier in the chapter, a DHCP server must be authorized within Active Directory before it can begin leasing IP addresses to clients. Again, the purpose of this is to eliminate the possibility that a DHCP server is mistakenly or maliciously introduced onto a network, especially if it has been misconfigured.

Authorizing a DHCP server is a relatively simple process. If you are unable to authorize a DHCP server, verify that the user account you are logged on has the required permissions. Only members of the Enterprise Admins group are permitted to perform this operation.

Multiple DHCP servers can exist on a network. However, you might encounter problems if you have a DHCP server configured as a standalone server and a DHCP server configured as a member server on the same subnet. When the standalone server detects the second DHCP server, it attempts to verify with a domain controller that it is authorized. Because the standalone server is not a member of the domain, it will fail to contact a domain controller and stop servicing DHCP client requests. To resolve the problem, the authorized DHCP server must be removed from the subnet.

# Verifying DHCP Reservation Configuration

As previously mentioned, client reservations are created so that certain DHCP clients can always be assigned the same IP address from a DHCP server. When you create the reservation, you specify the IP address to be leased and the MAC address of the DHCP client. If you find that a client for which a reservation has been configured is receiving a different IP address than intended, verify the configuration of the client reservation. To do so, right-click the appropriate client reservation within the Reservations container in the DHCP console and click Properties. From the Properties window, verify that you have correctly entered the MAC address of the DHCP client.

Keep in mind that DHCP servers do not share information. If there are multiple DHCP servers on the network, the client reservation must be configured on each one. This way, if one DHCP server is unavailable, the client can still be assigned the same IP address from another DHCP server.

# Conflict Detection

Conflict detection can be enabled on a DHCP server to reduce the chances of two clients being assigned the same IP address. When this feature is enabled, the DHCP server will use the ping process to test the availability of IP addresses before offering them to DHCP clients.

Before the DHCP server offers an IP address lease to a client, it will attempt to ping the IP address. If the DHCP server receives a successful response, the IP address is already in use on the network and the address will not be offered in a lease to a client. If the ping fails and times out, the IP address is available and the DHCP server proceeds to offer the address to lease.

To enable conflict detection:

1. Open the DHCP console.

2. Right-click your DHCP server and click Properties.

3. Select the Advanced tab.

4. In the Conflict detection attempts field, type in a number greater than 0 and less than 6. This determines how many times the DHCP server will attempt to ping an IP address before offering it as a lease.

5. Click OK.

# Examining the System Event Log and DHCP Server Audit Log to Find Related Events

Log files can provide administrators with valuable information when it comes to troubleshooting. You can use the system log within the Event Viewer to monitor and troubleshoot DHCP-related events. When an event occurs, such as the DHCP Server service being restarted, it is written to the log file and provides useful information, including a description of the event and when it occurred.

Windows Server 2003 also supports audit logging of the DHCP service. By default, the audit logs are stored in the %system%\system32\DHCP directory. Audit logging for a DHCP server can be enabled by right-clicking the appropriate DHCP server within the management console and selecting Properties. Using the General tab, auditing logging can be enabled or disabled. The default location of the audit logs can be changed by clicking the Advanced tab and editing the Audit log file path.

As events occur, they are written to a log file. Entries in the log contain an event ID, the date and time that the event occurred, as well as the IP address, hostname, and MAC address of the workstation that generated the event. Some of the common audit codes are as follows:

▶ *00*—The log was started.

▶ *01*—The log was stopped.

▶ *02*—The log was temporarily paused due to low disk space.

▶ *10*—A new IP address was leased to a client.

▶ *11*—A client renewed an existing lease.

▶ *12*—A client released an IP address.

▶ *13*—An IP address was found in use on the network.

▶ *14*—A client cannot lease an IP address because the address pool is exhausted.

▶ *15*—A lease request was denied.

▶ *30*—A DNS dynamic update request occurred.

▶ *31*—The DNS dynamic update failed.

▶ *32*—The DNS dynamic update was successful.

▶ *55*—The DHCP server was authorized to start on the network.

▶ *56*—The DHCP server was not authorized to start on the network.

> **NOTE**
>
> Do not limit your investigations of problems to just the DHCP's log files. Be sure to review the system, security, and application logs for related issues about the environment as a whole or the DHCP process itself that are not recorded by the DHCP server's internal audit system.

# Diagnosing and Resolving Issues Related to Configuration of DHCP Server and Scope Options

Scope options can be configured at different levels. The level at which scope options are configured determines which DHCP clients are affected. For example, configuring an option at the server level affects all clients, regardless of the IP subnet on which they reside.

One of the most common problems that can occur with DHCP options is that clients end up being assigned incorrect parameters. In such cases, you must verify the level at which the option has been configured. For example, configuring the router option at the server level when the network consists of multiple subnets results in some DHCP clients being configured with an incorrect gateway. In this case, the option needs to be configured at the scope level instead of the server level.

# Verifying Database Integrity

The Reconcile All Scopes option is useful when you need to fix any inconsistencies in the DHCP database, such as when not all IP address leases are being reflected in the DHCP database. Information in the database is compared with information stored in the Registry.

Selecting the Reconcile All Scopes option opens the Reconcile All Scopes dialog box. Click the Verify button to check the database for inconsistencies. Any errors are displayed.

# Compacting the DHCP Database

The DHCP database is automatically compacted. If there are Jet errors listed in Event Viewer or if the DHCP server is heavily used, you can manually compact the database using `Jetpack.exe`.

You can compact the DHCP database using the following steps:

1. Stop the DHCP Server service.

2. Open the command prompt and switch to the directory containing the DHCP database.

3. Type the following command: `jetpack.exe dhcp.mdb temp.mdb`

4. Restart the DHCP Server service.

# Exam Prep Questions

1. A DHCP server is running on your network. The range of IP addresses within the scope far exceeds the number of DHCP clients on the network. However, you notice that the number of IP address lease requests is very high. You need to determine the cause of the problem. What should you do first?

   ○ **A.** Check the Event Viewer for any DHCP-related messages.

   ○ **B.** Verify that the lease duration isn't configured with a low value.

   ○ **C.** Run System Monitor to view the performance of the server.

   ○ **D.** Run Network Monitor to capture DHCP-related traffic.

2. Your network consists of two subnets: SubnetA and SubnetB. Each subnet has its own DHCP server. You configure a scope on DHCP1 for SubnetA. Users are leasing a valid IP address but report that they cannot access any resources outside of their own subnet. How can you most easily solve the problem?

   ○ **A.** Activate the scope on DHCP1.

   ○ **B.** Configure the default gateway on each workstation.

   ○ **C.** Configure the 003 router option on DHCP1.

   ○ **D.** Configure the 006 DNS server option on DHCP1.

3. You recently installed the DHCP Server service on one of your member servers in the domain. You notice that the DHCP service is constantly being shut down and the server cannot lease IP addresses to DHCP clients. What is causing the problem to occur?

   ○ **A.** The DHCP server has not been configured with a scope.

   ○ **B.** The scope on the DHCP server has not been activated.

   ○ **C.** The DHCP server has not been authorized within Active Directory.

   ○ **D.** There is a DHCP server on the network with a duplicate scope.

4. You are the network administrator for your company. Servers are running Microsoft Windows Server 2003. Client computers are running Windows XP Professional.

   A DHCP server is used to assign IP addresses to clients and member servers on the network. Three of the member servers are configured as file servers. You need to ensure that these file servers lease the same IP address from the DHCP server. What should you do?

   ○ **A.** Exclude the IP addresses from the scope.

   ○ **B.** Create a separate scope for each of the file servers.

○  **C.** Create a client reservation for each file server.

○  **D.** Configure the DHCP options for the scope.

5. You are the network administrator for your organization. Servers are running Microsoft Windows Server 2003. Client computers are running Microsoft Windows XP Professional.

    You have recently deployed a DHCP server to centralize the administration of all IP addresses on the network. Before this, IP addresses were all manually configured. All users are successfully leasing IP addresses, but they now report that they can no longer print to the network interface printers. Upon examining the printers' properties, you notice they have been assigned incorrect IP addresses. What should you have done?

    ○  **A.** Defined separate scopes for each of the print devices

    ○  **B.** Created client reservations for the print devices

    ○  **C.** Excluded the IP addresses of the print devices from the scope

    ○  **D.** Created client exclusions for the print devices

6. Your network consists of multiple subnets connected by routers. You have finished installing a Windows Server 2003 DHCP server. You create the necessary scopes and configure the 003 router option to assign all clients the IP address of their local router. All clients successfully lease an IP address. However, you soon discover that users on Subnet A are the only ones capable of communicating outside their local subnet. What could be causing the problem?

    ○  **A.** All the scopes have not yet been activated.

    ○  **B.** The DHCP option is configured at the server level.

    ○  **C.** The DHCP server has not yet been authorized.

    ○  **D.** The 003 router option must first be activated.

7. You are the network administrator for your company. All servers are running Microsoft Windows Server 2003. Client computers are running Microsoft XP Professional.

    Several DHCP servers are being deployed in different domains throughout the forest. You want give another administrator the ability to authorize the DHCP servers. What should you do?

    ○  **A.** Add the user to the DNSUpdateProxy group.

    ○  **B.** Add the user to the Enterprise Admins group.

    ○  **C.** Add the user to the Domain Admins group.

    ○  **D.** Add the user to the local Administrators group on each DHCP server.

**8.** You are a junior network administrator. One of your tasks is to maintain a newly installed DHCP server. The scopes have not yet been created. The senior administrator documents all the required scopes and asks you to create them on the server. You notice that several DHCP options are to be configured, but it is not specified what type of scope options to configure. You are trying to recall how scope options are applied. Which of the following correctly lists the order in which they are applied to clients?

   ○  **A.** Server, scope, class, client

   ○  **B.** Server, class, scope, client

   ○  **C.** Server, scope, client, class

   ○  **D.** Scope, server, client, class

**9.** You are the network administrator for your organization. The DHCP servers are running Microsoft Windows Server 2003.

Your network supports three UNIX servers that provide name-resolution services. You have manually configured these three servers with IP addresses. All other member servers and client computers are DHCP clients. You want to avoid any IP address conflicts on the network. What should you do?

   ○  **A.** Configure client reservations for the three UNIX servers.

   ○  **B.** Exclude the three IP addresses from the scope.

   ○  **C.** Place the UNIX servers on a separate subnet.

   ○  **D.** Create a superscope for the three IP addresses.

**10.** You are the network administrator for your company. Servers are running Microsoft Windows Server 2003. Client computers have been upgraded to Windows XP Professional.

The network is divided into two subents. Each subnet hosts a DHCP server. You want to increase the fault tolerance so clients can obtain an IP address even if the local DHCP server is unavailable. What should you do?

   ○  **A.** Configure replication to occur between the two DHCP servers.

   ○  **B.** Nothing needs to be done because DHCP servers on the same network share scope information to provide fault tolerance.

   ○  **C.** Configure each server with a range of IP addresses for both subnets.

   ○  **D.** Configure all clients with the IP address of both DHCP servers.

**11.** You are the network administrator for your company. Servers are running Microsoft Windows Server 2003. Client computers have been upgraded to Windows XP Professional.

You are planning the subnet configuration for the network. The network currently needs to support 12 subnets with 12 hosts per subnet. The number of subnets is expected to reach 16 within the next year. You need to choose a subnet mask that will support this configuration. What should you do?

○ **A.** Use a subnet mask of 255.255.255.192.

○ **B.** Use a subnet mask of 255.255.255.224.

○ **C.** Use a subnet mask of 255.255.255.240.

○ **D.** Use a subnet mask of 255.255.255.248

**12.** You are the network administrator for a medium-sized company. The company is in the process of upgrading the existing network infrastructure. Servers are now running Microsoft Windows Server 2003. Client computers are still running Microsoft Windows 95 and configured with static IP addresses.

You have been instructed to implement dynamic IP addressing. You install Dynamic Host Configuration Protocol on a Windows Server 2003 server. The server is authorized and a scope is created and activated. Most of the client computers are configured for dynamic IP addressing.

You soon receive reports from a few users that there are IP address conflicts on the network. You do not know the specific IP addresses within the scope range that are still used for static IP addressing. You need to resolve the problem as quickly as possible.

What should you do?

○ **A.** Increase the number of conflict detection attempts.

○ **B.** Exclude the IP address from the DHCP scope.

○ **C.** Create a client reservation for the client computers with static IP addresses.

○ **D.** Change the start and end IP addresses for the scope.

# Answers to Exam Prep Questions

**1. B.** The first thing that should be verified is that a shorter lease duration has not been configured. Because the number of IP addresses exceeds the number of DHCP clients, the lease duration can be increased. After that has been verified, you can begin using the other tools to troubleshoot the problem if it continues. Therefore answers A, C, and D are incorrect. After you have verified that the lease duration is properly configured, you can choose to follow up using one of the other options.

2. **C.** If clients have not been configured with the IP address of the default gateway, they cannot access resources outside of their local subnet. Answer A is incorrect because the clients are already successfully leasing IP addresses from the server. Answer B would solve the problem but would not be the easiest solution; therefore, it is also incorrect. Answer D is incorrect because configuring the DNS server option allows clients to resolve hostnames but doesn't give them access outside of the local subnet.

3. **C.** If a DHCP server has not been authorized within Active Directory, it is considered to be a rogue server and the service will continue to shut down until it is authorized by a member of the Enterprise Admins group. Answers A, B, and D are incorrect because none of these problems would cause the DHCP service to shut down.

4. **C.** By creating a client reservation for each of the member servers, you ensure that they will always lease the same IP address from the DHCP server. Therefore, answers A, B, and D are incorrect.

5. **B.** To ensure that the IP address of the network interface printers did not change when the DHCP server was placed on the network, client reservation should have been defined. Answer A is incorrect because defining additional scopes does not address the problem. Answer C is incorrect because excluding the IP addresses means that the DHCP server will never offer them to DHCP clients. Answer D is incorrect because there is no such option in DHCP called a client exclusion.

6. **B.** Each subnet will have its own gateway, so the 003 router option should be configured at the scope level instead of the server level. Answers A and C are incorrect because all clients are successfully leasing IP addresses. Answer D is incorrect because DHCP options do not have to be activated.

7. **B.** To authorize DHCP servers throughout the forest, the user account that you log on with must be a member of the Enterprise Admins group. Therefore, answers A, C, and D are incorrect.

8. **A.** The correct order in which DHCP options are applied is server, scope, class, and then client. Therefore, answers B, C, and D are incorrect.

9. **B.** To ensure that the IP addresses of the UNIX servers are not leased to any DHCP clients, exclude the three IP addresses from the scope. Answer A is incorrect because client reservations are configured for the DHCP clients that need to lease the same IP address. Answer C is incorrect because placing the UNIX servers on a different subnet will have no affect on the IP addresses leased by the DHCP server. Answer D is incorrect because superscopes are created to support multinetted environments.

10. **C.** By configuring each DHCP server with a range of IP addresses from the remote subnet, you can provide some level of fault tolerance. Each server should be configured with 80% of the IP address for the local subnet and 20% of the IP address for the remote subnet, to avoid IP address conflicts. Answers A and B are incorrect because DHCP servers do not replicate, nor do they share scope information. Answer D is incorrect because clients are not configured with the IP address of DHCP servers.

11. **C.** The subnet mask of 255.255.255.240 will allow for a maximum amount of 16 subnets. This will meet the requirements for 12 subnets. Answers A and B are incorrect because these subnet masks do not allow for enough subnets. Answer D is incorrect because this subnet mask allows for more subnets that will ever be required. It will also not allow for the required number of hosts per subnet.

12. **A.** You should increase the number of conflict detection attempts. By default this value is set to zero. When this value is increased, the DHCP server will ping an IP address before leasing it to a DHCP client. If the ping is successful, the DHCP server will not lease the IP address. Answer B is incorrect. You should not exclude the static IP addresses from the scope. This would require more administrative effort to identify the static IP addresses and then exclude them from the scope. Answer C is incorrect. You should not create client reservations. A client reservation is created when a DHCP client requires the same IP address. The DHCP server always leases the same IP addresses to the DHCP client. Answer D is incorrect. You should not alter the range of IP addresses in the scope because you do not know the IP addresses that are still statically configured on client computers.

# Need to Know More?

Search the online version of TechNet and the Windows Server 2003 Resource Kit using keywords such as "DHCP," "IP Addresses," and "Dynamic Updates."

Williams, Robert; Walla, Mark *The Ultimate Windows Server 2003 System Administrator's Guide*. Addison-Wesley Professional, 2003. ISBN: 0201791064.

Habraken, Joe. *Sams Teach Yourself Microsoft Windows Server 2003 in 24 Hours*. Sams, 2003. ISBN: 0672324946.

Abbate, Andrew; Kovach, Eric; Morimoto, Rand; Roberts, Ed. *Microsoft Windows Server 2003 Insider Solutions*. Sams, 2003. ISBN: 0672326094.

CHAPTER THREE

# Managing Name Resolution

---

## Terms you'll need to understand:

- ✓ Windows Internet Naming Service (WINS)
- ✓ WINS Proxy Agent
- ✓ LMHOSTS
- ✓ Tombstoning
- ✓ Persistent Connections
- ✓ Push/pull partner
- ✓ Hostnames
- ✓ Domain name system (DNS)

- ✓ Recursive and iterative queries
- ✓ Primary, secondary, and stub zones
- ✓ Dynamic update
- ✓ Delegation
- ✓ Caching-only server
- ✓ Root name server
- ✓ Resource records

---

## Techniques you'll need to master:

- ✓ Understanding NetBIOS name resolution methods
- ✓ Installing and configuring WINS
- ✓ Configuring a WINS proxy agent
- ✓ Configuring replication between WINS servers
- ✓ Managing and monitoring a WINS server
- ✓ Installing and configuring the DNS Server service

- ✓ Configuring zones
- ✓ Understanding a caching-only server
- ✓ Understanding DNS zone types
- ✓ Managing zones and resource records
- ✓ Implementing a delegated zone for DNS
- ✓ Monitoring a DNS server

Each machine on a computer network is assigned a unique network address. Computers communicate with one another across networks by connecting to these network addresses. These numbers, also known as Internet Protocol (IP) addresses, consist of four groups of numbers, or octets, and can be difficult for people to remember. To solve this dilemma, a system was developed whereby people can use "friendly" names that are then translated automatically into IP addresses that computers use to locate each other and to communicate. These friendly names are called *hostnames*, and each machine is assigned one. Groups of these hosts form a *domain*. The software that translates these names to network addresses is called the *Domain Name System (DNS)*.

Before the advent of DNS, HOSTS files were used for name resolution, but as the Internet quickly grew in size and popularity, HOSTS files became impossible to maintain and keep current. When the Internet community realized there was a need for a more manageable, scalable, and efficient name-resolution system, DNS was created. Since that time, DNS servers have been used on the Internet almost exclusively.

Before the introduction of Windows 2000, Network Basic Input/Output System (NetBIOS) names were used to identify computers, services, and other resources on Windows-based machines. In the early days of Windows networks, LMHOSTS files were used for NetBIOS name resolution. Later, these names were often resolved to IP addresses using a NetBIOS Name Server (NBNS). Microsoft's version of the NBNS was called Windows Internet Naming Service (WINS). With Windows 2000 and Windows Server 2003, hostnames are used instead of NetBIOS names. In a Windows Server 2003 domain, DNS is used to resolve hostnames and locate resources such as network services.

This chapter introduces the Windows Server 2003 implementation of WINS and DNS. You'll learn how to install and configure both name resolution services, as well as how to maintain and monitor them. Having a thorough understanding of the topics presented here is important to both the exam and on-the-job success.

# Introduction to NetBIOS Name Resolution

Some clients still rely on NetBIOS names to communicate with other hosts on a network. A NetBIOS name is a 16-character name where the first 15 characters identify a unique host and the 16th character identifies a service or application running on the host such as the Workstation or Server service. Table 3.1 outlines common hexadecimal values used to identify services running on a computer.

**TABLE 3.1   Node Types**

| Node Type | Description |
|-----------|-------------|
| <00H> | Registered by the Workstation service |
| <1CH> | Indicates a domain name that can be used to locate domain controllers |
| <06H> | Registered by a computer running Routing and Remote Access |
| <1BH> | Registered by each domain controller functioning as the domain master browser |
| <20H> | Registered by a WINS client running the Server service |
| <21H> | Registered by the RAS client running on a WINS client |

As with domain names, NetBIOS names must be resolved to an IP address before two hosts can communicate. There are a number of different methods available for name resolution and the method employed will depend on the environment.

# Name Resolution Methods

The three standard ways of resolving NetBIOS names to IP addresses are through a local broadcast, using the local cache, or by using a NetBIOS name server.

With a local broadcast, a broadcast is sent out on the network requesting the IP address of a specific host. The obvious disadvantage to this method is the increase in traffic.

All hosts maintain a local cache that can be used for name resolution. Each time a host resolves a NetBIOS name to an IP address, the record is added to the local cache and remains valid for 10 minutes. By default, all clients will check their local cache before using any of the other resolution methods available.

The third option is to use a NetBIOS name server (such as a WINS server) to resolve names to IP addresses.

In a Microsoft environment, several other methods for resolving names are also available such as DNS servers, HOSTS files, and LMHOSTS files.

Depending on the requirements of an environment, clients can be configured to use a single method for name resolution or they can use a combination of methods. The exact method a client uses to resolve NetBIOS names is determined by their node type. For example, if a client is configured as an M-Node, it will attempt to resolve a NetBIOS name by first performing a local broadcast. If this is unsuccessful, it will then try to resolve the name using a NetBIOS name server. You can check the node type a client is configured for by typing `ipconfig/all` at the command prompt. The node type can be changed within the local Registry. Table 3.2 summarizes the four different node types.

> **TIP**
>
> Remember that before performing a broadcast or contacting a WINS server, the host will attempt to resolve a NetBIOS name using its local cache.

> **EXAM ALERT**
>
> Be prepared to encounter exam questions pertaining to the NetBIOS node types. Make sure you are familiar with what methods of resolution are used for each type and in what order.

**TABLE 3.2    Node Types**

| Node Type | Description |
| --- | --- |
| B-Node | A broadcast is used for NetBIOS name registration and resolution. |
| P-Node | A NetBIOS name server is used for name registration and resolution. |
| M-Node | A broadcast is attempted first for name resolution. If this method fails, a NetBIOS name server is contacted. |
| H-Node | A NetBIOS name server is attempted first for name resolution. If this fails a broadcast is used. |

> **EXAM ALERT**
>
> A Windows Server 2003 or Windows XP client that is configured as a DHCP client automatically uses H-Node for NetBIOS name resolution. This means the client will attempt to resolve NetBIOS names using a WINS server first before using a local broadcast (after checking the local cache). The client will resolve names in the following order: local cache, WINS, broadcast, LMHOSTS, HOSTS, DNS.

## LMHOSTS Files

As already mentioned, one of the ways in which NetBIOS names can be resolved is through the use of a text file known as an LMHOSTS file. One of the benefits of using an LMHOSTS file is that entries from the file can be preloaded into the local cache to facilitate name resolution (because this is the method a client will use to resolve a NetBIOS name). So if a client cannot resolve a NetBIOS name using any of the methods described previously, it can parse the LMHOSTS file to see whether a record exists.

> **TIP**
>
> Remember that in order for clients to resolve names using an LMHOSTS file, they must be configured to do so (refer to the section "Configuring WINS Clients" for more information).

The LMHOSTS file can be found in the `%systemroot%\system32\drivers\etc` directory. When configuring records within the file, there are several directives that can be used which are outlined in Table 3.3.

**TABLE 3.3  Predefined Directives That Can Be Used Within an LMHOSTS File**

| Predefined Keyword | Description |
| --- | --- |
| #Pre | Defines which entries within the file should be loaded into the local cache. |
| #DOM:*domain_name* | Indicates the record is for a domain controller. |
| #Begin_Alternate | Specifies a list of other locations for an LMHOSTS file. |
| #End_Alternate | |
| #inlcude | Loads entries from a separate LMHOSTS file separate from the default file on the local computer. This option is most often used to specify a centrally located LMHOSTS file. |
| #MH | Adds multiple entries for a multihomed computer. |

**EXAM ALERT**

Be sure you are familiar with the different directives that can be used within an LMHOSTS file and what their purposes are.

# Introduction to WINS

The Windows Internet Naming Service (WINS) provides a dynamic database to register NetBIOS names and resolve them to IP addresses. Clients can dynamically register their NetBIOS names with a WINS server, and query the WINS server when they need to resolve a NetBIOS name to an IP address.

WINS solves the problem of registering and resolving NetBIOS names in a routed environment. In a nonrouted environment, NetBIOS names can be registered and resolved using local broadcasts. However, in a routed environment this poses a problem because routers are not normally configured to forward broadcasts between subnets.

By using WINS, name registration and renewal requests can be directed to a WINS server, thereby allowing name registration and renewal across subnets.

There are a number of other benefits to implementing a WINS server on the network including the following:

- ▶ It provides a dynamic database for registering NetBIOS names and resolving them to an IP address.

- ▶ It centralizes the management of NetBIOS names to IP addresses and eliminates the need for LMHOSTS files.

- ▶ It reduces the amount of broadcast traffic on the network. Clients can directly query the WINS server for name registration and resolution instead of performing a broadcast.

- ▶ It allows pre–Windows Server 2003 clients to locate domain controllers that are not on their local subnet.

# Installing WINS

WINS is not a service that is installed by default. It can be added afterward through the Add or Remove Programs applet in the Control Panel.

To install WINS:

1. Point to Start, Settings, and click Control Panel.

2. Double-click the Add or Remove Programs applet. Click Add/Remove Windows Components.

3. In the list of components, select Networking Services and click Details.

4. Click Windows Internet Name Service (WINS) and click OK.

# Configuring a WINS Server

You can configure and manage a WINS server through the WINS management console. Click Start, Administrative Tools, and then WINS.

Within the WINS console, right-click the WINS server and click Properties. You can configure several options from the Properties dialog box.

Using the General tab, you can configure how often server statistics are updated (you can also disable this option) and specify a location to back up the WINS database.

From the Intervals tab, the rate at which records are renewed, deleted, and verified can be configured (see Figure 3.1). Table 3.4 summarizes the configurable options.

**FIGURE 3.1** Configuring the rate at which records are renewed, deleted, and verified.

## TABLE 3.4  Zone Property Tabs

| Option | Description |
|---|---|
| Renew Interval | Specifies the number of days before a WINS client must renew its registered NetBIOS name. |
| Extinction Interval | Specifies the amount of time before a record marked as released is marked as extinct. |
| Extinction Timeout | Specifies the amount of time before a record marked as extinct is removed from the WINS database. |
| Verification Interval | Specifies the amount of time before a WINS server must verify any records that have been replicated from a replication partner. |

**NOTE**

The process of deleting records marked as extinct is known as scavenging. Using the Scavenge Database option allows an administrator to manually initiate the scavenging process.

The Database Verification tab enables you to configure when and how often the WINS server should verify the records within its database.

The Advanced tab has several configurable options (see Figure 3.2). You can enable logging so WINS-related events are written to the System Log. Burst Handling can be enabled or disabled, which enables you to configure the number of requests a WINS server can successfully respond to without actually registering the name within the database. You can also specify the location of the WINS database and configure the version number.

**FIGURE 3.2** Configuring Advanced server options.

# WINS Replication

Consider the following scenario: Two subnets exist on a physical network each with its own WINS server. Clients on each subnet register their names with their local WINS server. When a host on subnet A attempts to communicate with a host on subnet B, they will be unable to resolve the name to an IP address. This is due to the fact that the local WINS server will not have an entry in its database for the host on subnet B.

In a WINS environment, replication must be configured between WINS servers to facilitate network communication between hosts on different subnets. WINS servers can be configured as push partners, pull partners, or both depending on how you want replication to occur.

Push partners notify other WINS servers when changes are made to its database, whereas pull partners request database changes from other WINS servers. In order to accomplish one-way replication one of these partnerships (either a push or pull) must be configured.

When considering whether to configure push or pull partners, keep the following points in mind:

- ▶ If WINS servers are connected by slow links, configure a pull partner so replication can be scheduled.

- ▶ If WINS servers are connected by fast links, configure a push partner so replication can occur when changes are made to the database.

# Configuring WINS Replication

WINS servers can be configured for replication using the WINS management console. To configure replication, follow these steps:

1. Within the WINS management console, right-click Replication Partners and select New Replication Partner.

2. Enter the name or IP address of the WINS server you want to add as a replication partner. Click OK.

3. Right-click the WINS server that was added as a replication partner and click Properties.

4. From the Advanced tab within the WINS server's properties window, use the drop-down list to select the replication partner type. Click OK.

If you do not want to manually set up WINS replication partners, you can configure WINS servers to automatically find one another and configure themselves for replication. They do so by multicasting to the IP address of 224.0.1.24. When WINS servers locate each other they automatically configure themselves as push/pull replication partners. This automatic discovery option can be enabled by right-clicking Replication Partners within the WINS management console and clicking Properties. From the Replication Partners Properties window, select the Advanced tab and choose the Enable Automatic Partner Configuration option.

# Forcing Replication

The replication of WINS records between WINS servers normally occurs in any of the following situations:

- ▶ When a WINS server starts up

- ▶ When the number of changes to the database reaches a certain number
- ▶ At specific intervals configured by an administrator

Sometimes, however, you may need to update the WINS database immediately. Within the WINS management console, administrators have the option of forcing replication to occur between WINS partners. To force replication between replication partners, click Replication Partners, right-click the server you want to replicate with, and select either Start Push Replication or Start Pull Replication.

## Persistent Connections

One of the features introduced in Windows 2000 and supported by Windows Server 2003 is persistent connections between WINS replication partners. In previous versions of Windows, WINS servers disconnected from one another when replication was complete. Each time the replication process occurred, a new connection needed to be established requiring more processor cycles. In other words, it's inefficient, especially if the WINS servers are connected with high-speed links. To make the replication process more efficient, administrators could configure replication to occur after a large number of changes occurred to the database, as opposed to having to reestablish a connection for a small number of changes. In any case, replication was slow and it was not uncommon to find inconsistencies in the WINS database.

With persistent connections, WINS servers no longer close connections after replication is complete. Not only does this increase the speed and efficiency of replication, as changes can be sent without having to wait for a connection to be established, but it also makes for more consistency within the WINS database.

# Managing and Monitoring WINS

Most management and monitoring tasks can be performed within the WINS management console. Most of the maintenance tasks performed will be to the WINS database, such as ensuring it is backed up in the event it becomes corrupt, and ensuring the database remains consistent over a period of time.

## Backing Up and Restoring the WINS Database

Through the WINS management console, you can configure a WINS server to periodically back up its local database. From the WINS server properties window, you can specify a backup location. You can also right-click the WINS server and select the Backup database option.

After you specify a backup location the WINS server will create the Wins_bak\NewFolder within the location you specify and back up the local database to this location every three hours. You also have the option of selecting whether the WINS server should perform a backup when the server is shut down.

If you have a backup of the WINS database, you can restore it by right-clicking the WINS server, choosing the Restore Database option, and specifying the location of folder where the database was backed up to. Keep in mind that before you perform a restore, the WINS service must be stopped. If the WINS service is running, the option to restore the database will not be available.

# Server Statistics

Viewing the statistics of a WINS server can provide an administrator with a general idea of what is happening. Within the WINS management console, you can right-click the WINS server and select the Display Server Statistics option. Some of the information provided includes when the server was last started, when replication last took place, and the number of name queries resolved.

# Tombstoning

Records that are deleted or marked as extinct on one server can cause inconsistencies to the database of its replication partners. For example, a record that was deleted from the database on one server can easily still appear within the database of a replication partner.

Windows Server 2003 supports a feature known as tombstoning. After a record is marked as tombstoned it is no longer considered to be active on the local WINS server. The record remains within the local database for replication purposes. When a tombstoned record is replicated, all replication partners mark the record as being tombstoned and it becomes extinct, eventually being removed from the database.

Records within the WINS database can be manually deleted or tombstoned using the following process:

1. Within the WINS console, right-click the Active Registrations container and click either the Find by Name or Find by Owner option to locate the appropriate record.

2. If you select Find by Name, type in the NetBIOS name you are searching for. If you select Find by Owner, specify whether to have all entries

in the local WINS database displayed or records from a specific WINS server. Click Find Now.

3. In the Details pane right-click the appropriate record and click Delete.

4. Within the Delete Record dialog box select one of the following options: Delete the Record Only from this Server or Replicate Deletion of the Record to Other Servers (Tombstone).

# Verifying Database Consistency

With multiple WINS servers configured for replication, a WINS database can become inconsistent over a period of time. Using the Verify Database Consistency and Verify Version ID Consistency options, an administrator can periodically perform database consistency checks. Checking the WINS database for inconsistencies will force the local WINS server to check all names replicated from other WINS servers and compare them with the local versions on the servers that own the records. The WINS server will then update its local records.

# Configuring WINS Clients

In order for clients to dynamically register their NetBIOS names with a WINS server and use the server for name resolution, they must be configured with the IP address of the WINS server. A WINS client can be running any of the following platforms:

► Windows Server 2003

► Windows XP

► Windows 2000

► Windows NT 3.51 and later

► Windows 95

► Windows 98

► Windows for Workgroups 3.11 running MS TCP/IP32

► Microsoft Network Client 3.0 for MS-DOS

► LAN Manager 2.2c for MS-DOS

There are two methods available for configuring clients with the IP address of the WINS server. You can use a DHCP server or you can configure each client manually.

If you opt to use DHCP, clients will require no configuration as they are enabled for DHCP by default. But you will have to configure the DHCP server to assign the IP Address of the WINS server to DHCP clients. To do so, configure the 044 WINS/NBNS server and the 046 WINS/NBT Node type DHCP options. You can do so by configuring the scope options within the DHCP management console (refer to Chapter 2, "Managing IP Addressing," for instructions on how to configure scope options).

The first option specifies the IP address of the WINS server. The second option specifies the node type or methods clients use to resolve NetBIOS names and in what order.

Clients can also be configured manually by an administrator, which means visiting each workstation and typing in the IP address of the WINS server. To manually configure a Windows XP client for WINS, follow these steps:

1. Point to Start, Settings, and click Network Connections.

2. Right-click the Local Area Connection and click Properties.

3. From the list of components select Internet Protocol (TCP/IP) and click Properties.

4. From the Internet Protocol (TCP/IP) Properties window, select the Advanced button and click the WINS tab.

5. Click the Add button and type in the IP address for the WINS server. Repeat the process for additional WINS servers on the network. Click OK.

There are several other configurable options available on the WINS tab, which are summarized as follows:

▶ *Enable LMHOSTS Lookup*—This option is selected by default and it enables the client to use an LMHOSTS file to resolve NetBIOS names to IP addresses. The Import LMHOSTS button allows you to import an existing file into the LMHOSTS file on the client computer.

▶ *Enable NetBIOS over TCP/IP*—This option specifies that the local area connection uses NetBIOS over TCP/IP and WINS. This setting should be enabled if the computer must communicate using computer names or with pre–Windows 2000 clients.

▶ *Disable NetBIOS over TCP/IP*—This option disables NetBIOS over TCP/IP and WINS for the local area connection. On a network that runs only Windows 2000, this option can be selected.

▶ *Use NetBIOS Setting from the DHCP Server*—Select this option to have the client obtain WINS information from a DHCP server. If the client is configured to receive its IP address from a DHCP server, this option is selected by default.

# Configuring Static Mappings

In some cases there may be clients on the network that are unable to dynamically update their NetBIOS name with a WINS server. In these instances, a static mapping can be manually added to the WINS database by an administrator. After a static mapping is created, it does not need to be renewed, nor does it expire. The entry must be manually deleted by an administrator.

To configure a static mapping:

1. Click Start, point to Programs, Administrative Tools, and click WINS.

2. Within the WINS management console, right-click Active Registrations and select New Static Mapping.

3. In the New Static Mapping dialog box, type in the computer name (NetBIOS name) for the host.

4. If required, type in the NetBIOS scope.

5. Using the drop-down arrow, select the type of entry you are creating.

6. Type in the IP address of the host. Click OK.

Keep in mind that if the client for which you created a static mapping is also a DHCP client, a client reservation should be created for it so it is leasing the same IP address all the time. If the client leases an IP address different from the IP address listed in the WINS database, the name will be resolved to the incorrect IP address.

# WINS Proxy

Clients that do not support WINS may resolve NetBIOS names using a broadcast. For routed IP networks, this method of name resolution becomes difficult if not impossible all together. In these situations, you can configure what is known as a WINS proxy agent.

A *WINS proxy* is a computer on a local subnet that listens for name resolution broadcasts. After the WINS server receives a broadcast, it queries the WINS server on behalf of the non-WINS client and returns the results. In terms of

NetBIOS name registration, the WINS proxy also listens for name registration broadcasts on the local subnet. When a non-WINS client attempts to register its NetBIOS name, the WINS proxy queries the WINS server to ensure that the name has not already been registered by another host.

To configure a computer to act as a WINS proxy, you must edit the local Registry. To do so, navigate to `HKEY_LOCAL_MACHINE\system\currentcontrolset\services\netbt\parameters` and change the value for the EnableProxy to 1.

# DNS Concepts

At one time or another, most of us have typed a universal resource locator (URL) to get to one of our favorite websites. Before you can view the website stored on a web server, that URL you typed must be resolved to an IP address, and this is where DNS servers come into play.

You might have also heard the term *fully qualified domain name (FQDN)*. An FQDN contains both the hostname and a domain name. It uniquely identifies a host within a DNS hierarchy. For example, www.bayside.net is an FQDN. Every FQDN is broken down into different levels, each separated by a period. In the preceding example, .net is the top-level domain and bayside is the second-level domain. The top-level domain normally identifies the type of organization, such as a government organization (gov) or an educational organization (edu). The second-level domain indicates a specific domain within that top-level namespace, whereas the third level might indicate a specific host within that domain. In all cases, DNS servers are used to resolve FQDNs to IP addresses.

## DNS Queries

A DNS query is a request for name resolution. Name resolution requests can be initiated by both DNS clients and DNS servers. A DNS client sends a query to a DNS server and a DNS server can send a query to another DNS server on behalf of a client.

DNS can use two different processes to resolve queries: recursive and iterative. With a *recursive query*, the DNS client requires the DNS server to respond with the IP address of the request or an error message that the requested name does not exist. The DNS server cannot refer the client to another DNS server if it cannot map the request to an IP address. When a DNS server receives a recursive request, it queries other DNS servers until it finds the information or until the query fails.

With an *iterative query*, the DNS server uses zone information and its cache to return the best possible answer to the client. If the DNS server does not have the requested information, it can refer the client to another DNS server. An iterative query is typically performed by a DNS server once it has received a recursive query from a DNS client.

For example, when a DNS client enters www.bayside.net into a browser, the following process occurs:

1. A DNS client sends a recursive query to the local DNS server.

2. Before forwarding the request to a root server, the DNS server checks its local cache to determine whether the name has recently been resolved. If there is an entry in the local cache, the IP address is returned to the client.

3. If no entry exists in the cache for the hostname, an iterative query is sent by the DNS server to a root name server.

4. The *root name server* refers the DNS server to a name server responsible for the first-level domain within the hostname. For example, the root name server would refer the request to the bayside.net DNS server.

5. The original DNS server is referred to second-level DNS servers, and then third-level DNS servers, until one of them can resolve the hostname to an IP address and return the results back to the client.

# DNS Forwarders

DNS servers often must communicate with DNS servers outside of the local network. A *forwarder* is an entry that is used when a DNS server receives DNS queries that it cannot resolve locally. It then forwards those requests to external DNS servers for resolution.

By configuring forwarders, you can specify which DNS servers are responsible for handling external traffic. Otherwise, all DNS servers can send queries outside of the local network, possibly exposing DNS information to untrusted hosts on the Internet. Configuring forwarding adds another level of security to the network because only servers identified as forwarders are permitted to forward queries outside the local network.

Additionally, if all DNS servers were allowed to forward queries outside the network, the result could be a large amount of unnecessary network traffic. This can become an important issue if the Internet connection is slow, costly, or already heavily used. Because a forwarder receives queries from local DNS servers, it builds up a large amount of cache information. This means that many of the queries received by the forwarder can be resolved from the cache instead of forwarding the requests outside the local network. This is obviously more efficient in terms of network traffic.

When a DNS server configured to use forwarding receives a DNS query from a DNS client, the following process occurs:

1. The DNS server first attempts to resolve the request using its zone information and information within its local cache.

2. If the request cannot be resolved locally, the DNS server sends a recursive query to the DNS server designated as the forwarder.

3. The forwarder attempts to resolve the query. If the forwarder does not respond, the DNS server attempts to resolve the request by contacting the appropriate DNS server, as specified in the root hints. (Root hints list authoritative root servers for the Internet.)

# Conditional Forwarder

A DNS server can be configured to send all queries that it cannot resolve locally to a forwarder, and you can also configure *conditional forwarders*. With conditional forwarders, DNS servers are configured to forward requests to different servers based on the DNS name within the query. When configuring conditional forwarding, you must specify the following information:

▸ The domain name for which queries will be forwarded

▸ The IP address of the DNS server for which unresolved queries for a specified domain should be forwarded

> **EXAM ALERT**
>
> You cannot configure a DNS server as a forwarder if a root zone exists. If you plan to configure your DNS server as a forwarder, you must delete the root zone. Open the forward lookup zone in the DNS console. The root zone entry is identified as ".". To delete the root DNS zone, right-click this entry and click Delete.

# DNS Server Caching

Caching is designed to improve response times. A DNS server caches the queries that it resolves to improve response time and reduce network traffic.

When performing a recursive query on behalf of a client, the DNS server caches all the information it receives from other DNS servers. Information is kept in the cache for a specified amount of time known as the *Time to Live* (TTL). The TTL is set by the administrator for the primary zone.

When the data is cached, the TTL begins to count down. After the TTL expires, the data is deleted from the cache.

DNS clients also maintain a cache. If a DNS server resolves a query from its cache, it returns the remaining TTL for the data to the DNS client. The DNS client in turn, caches the information and uses the TTL to determine when the entry expires.

# Implementing Windows 2003 DNS Server Roles

You can configure a DNS server in one of three possible roles. The role the server plays depends on the configuration of *zone files* and how they are maintained. The zone files contain configuration information for the zone as well as the resource records.

> **NOTE**
>
> A zone file contains the *resource records* for a portion of the DNS namespace. Resource records map hostnames to IP addresses. Both of these topics are covered later in this chapter, in the section "Creating Resource Records."

The three possible DNS server configuration roles are as follows:

- ▶ Caching-only server
- ▶ Primary server
- ▶ Secondary server

Keep in mind when you are planning DNS server roles that a single DNS server can perform multiple roles. For example, a DNS server can be the primary server for one zone and at the same time be a secondary server for another DNS zone.

## Caching-Only Server

All DNS servers maintain a cache.dns file that contains a list of all Internet root servers. Any time a DNS server resolves a hostname to an IP address, the information is added to the cache file. The next time a DNS client needs to resolve that hostname, the information can be retrieved from the cache instead of the Internet.

*Caching-only servers* do not contain any zone information, which is the main difference between them and primary and secondary DNS servers. The main purpose of a caching-only server (other than providing name resolution) is to build the cache file as names are resolved. They resolve hostnames, cache the information, and return the results to the client. Because these servers hold no zone information, either hostnames are resolved from the cache or else another DNS server is required to resolve them.

Caching-only servers are useful when you need to reduce network traffic. Again, because there is no zone information, no zone transfer traffic is generated (meaning that no information is replicated between DNS servers). Hostname traffic is also reduced as the cache file is built up because names can be resolved locally using the contents of the local DNS server's cache.

> **EXAM ALERT**
>
> It's important to understand when caching-only servers should be implemented. Caching-only servers are useful when there are remote locations that have slow WAN links. Configuring a caching-only server in these locations can reduce WAN traffic that would normally be generated between primary and secondary DNS servers, and can speed up hostname resolution after the cache file has been established.

# Primary Server

A primary DNS server hosts the working (writable) copy of a zone file. If you need to make changes to the zone file, it must be done from the server that is designated as the primary server for that zone. For those of you who are familiar with Windows NT 4.0, this is similar to how the primary domain controller (PDC) maintains the working copy of the directory database. After a server has been configured as a primary DNS server for a zone, it is said to be authoritative for that domain. Also, a single DNS server can be the primary DNS server for multiple *zones*.

# Secondary Server

A secondary server gets all its zone information from a master DNS server. The secondary DNS server hosts a read-only copy of the zone file, which it gets from the primary server or another secondary DNS server. Through a process known as a *zone transfer*, the master DNS server sends a copy of the zone file to the secondary server.

> **NOTE**
>
> Pre–Windows 2000 implementations of DNS supported only full transfers, in which an update to the zone file resulted in the entire zone database being transferred to the secondary servers. Windows Server 2003 (as well as Windows 2000 DNS) supports incremental zone transfers, so the secondary servers can synchronize their zone files by pulling only the changes. This results in less network traffic.

For example, if Server2 is configured as a secondary server for bayside.net, Server2 would get all of its zone information from Server1, the primary DNS server for the zone. Any changes that need to be made to the zone file would have to be done on Server1. The changes would then be copied to Server2. As already mentioned, a DNS server can be both a primary and a secondary server at the same time. Using this example, Server2 could also be configured as the primary server for riverside.net, and, to provide fault tolerance for the zone file, Server1 could be configured as a secondary server for this zone.

Secondary DNS servers provide the following benefits:

▶ *Fault tolerance*—Because the secondary server has a copy of the zone file, name resolution can continue if the primary DNS server becomes unavailable.

▶ *Reduction in name-resolution traffic*—Secondary servers can be placed in remote locations with a large number of users. Clients can then resolve hostnames locally instead of having to contact a primary DNS using a WAN link.

▶ *Load balancing*—Name-resolution services for a zone can be provided by the secondary server as well, thereby reducing the load placed on the primary DNS server.

# Installing DNS

DNS can be installed in several ways. It can be added during the installation of Windows Server 2003, after installation using the Configure Your Server Wizard, or through the Add or Remove Program applet in the Control Panel. DNS can also be installed when promoting a server to a domain controller using the DCPROMO command.

The only real requirement for installing DNS is Windows Server 2003. It cannot be installed on a computer running Windows XP. Also, if you are using Dynamic Host Configuration Protocol (DHCP) on the network to assign IP addresses, it's generally a good idea to configure the DNS server with a static IP address that is outside the range of addresses included in the DHCP scope.

To install the DNS Server service using the Add or Remove Program applet within the Control Panel, perform the following steps:

1. Click Start, point to Control Panel, and click Add or Remove Programs.

2. Click Add/Remove Windows Components.

3. Highlight Networking Services from the Components list and click the Details button.

4. From the list of components, select Domain Name System (DNS). Click OK and then click Next.

5. After the necessary files are copied, click Finish.

6. Close the Add or Remove Programs applet.

# Configuring DNS Server Options

When DNS is installed, the DNS management console is added to the Administrative Tools menu. From the management console, you can manage all aspects of a DNS server, from configuring zones to performing management tasks.

A number of options can be configured for a DNS server. By right-clicking the DNS server within the management console and selecting the Properties option, the properties window for the server is displayed (see Figure 3.3).

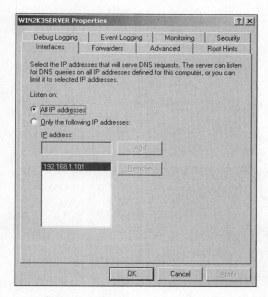

**FIGURE 3.3** After installing the DNS service, you can configure DNS server options through the server's Properties dialog box.

The available tabs from the DNS server Properties sheet and their uses are summarized as follows:

▶ *Interfaces*—Using this tab, you can configure the interfaces on which the DNS server will listen for DNS queries.

- ▶ *Forwarders*—From this tab, you can configure where a DNS server can forward DNS queries that it cannot resolve.

- ▶ *Advanced*—This tab allows you to configure advanced options, determine the method of name checking, determine the location from which zone data is loaded, and enable automatic scavenging of stale records.

- ▶ *Root Hints*—This tab enables you to configure root name servers that the DNS server can use and refer to when resolving queries.

- ▶ *Debug Logging*—From this property tab, you can enable debugging. When this option is enabled, packets sent and received by the DNS server are recorded in a log file. You can also configure the type of information to record in the file.

- ▶ *Event Logging*—The Event Logging tab enables you to configure the type of events that should be written to the DNS event log. You can log errors, warnings, and all events. You can also turn off logging by selecting No Events.

- ▶ *Monitoring*—The Monitoring tab can be used to test and verify the configuration by manually sending queries against the server. You can perform a simple query that uses the DNS client on the local server to query the DNS service to return the best possible answer. You can also perform a recursive query in which the local DNS server can query other DNS servers to resolve the query.

- ▶ *Security*—This tab enables you to assign permissions to users and groups for the DNS server.

**EXAM ALERT**

Windows Server 2003 DNS supports fast zone transfers. This feature is not supported by DNS servers running BIND versions older than 4.9.4. This feature must be enabled on the Advanced tab to support zone transfers with DNS servers running older versions of BIND.

# Advanced DNS Server Options

There are several options that can be configured using the Advanced tab of the DNS server's properties window. Generally, the default settings should be acceptable and require no modifications. The advanced settings that can be configured are summarized in the following list:

- ▶ *Disable Recursion*—This determines whether the DNS server uses recursion. If recursion is disabled, the DNS server will always use referrals, regardless of the type of request from clients.

- ▶ *BIND Secondaries*—This determines whether fast transfers are used when transferring zone data to a BIND server. Versions of BIND earlier than 4.9.4 do not support fast zone transfers.

- ▶ *Fail on Load if Bad Zone Data*—This option determines whether the DNS server continues to load a zone if the zone data is determined to have errors. By default, the DNS server will continue to load the zone.

- ▶ *Enable Round Robin*—This option determines whether the DNS server will rotate and reorder a list of resource records when multiple resource records exist for a query answer.

- ▶ *Enable Netmask Ordering*—This determines whether the DNS server reorders host (A) records within the same resource record set in response to a query based on the IP address of the source query.

- ▶ *Secure Cache Against Pollution*—This determines whether the DNS server attempts to clean up responses to avoid cache pollution. This option is enabled by default.

# Configuring DNS Zone Options

After you have installed the DNS Server service, your next step is to create and configure zones (unless the DNS server is not authoritative for any zones).

A *zone* is basically an administrative entity. A zone is nothing more than a portion of the DNS database that is administered as a single unit. A zone can contain a single domain or span multiple domains. The DNS server that is authoritative for a zone is ultimately responsible for resolving any requests for that particular zone. The zone file maintains all the configuration information for the zone and contains the resource records for the domains in the zone.

Each new zone consists of a forward lookup zone and an optional reverse lookup zone. A *forward lookup zone* maps hostnames to IP addresses. When a client needs the IP address for a hostname, the information is retrieved from the forward lookup zone. A *reverse lookup zone* does the opposite. It allows for reverse queries, or mapping of an IP address back to a hostname. Reverse queries are often used when troubleshooting with the NSLookup command.

## Zone Types

Windows Server 2003 supports four types of zones:

- ▶ *Standard primary zone*—This type of zone maintains the master writable copy of the zone in a text file. An update to the zone must be performed from the primary zone.

▶ *Standard secondary zone*—This zone type stores a copy of an existing zone in a read-only text file. To create a secondary zone, the primary zone must already exist, and you must specify a master name server. This is the server from which the zone information is copied.

▶ *Active Directory–integrated zone*—This zone type stores zone information within Active Directory. This enables you to take advantage of additional features, such as secure *dynamic updates* and replication. Active Directory–integrated zones can be configured on Windows Server 2003 domain controllers running DNS. Each domain controller maintains a writable copy of the zone information, which is stored in the Active Directory database.

▶ *Stub zone*—This type of zone is new in Windows Server 2003. A stub zone maintains only a list of authoritative name servers for a particular zone. The purpose of a stub zone is to ensure that DNS servers hosting a parent zone are aware of authoritative DNS servers for its child zones. One of the advantages of stub zones is that they create a dynamic relationship between the parent and child. Compared to delegation, which points to a single IP address, stub zones allow much more flexibility for the administrator because changes in the child zone are automatically reflected in the stub without making changes to the configuration.

## Stub Zones Versus Conditional Forwarding

A *stub zone* is an actual zone that would exist on the DNS server that contains just the SOA record for the zone it refers to and the DNS server's records and glue records (host A records). The stub zone replicates from the master DNS server in the zone it refers to and will keep current with DNS servers for that zone/domain. It is more work to set up than conditional forwarding and requires permission from the administrator of the other domain because it does zone transfers with it. However, it is more reliable in keeping current with the DNS servers in the zone.

Stub zones provide a way for DNS servers hosting a parent zone to maintain a current list of the authoritative DNS servers for the child zones. As authoritative DNS servers are added and removed, the list is automatically updated.

Conditional forwarding, on the other hand, is used to control where a DNS server forwards queries for a specific domain. A DNS server on one network can be configured to forward queries to a DNS server on another network without having to query DNS servers on the Internet.

**EXAM ALERT**

Stub zones provide an advantage over conditional forwarding because the information in a stub zone is dynamic, whereas the list of conditional forwards must be updated by a DNS administrator.

## Creating Zones

After the DNS service is installed, you can manage it using the DNS management console. From this management console, you can begin configuring a DNS server by creating zones. To create a new zone, follow these steps:

1. Click Start, point to Administrative Tools, and click DNS. This opens the DNS management console.

2. Right-click the DNS server and click New Zone. The New Zone Wizard opens. Click Next.

3. Select the type of zone you want to create: primary zone, secondary zone, or stub zone. You also have the option of storing the zone within Active Directory, if it is available. (The option to store information within Active Directory is available only if Active Directory is installed on the local machine.) Click Next.

4. Select the type of zone you want to create: a forward lookup zone or a reverse lookup zone. Click Next.

5. If you select a forward lookup zone, the Zone Name page appears. Type the name for the zone, such as bayside.net. Click Next.

6. If you selected to create a reverse lookup zone, type the network ID (see Figure 3.4). This is used to create the in-addra.arpa domain, with subdomains named using the network ID of the IP address. DNS uses the reverse lookup zone for performing address-to-name translations. For example, a network ID of 192.168.1 would be translated into 1.168.192.in-addra.arpa. Click Next.

7. In the Zone File screen, select whether to create a new zone file or to use an existing one (see Figure 3.5). This option appears when creating a forward or reverse lookup zone. Click Next.

8. Specify how the DNS zone will receive updates from DNS client computers. Three options are available, as shown in Figure 3.6. If the zone is Active Directory–integrated, you can allow secure updates only. You can allow both nonsecure and secure updates, or you can turn off dynamic

updates so that the resource records must be manually updated. Dynamic updates are covered in more detail later in the chapter in the section "Dynamic Updates."

9. Click Finish.

**FIGURE 3.4** If you are creating a reverse lookup zone, you must supply the network ID.

**FIGURE 3.5** You must provide a filename for the zone file or select an existing file.

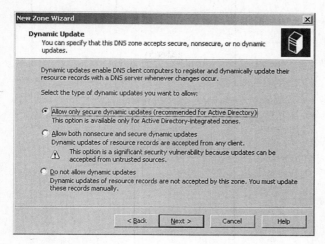

## Creating Resource Records

After a zone has been created, it can be populated with resource records. Remember, if your clients are all running Windows Server 2003, Windows XP, or Windows 2000 and the zone is configured for dynamic updates, the clients can add and update their own resource records. You can also manually add resource records to a zone file through the DNS management console. A number of resource records can be created. To view all the resource records supported by Windows Server 2003 DNS, right-click a zone and select Other New Records (see Figure 3.7).

The following list summarizes some of the more common resource records you might encounter:

▶ *Host Address (A) record*—Maps a DNS name to an IP address. An A record represents a specific device on the network.

▶ *Start of Authority (SOA) record*—Identifies the primary DNS server for the zone. This is the first resource record in a zone file.

▶ *Mail Exchanger (MX) record*—Routes messages to a specified mail exchanger for a specified DNS domain name.

▶ *Pointer (PTR) record*—Points to a location in the DNS namespace. PTR records map an IP address to a DNS name and are commonly used for reverse lookups.

▶ *Alias (CNAME) record*—Specifies another DNS domain name for a name that is already referenced in another resource record.

▶ *Service Locator (SRV) record*—Used to identify network services offered by hosts, the port used by the service, and the protocol. SRV records are used to locate domain controllers in an Active Directory domain.

As already mentioned, resource records can be created using the DNS management console. To create a new host record, simply right-click the zone in which you want to create the record and select the New Host (A) option. In the New Host dialog box, type the name and IP address for the host. To automatically create a pointer record, select the Create Associated Pointer (PTR) Record check box (see Figure 3.8).

**FIGURE 3.8**  You can add a new host record via the DNS management console.

To create additional resource records, simply select the type of record you want to create and fill in the required information.

> **NOTE**
>
> The NSLookup command can be used to determine the hostname associated with a specific IP address. To use the NSLookup command, PTR records must exist.

## Configuring DNS Simple Forwarding

As you learned earlier in the chapter, a DNS server can be configured to send all queries that it cannot resolve locally to a forwarder. To configure DNS forwarders, follow these steps:

1. Within the DNS management console, right-click the DNS server and click Properties.

2. From the Properties window for the DNS server, click the Forwarders tab.

3. Under DNS Name, select a domain name. To add a new domain name, click the Add button.

4. Under the Selected Domain's Forwarder IP Address list, type the IP address of the forwarder and click Add.

# Managing DNS

After DNS is installed, it can be managed using the DNS management console. Management tasks include configuring zone settings, creating and managing resource records, and monitoring the status and performance of DNS. The following sections discuss some of the common management tasks associated with DNS.

## Managing DNS Zone Settings

After a zone has been successfully added to your DNS server, you can configure it via the zone's properties dialog box. To do so, right-click the zone from within the DNS management console and click Properties. The Properties dialog box for the zone displays six tabs, as shown in Figure 3.9. If Active Directory is not installed, only five tabs are available (the Security tab is not present).

**FIGURE 3.9** You can configure a zone through its Properties dialog box.

The following list summarizes each of the tabs for a DNS zone's properties:

▶ *General*—View the status of the zone, change the type of zone, change the zone filename, change the replication scope for a zone, and configure dynamic updates. You can also set the aging and scavenging properties for the zone.

▶ *Start of Authority (SOA)*—Configure the zone transfer information and the email address of the zone administrator. The serial number is used to determine whether a zone transfer is required. Each time a change is made this number is incremented by 1. By using the Increment button, you can increase the value, thereby forcing a zone transfer.

▶ *Name Servers*—Specify the list of secondary servers that should be notified when changes to the zone file occur.

▶ *WINS*—Enable the DNS server to query the list of WINS servers for name resolution.

▶ *Zone Transfers*—Configure which secondary servers can receive zone transfers. You can specify any server, only those listed on the Name Servers tab, or the ones configured from this property sheet. Clicking the Notify button enables you to configure which secondary servers will be notified of changes.

▶ *Security*—If the zone is Active Directory–integrated, the Security tab is available and can be used to configure permissions to the zone file. This is where you can control who can perform dynamic updates.

## Changing Zone Types

Using the General tab from the Zone Properties dialog box, you can change the current zone type (see Figure 3.10). To do so, click the Change button beside the zone type. You have the option of changing a primary or secondary zone to an Active Directory–integrated zone or changing an Active Directory–integrated zone to a primary zone or secondary zone.

**FIGURE 3.10** You can change the zone type via a zone's Properties dialog box.

Before you attempt to change the zone type, be aware of the following points:

▶ The option to store zone information within Active Directory is available only when the DNS server is also configured as a domain controller.

▶ If you convert to a secondary zone or a stub zone, you must specify the IP address of the server from which the zone information will be retrieved.

▶ Changing a secondary zone to a primary zone affects such things as dynamic updates, the use of the DNS Notify option, and zone transfers.

▶ When the option to store information within Active Directory is cleared, zone information is deleted from Active Directory and copied into a text file on the local DNS server in the %systemroot%/system32/DNS folder.

▶ Because the purpose of a stub zone is to maintain information about only authoritative name servers for the zone, it is not recommended that a stub zone be converted to a primary zone because primary zones can contain a number of other records rather than just those for authoritative name servers.

# Dynamic Updates

Windows 2003 Server, Windows XP, and Windows 2000 clients can interact directly with a DNS server. With dynamic updates, clients can automatically register their own resource records with a DNS server and update them as changes occur. Resource records are the entries within the DNS server database files. Each resource record contains information about a specific machine, such as the IP address or specific network services running. The type of information within a resource record depends upon the type of resource record that is created. For example, an A (address) record contains the IP address associated with a specific computer; it's used to map a hostname to an IP address.

Dynamic updates greatly reduce the administration associated with maintaining resource records. Dynamic updates eliminate the need for administrators to manually update these records. In terms of DHCP, with a short lease duration configured, the IP address assigned to DNS clients can change frequently. If dynamic updates are not enabled, an administrator can end up spending a lot of time updating zone information. In addition, there is always the chance for human error when done manually.

Dynamic updates provide the following advantages:

▶ DHCP servers can dynamically register records for clients. This is particularly important because DHCP servers can perform updates on behalf of clients that do not support dynamic updates, such as Windows 95, 98, or NT4 clients.

▶ The administrative overhead is reduced because A records and PTR records can be dynamically updated by Windows DNS clients that support this option.

▶ The SRV records required to locate domain controllers can be dynamically registered.

**EXAM ALERT**

To implement dynamic updates on a network with pre–Windows 2000 clients, a DHCP server and a DNS server are required on the network. The DHCP and DNS servers must be running Windows Server 2003 or Windows 2000 because Windows NT 4.0 DNS servers don't support dynamic updates. A DHCP server is required to perform dynamic updates on behalf of clients that do not support this feature, such as Windows 95 clients.

By default, any Windows Server 2003, Windows XP, or Windows 2000 client can update its own records with the DNS server. The DHCP client service attempts to update records with the DNS server when any of the following events occur:

▶ The workstation is rebooted.

▶ The client records are manually refreshed using the `ipconfig /registerDNS` command.

▶ A statically configured IP address is modified.

▶ The IP address leased from a DHCP server changes or is renewed. An IP address can be manually renewed using the `ipconfig /renew` option.

Let's take a look at an example of what happens when a Windows XP DNS client performs a dynamic update. Assume that you change a bayside.net workstation's computer name from computer1 to computer2. Upon changing the computer name, you are required to restart before the changes take effect. When the workstation restarts, the following process occurs:

1. The DHCP client service sends a query to an authoritative DNS server for the domain using the new DNS domain name of the workstation.

2. The DNS server that is authoritative for the workstation's domain responds to the request with information about the primary DNS server for the domain.

3. The client sends a dynamic update request to the primary DNS server.

4. The update request is processed by the primary DNS server. The old host and pointer records are removed and replaced with the updated ones.

5. The master name server randomly notifies any secondary servers that a change to the zone file has occurred.

6. Secondary servers request the zone transfer update to the zone file according to the frequency configured on the zone's Start of Authority tab.

Dynamic updates are configured on a per-zone basis. To configure a zone for dynamic update, right-click the zone within the DNS management console and click Properties. In the Properties dialog box, ensure that the General tab is selected. To enable dynamic updates, select one of the following options:

▶ *None*—Select this option to disable dynamic updates for the zone. Doing this means that the zone file must be manually updated.

▶ *Nonsecure and Secure*—Select this option to allow nonsecure updates (anyone can perform the update) as well as secure updates (only certain users can perform the update).

▶ *Secure Only*—Select this option to enable dynamic updates for those users and groups authorized to do so because they have accounts in Active Directory and have been granted permission to update their records. This option is available only for zones that store information within Active Directory. You can use the Security tab from the zone's Properties window to configure who can perform dynamic updates.

---

**EXAM ALERT**

When configuring dynamic updates, remember that the zone must be standard primary (information is stored locally in files) or Active Directory–integrated (information is stored on all DCs). Also, to use secure updates, the zone must be Active Directory–integrated. This feature is not supported by standard primary zones.

---

## Secure Updates

Windows Server 2003 supports secure dynamic updates for zones that store information within Active Directory. With secure updates, only those clients authorized within the domain are permitted to update resource records. This means that the DNS server accepts updates only from clients that have accounts within Active Directory. Any computers that do not have accounts are not permitted to register any records, thereby eliminating the chance that unknown computers will register with the DNS server. Secure updates for a zone can be configured by selecting the Secure Only option.

The benefit of selecting this option is obviously an increase in security. The resource records and zone files can be modified only by users who have been authorized to do so. This also provides administrators with a finer granularity of control because they can edit the access control list (ACL) for the zone and specify which users and groups can perform dynamic updates. You edit the ACL for a zone by right-clicking the zone, selecting Properties, and choosing the Security tab.

## Zone Transfers

Secondary servers get their zone information from a master name server. The master name server is the source of the zone file; it can be a primary server or another secondary server. If the master name server is a secondary server, it must first get the updated zone file from the primary server. The process of replicating a zone file to a secondary server is referred to as a *zone transfer*. Zone transfers occur between a secondary server and a master name server in the following situations:

▶ When the master name server notifies the secondary server that changes have been made to the zone file. When the secondary server receives notification, it requests a zone transfer. If multiple secondary servers exist, they are notified at random so that the master name server is not overburdened with zone transfer requests.

▶ When the refresh interval expires and the secondary server contacts the primary name server to check for changes to the zone file.

▶ When the DNS server service is started on a secondary server.

▶ When a zone transfer is manually initiated through the DNS management console on a secondary server.

Windows Server 2003 DNS (as well as Windows 2000 DNS) supports two types of zone transfers. Pre–Windows 2000 implementations of DNS supported a *full zone transfer (AXFR)* only, in which the entire zone file is replicated to the secondary server. This type of zone transfer is supported by most implementations of DNS. If the secondary server's zone file is not current, which means that changes were made, the entire zone file is replicated. The second type of zone transfer is known as an *incremental zone transfer (IXFR)*, in which only the changes made to a zone file are replicated to the secondary server, thereby reducing the amount of network traffic. Frequency of zone transfers is configured on the Start of Authority tab.

The following list summarizes the configurable options for zone transfers. You can find these options on the SOA tab from the properties window for a zone:

▶ *Serial Number*—Lists the number used to determine whether the zone file has changed. Each time a change is made, this number is incremented by 1. You can force a zone transfer by manually increasing this number.

▶ *Primary Server*—Lists the hostname of the primary DNS server for the zone.

▶ *Responsible Person*—Lists the email address of the person responsible for administering the zone.

▶ *Refresh Interval*—Determines how often the secondary server polls the primary server for updates. Consider increasing this value for slow network connections.

▶ *Retry Interval*—Specifies how often the secondary server attempts to contact the primary server if the server does not respond.

▶ *Expires After*—Specifies when zone file information should expire if the secondary server fails to refresh the information. If a zone expires, zone data is considered to be potentially outdated and is discarded. Secondary master servers do not use zone data from an expired zone.

▶ *Minimum (Default) TTL*—Specifies how long records from the zone should be cached on other servers.

▶ *TTL for this Record*—Specifies how long DNS servers are allowed to store a record from the zone in their cache before it expires.

---

**NOTE**

When zone information is stored within Active Directory, zone updates are replicated differently than in a standard primary/secondary scenario. DNS notification is no longer needed, and configuring a notify list is unnecessary. Instead, the DNS servers that store information within Active Directory poll Active Directory at 15-minute intervals to check for updates.

---

## Zone Delegation

*Delegation* is the process of designating a portion of the DNS namespace for another zone. It gives administrators a way of dividing a namespace among multiple zones. For example, an administrator might place the bayside.net domain in one zone and place the sales.bayside.net subdomain in another delegated zone. The bayside.net zone would contain all the records for the sales subdomain if it is not delegated. Through delegating, the bayside.net zone contains only information for bayside.net, as well as records to the authoritative name servers for the sales.bayside.net zone. The host entries for any machines in sales.bayside.net are contained only on the delegated server.

In any case, when deciding whether to delegate, keep the following points in mind:

▶ Zone delegation allows you to delegate management of part of the DNS namespace to other departments or locations.

▶ Zone delegation allows you to distribute a large DNS database across multiple servers for load balancing, faster name resolution, and increased performance.

▶ Zone delegation allows you to extend the namespace for business expansion; that is, it is scalable with business needs.

---

**NOTE**

To facilitate the delegation of zones, you need the appropriate delegation records that point to authoritative name servers for the new zone(s).

---

You can use the following procedure to delegate a zone:

1. From within the DNS management console, right-click the domain you want to delegate and select New Delegation. The New Delegation Wizard opens. Click Next.

2. Type a name for the delegated domain in the Delegated Domain text box. Click Next.

3. Specify the name servers that will host the delegated domain by clicking the Add button. The New Resource Record screen appears, allowing you to specify the name and IP address of the name servers. Click OK. Click Next.

4. Click Finish.

# Managing DNS Record Settings

After resource records have been created, they can be managed through the management console. Tasks associated with resource records include modifying the resource records, deleting existing records, and configuring security.

## Modifying Resource Records

If you have manually created resource records within a zone, at some point you might need to modify them, such as change the IP address associated with a particular hostname. This won't be an issue if you are using dynamic updates because DNS clients (running the appropriate platform) can update this information on their own.

You can modify a resource record within the DNS management console by selecting the appropriate zone, right-clicking the resource record, and clicking Properties (see Figure 3.11). For example, you can change the hostname, domain name, and IP address of a Host (A) record.

## Deleting Resource Records

You can delete resource records within a zone file at any time. For example, if you manually create resource records for a server and remove it from the network, you will want to delete the records from the zone file. Deleting a record is a simple process. Simply right-click the record within the zone and click the Delete option. Click Yes to confirm your actions.

**FIGURE 3.11** You can modify the properties of a resource record through the management console.

## Modifying Security for Records

Each record has an associated ACL that can be edited. Doing so enables you to specify which users and groups are permitted to securely update the record and change their permissions. You can modify the security by opening the Properties window for a record and selecting the Security tab (see Figure 3.12).

**FIGURE 3.12** You modify security for a record on its Security tab.

# Managing DNS Server Options

Most management tasks performed on a DNS server are done through the DNS management console. When you highlight your DNS server within the DNS management console and click the Action menu, you see a number of options that can be used to manage different aspects of DNS. Some of the options available are summarized as follows:

▶ *Set Aging/Scavenging for All Zones*—Use this option to configure refresh intervals for resource records. This enables you to refresh resource records on a set schedule. Refreshing periodically keeps bad records, such as invalid URLs, out of the database.

▶ *Scavenge Stale Resource Records*—Use this option to manually scavenge stale resource records. Stale resource records can accumulate within a zone over a period of time. For example, if a computer registers its own resource record and is shut down improperly, the record might not be removed from the zone file. Scavenging stale resource records can eliminate any problems, such as outdated information.

▶ *Update Server Data Files*—Use this option to write all changes to the zone file stored within Active Directory to a zone file on the disk.

▶ *Clear Cache*—Use this option to clear the contents of the name server's cache.

▶ *Launch NSLookup*—Use this option to open the command prompt from which you can use the NSLookup command.

# Monitoring DNS

You should monitor your DNS servers on a regular basis. Obviously, in large enterprise environments, you will want to monitor DNS servers more frequently than for small businesses. Because DNS servers play such an important role for a Windows Server 2003 domain, it's important that solid performance is maintained.

## System Monitor

The tool most often used to monitor how services are performing is the System Monitor tool, located within the Performance console. When you install DNS, several counters are added specifically for monitoring this service (see Figure 3.13).

**FIGURE 3.13** DNS-specific counters are added to the System Monitor tool for monitoring DNS activity.

The following list outlines some of the common DNS performance counters:

▶ *Caching Memory*—Monitors the total caching memory used by the DNS server

▶ *Dynamic Update Received/Sec*—Determines the number of dynamic update requests received by the server per second

▶ *Dynamic Update Requests*—Counts the total number of dynamic updates received by the server

▶ *Recursive Queries*—Monitors the total number of recursive queries received by the server

▶ *Total Queries Received*—Calculates the total number of queries received by the server

# Event Viewer

If logging is enabled, DNS-related events can be written to the DNS log. As already mentioned, logging can be enabled using the Event Logging tab from the DNS server's Properties window. By default, all DNS-related events are written to the log. You can choose to log errors only or to log both errors and warnings. By selecting the No Events option, you can disable event logging.

You can use the Event Viewer, located on the Administrative Tools menu, to view events. When the Event Viewer is open, click the DNS log. Any DNS-related events are displayed within the right pane (see Figure 3.14). To view more detailed information about an event, double-click the event within the

**FIGURE 3.14**   DNS events are logged in the Event Viewer's DNS log.

right pane. The Properties window for the event displays information such as the date and time the event occurred, the type of event, the user and computer under which the event occurred, and an event ID. A basic description of the event is also provided.

# DNS Debug Logging

If you want to collect detailed information about how your DNS server is functioning, you can enable DNS debug logging. Once you do, DNS data will be collected and stored in the DNS.log file. Using the Debug Logging tab from the DNS server's properties window, you can choose the type of information that you want logged. For example, you can have all incoming and outgoing packets using TCP logged.

DNS debug logging is not enabled by default. Because it can be resource-intensive and affect server performance, it should only be enabled on a temporary basis.

# Replication Monitor

As mentioned earlier in the chapter, zone information can be stored within Active Directory if DNS is installed on a domain controller. This also means that zone updates can be included in Active Directory replication.

Using a tool called Replication Monitor, you can monitor the status of Active Directory replication between domain controllers. If zone information is stored within Active Directory, this also enables you to monitor replication between DNS servers.

Replication Monitor is not installed by default. It can be added by browsing to the `i386\Support\Tools` directory on the Windows Server 2003 CD and running setup. After it is installed, it can be launched from the command prompt using the `Replmon` command.

# Troubleshooting DNS

Many of the DNS problems that a network administrator encounters result from missing or incorrect resource records. There are several different tools available that can be used to troubleshoot problems with resource records. These include the following:

- Nslookup
- Dnslint
- Dnscmd

You can run NSLOOKUP with an IP address for a system that you know is outside of your local LAN, or an address that would normally be handled by DNS. NSLOOKUP does the reverse of standard DNS, and should tell you the FQDN that DNS is returning for that particular IP address. If it fails to do so, you need to check DNS connectivity by PINGing the DNS server from a client. You also need to check and make sure that the results of NSLOOKUP are actually valid and true; if they're not, there's a problem with the DNS database and requires some reconfiguration.

NSLOOKUP can be run in two different modes: interactive and noninteractive. If you are looking for a single piece of information, use NSLOOKUP in noninteractive mode. For example, type **NSLOOKUP 192.168.0.1** to find the name of the computer. If you need to look up more than one piece of information, use interactive mode.

The Dnslint command-line utility is included in the support tools. It is used to verify the existence and consistency of DNS records. For example, if clients are unable to log on to an Active Directory domain, you can use the command-line utility to verify the existence and the accuracy of the SRV records.

Dnslint will verify the following information and generate a report in HTML format:

- Verifies that all authoritative DNS servers for a domain are responding to queries.

- ▶ Verifies that all authoritative DNS servers have synchronized zone data.
- ▶ Verifies resource records associated with delegation.

Dnscmd is another command-line utility included in the Windows Server 2003 support tools. It can be used to perform various DNS administrative tasks from the command prompt window. You can use the command to perform the following tasks:

- ▶ View and change the properties of a DNS server, zone, or resource record.
- ▶ Create and delete zones and resource records.
- ▶ Force replication events.

# Exam Prep Questions

1. You are the network administrator for your company. All servers are running Microsoft Windows Server 2003. Client computers are running Windows XP Professional.

   Two DNS servers are currently configured on the network that are connected by high-speed WAN connections. Both servers are configured with identical hardware.

   Currently, one server is configured as a primary server and the other is configured as a secondary server. Both DNS servers are upgraded to domain controllers.

   You want to be able to perform updates to the zone data from either DNS server. What should you do?

   ○ **A.** In the Properties dialog box for the DNS server, select the General tab and click the Change button beside the zone type. Select the option to store the zone in Active Directory.

   ○ **B.** In the Properties dialog box for the zone, select the Zone Type tab and click the Change button. Select the Active Directory–Integrated option.

   ○ **C.** In the Properties dialog box for the zone, select the General tab and click the Change button beside the zone type. Select the option to store the zone in Active Directory.

   ○ **D.** In the Properties dialog box for the DNS server, select the Zone Type tab and click the Change button. Select the Active Directory–Integrated option.

2. You are the network administrator for your company. All servers are running Microsoft Windows Server 2003. Client computers are running Windows XP Professional.

   You have just finished installing the DNS service on a Windows Server 2003 member server in the bayside.net domain. You need to add a record into the zone file to identify the mail server in the domain.

   What should you do?

   ○ **A.** Create a PTR record on the DNS server.

   ○ **B.** Create an A record on the DNS server.

   ○ **C.** Create a CNAME record on the DNS server.

   ○ **D.** Create an MX record on the DNS server.

3. You are the network administrator for your company. Servers have been upgraded to Microsoft Windows Server 2003. Client computers are running Microsoft Windows XP Professional.

The DNS service has been installed on a member server within the company domain. You want to provide fault tolerance for your zone so that name resolution can still continue if the DNS server goes offline. You plan to add another DNS server to the domain. You need to configure the new DNS server role in the appropriate role.

What should you do?

- ○ **A.** Configure the new server as a secondary DNS server.
- ○ **B.** Configure the new server as a Master name server.
- ○ **C.** Configure the new server as a caching-only server.
- ○ **E.** Configure the new server as a DNS forwarder.

4. You are the network administrator for the Bayside Co. All servers are running Microsoft Windows Server 2003.

Bayside has seven offices located in different parts of the United States. The central office hosts the primary DNS server. All branch office locations have their own DNS servers configured as secondary servers.

The offices are currently connected by slow WAN links, with no plans to upgrade them. The annual budget allows for the addition of a second DNS server at each of the locations. However, you do not want any more traffic generated from zone transfers on the WAN or the local networks.

What should you do?

- ○ **A.** Configure the new servers as Standard primary DNS servers.
- ○ **B.** Configure the new servers as Standard secondary DNS servers.
- ○ **C.** Configure the new servers as Master name servers.
- ○ **D.** Configure the new servers as Caching-only servers.

5. You are the network administrator for an insurance company. You have upgraded all servers to Microsoft Windows Server 2003. Client computers are running Microsoft Windows XP Professional.

You are trying to determine the hostname associated with the IP address of 192.168.0.20 using the NSLookup command from Wrk02, but you are unsuccessful.

You know the IP address is assigned with Wrk01 and you can successfully resolve other hostnames on the network using this command.

What is most likely the cause of the problem?

- ○ **A.** There is no A record for Wrk01.
- ○ **B.** There is no A record for Wrk02.

    ◯  **C.** There is no PTR record for Wrk01.

    ◯  **D.** There is no PTR record for Wrk02.

6. You are the network administrator for the Bayside Company. Domain controllers are running Microsoft Windows Server 2003. Client computers are running Microsoft Windows XP Professional.

    A client reports that he is having problems resolving certain hostnames to IP addresses from his computer. You verify that changes have recently been made to some resource records in the zone file. You suspect there are outdated entries in the client resolver cache. The problem is not affecting any other clients on the network

    What should you do?

        ◯  **A.** Uninstall the DNS server service.

        ◯  **B.** Delete the `cache.dns` file.

        ◯  **C.** Use the `ipconfig /flushdns` command on the client computer.

        ◯  **D.** Use the Clear Cache option from the Action menu within the DHCP console.

7. You are the network administrator for your organization. You have installed the DNS service on all the Windows Server 2003 domain controllers in the company domain.

    Zone information is stored within Active Directory. You want to verify that zone data is being updated between DNS servers.

    Which tool can you use to verify this?

        ◯  **A.** System Monitor

        ◯  **B.** Replication Monitor

        ◯  **C.** DNS management console

        ◯  **D.** DNS Debug logging

8. You are the network administrator for a small accounting firm. Domain controllers and member servers are running Microsoft Windows Server 2003. Client computers are running Microsoft Windows XP Professional.

    You install the DNS service on two member servers. You need to enable the zone for secure updates. When you open the Property window for the zone, you do not see the Secure Only option.

    What could be causing the problem?

        ◯  **A.** You are not logged on as the administrator.

        ◯  **B.** You do not have permission to dynamically update the zone database.

    ○  **C.** The DNS service is not running on domain controllers.

    ○  **D.** The zone is configured as a primary zone.

**9.** You are the network administrator for the Bayside Company. All servers have been upgraded to Microsoft Windows Server 2003.

You have delegated the sales.bayside.net zone to another DNS server on the network. You want to ensure that the name server for bayside.net is notified anytime a new authoritative name server is added to the sales.bayside.net zone.

What should you do?

    ○  **A.** Using the Name Servers tab from the sales.bayside.net zone, configure the DNS server to notify the DNS server in the parent domain of any changes.

    ○  **B.** Configure a stub zone on the DNS server within the parent domain.

    ○  **C.** Configure a DNS server within the bayside.net zone to be a secondary server to the sales.bayside.net zone.

    ○  **D.** Configure all zones to store information within Active Directory.

**10.** You are the network administrator for a large insurance company. The primary DNS server is located in the head office.

One of the branch locations has a large number of users. You install a secondary DNS server in this location to decrease name resolution response time.

The WAN link between the branch office and the head office is heavily used.

You want to decrease the number of times that the secondary DNS server checks for zone updates.

What should you do?

    ○  **A.** In the Properties dialog box for the DNS server, select the Zone Transfers tab and increase the refresh interval.

    ○  **B.** In the Properties dialog box for the zone, select the Start of Authority (SOA) tab and increase the refresh interval.

    ○  **C.** In the Properties dialog box for the zone, select the Start of Authority (SOA) tab and increase the retry interval.

    ○  **D.** In the Properties dialog box for the zone, select the General tab and increase the retry interval.

**11.** You are the network administrator for your company. All servers have been upgraded to Microsoft Windows Server 2003. Client computers are running Microsoft Windows XP Professional.

You have installed the DNS service on DNSSRV01. You want to configure this DNS server to forward queries that it cannot resolve to another DNS server on the network.

You log on to DNSSRV01 using a user account that belongs to the DNS Admins group. When you display the Forwarders tab in the properties of SRV1 in the DNS console, the option to enable forwarders is unavailable.

What should you do?

- ○ **A.** Add your user account to the Enterprise Admins group.

- ○ **B.** Configure DNSSRV01 as a secondary DNS server.

- ○ **C.** Enable Round Robin on DNSSRV01.

- ○ **D.** Delete the root DNS zone on DNSSRV01.

**12.** You are the network administrator for a large company. All network servers are running Microsoft Windows Server 2003. Client computers are running a mixture of Microsoft Windows 95 and Microsoft Windows 2000 Professional.

Your company, contoso.com, has just acquired another company, nwtraders.com. You want to keep the existing network infrastructure. Each domain will maintain its own DNS servers.

You want DNS01, the DNS server for contoso.com, to send DNS queries for hosts in nwtraders.com to DNS01, the DNS server for nwtraders.com domain.

What should you do?

- ○ **A.** Open the properties window for contoso.com. Use the Forwarders tab to configure DNS01 to forward all name resolution requests to DNS02.

- ○ **B.** Open the properties window for DNS01. Use the Forwarders tab to config- ure DNS01 to forward all name resolution requests to DNS02.

- ○ **C.** Open the properties window for DNS01. Use the Forwarders tab to config- ure DNS01 to forward all name resolution requests for nwtraders.com to DNS02.

- ○ **D.** Open the properties window for contoso.com. Use the Forwarders tab to configure DNS01 to forward all name resolution requests for nwtraders.com to DNS02.

**13.** You are the network administrator for the Bayside Company. You have upgraded all servers to Microsoft Windows Server 2003. Client computers are running Microsoft Windows XP Professional.

All computers are members of a single Active Directory domain called bayside.net. The company website is hosted on three different web servers. The web servers are config- ured with identical hardware and each one is assigned a unique IP address.

You want traffic to the company website distributed evenly across all three web servers. You open the properties windows for the DNS server.

Which option should you select?

14. You are the network administrator for bcdtrain.com. The network has recently been upgraded to Microsoft Windows Server 2003. Client computers have been upgraded to Microsoft Windows XP Professional.

A new Domain Name System (DNS) server, DNS-01, has been added to the network. This server is configured as the primary DNS server for the bcdtrain.com domain. There is an existing legacy UNIX server on the network, DNS-02, that you configure as a secondary DNS server. You determine that this server is running a version of BIND older than 4.9.4.

You soon discover that DNS-02 is not receiving zone transfers from DNS-01.

What should you do?

- ○ **A.** Disable the BIND secondaries option on DNS-01.
- ○ **B.** Enable the BIND secondaries option on DNS-01.
- ○ **C.** Disable the BIND secondaries option on DNS-02.
- ○ **D.** Enable the BIND secondaries option on DNS-02.

15. You are a network administrator for your company. The network consists of server computers running Microsoft Windows Server 2003 and client computers running Microsoft Windows XP Professional.

The DNS service is installed on SRV01. It hosts a zone file called contoso.com. SRV02 is configured as an FTP server. The following resource records exist in the zone file for SRV02.

Host (A)

Alias (CNAME)

Service Location (SRV)

Well Known Service (WKS)

You decide to change SRV02 to use Transmission Control Protocol (TCP) port 1021 as the control port for FTP.

You need to ensure that the port is defined correctly in DNS.

Which resource record should you update?

- ○ **A.** Host (A)
- ○ **B.** Alias (CNAME)

    ○  **C.**  Service Locator (SRV)

    ○  **D.**  Well Known Service (WKS)

16. You are the network administrator for your company. All servers are running Microsoft Windows Server 2003.

    The network consists of several subnets. All clients are WINS-enabled and capable of updating their records dynamically. Each of the subnets has its own WINS server. One of the subnets contains two UNIX servers. Hosts on the local subnet can communicate with the UNIX servers; however, hosts on other subnets are unsuccessful. Clients can resolve NetBIOS names for hosts on other subnets.

    Clients on all subnets need to be able to resolve the NetBIOS names of the UNIX servers.

    What should you do?

        ○  **A.**  On each of the subnets, configure a secondary WINS server on each subnet.

        ○  **B.**  Configure the WINS servers as replication partners.

        ○  **C.**  Configure the WINS servers to back up their local databases.

        ○  **D.**  Configure static mappings for the two UNIX servers.

17. You are the network administrator for your company. All servers are running Microsoft Windows Server 2003.

    The network has a mixture of WINS and non-WINS clients. Three of the seven subnets contain WINS servers. Several users report that they are unable to browse hosts on other subnets. Upon investigating the reports, you discover that the problem is only affecting non-WINS clients.

    What should you do?

        ○  **A.**  Configure static mappings for the non-WINS clients.

        ○  **B.**  Install a WINS proxy on each subnet that does not have a local WINS server.

        ○  **C.**  Configure replication between the three WINS servers.

        ○  **D.**  Configure a DHCP relay agent on each subnet.

# Answers to Exam Prep Questions

1. **C.** To change the zone type, right-click the zone within the DNS management console and click Properties. In the Properties dialog box, make sure the General tab is selected and click the Change button beside the zone type. Select the option to store the zone within Active Directory. Answer A is incorrect because the zone type is configured at

the zone level. Answers B and D are incorrect because there is no Zone Type tab available in either the server's Properties dialog box or the zone's Properties dialog box. There is also no option known as Active Directory Integrated.

2. **D.** Mail servers are identified within a zone file using Mail Exchanger (MX) records. Answer A is incorrect because PTR records are used to associate an IP address with its hostname. Answer B is incorrect because A records are used to map hostnames to IP addresses. Answer C is incorrect because CNAME records are used to assign alias names to those names that are already referenced in another record.

3. **A.** The new server should be configured as a secondary server. It will then maintain a copy of the DNS zone file. If the original DNS server goes offline, name resolution can still occur. Answer B is incorrect because master name servers are the source of the zone file for secondary servers. Answer C is incorrect because caching-only servers do not hold any zone information. Answer D is incorrect. A DNS forwarder is not a specific DNS role. When a DNS server is configured as a forwarder, it can forward requests that it cannot resolve to a specific DNS server.

4. **D.** By configuring caching-only servers within each location, you can decrease the name resolution response time for users. Because the caching-only servers do not maintain any zone information, no traffic is generated from zone transfers. Therefore, answers A, B, and C are incorrect.

5. **C.** If the hostname cannot be resolved using the `NSLookup` command, adding a PTR to the zone file will allow you to resolve the IP address to a hostname. Answer B is incorrect because Wrk02 is not the hostname being resolved. Answers A and B are incorrect because A records are used to map hostnames to IP addresses, not vice versa.

6. **C.** By executing the `ipconfig /flushdns` command, you can delete the contents of the client resolver cache on the client computer. Although uninstalling the service would clear the contents of the cache, it's not the easiest way to perform the task; therefore, answer A is incorrect. Answer B is incorrect because deleting the file will completely remove it. Answer D is incorrect because this option is used to clear the contents of the cache file on the DNS server. However, the problem is not affecting any other DNS clients, which indicates that the problem likely resides with the cache on the DNS client.

7. **B.** If the support tools have been installed, you can use Replication Monitor to ensure that replication between DNS servers is occurring on a regular basis. Answer A is incorrect because System Monitor is used to monitor the real-time performance of a DNS server. Answer C is incorrect because the DNS management console is used to configure and manage a DNS server but cannot be used to monitor DNS replication. Answer D is incorrect. DNS debug logging is used to collect detailed information about how a DNS server is operating.

8. **C.** The Secure Only option is available only if the DNS service is installed on a domain controller. Therefore, answers A, B, and D are incorrect. Answer A is incorrect because this would not make the Secure Updates option unavailable. Answer B is incorrect

because dynamic updates are performed when a computer or server updates resource records. Answer D is incorrect because primary and stub zones can be configured for secure updates.

9. **B.** By configuring an authoritative DNS server within bayside.net to host a stub zone for the sales.bayside.net zone, any updates made to the authoritative name server resource records will be updated within the parent zone as well. None of the other options provided remedy this scenario effectively; therefore, answers A, C, and D are incorrect.

10. **B.** To increase the rate at which the secondary server polls for updates, select the Start of Authority (SOA) tab from the zone's Properties dialog box and increase the refresh interval. Answer A is incorrect because the interval at which a secondary server polls for updates is configured at the zone level. Answer C is incorrect because the retry interval defines how often the secondary server continues to poll if the server does not respond. Answer D is incorrect because you must configure the refresh interval, and it must be done from the Start of Authority (SOA) tab.

11. **D.** If a root DNS zone exists on the DNS server, you will not be able to configure a DNS forwarder. You must delete this file before you can proceed. Answer A is incorrect because you do not need to be a member of the Enterprise Admins group to manage a DNS server. Answer B is incorrect because changing the DNS role of the server will not determine whether the DNS server can be a forwarder. Answer C is incorrect because the round robin feature is used to load balance queries across multiple DNS servers.

12. **C.** You should open the properties window for the DNS server called DNS01. Select the Forwarders tab and configure the DNS server to forward any name resolution requests for hostnames in the nwtraders.com domain to DNS02. Answers A and D are incorrect because DNS forwarders are not configured at the zone level. Forwarding must be configured at the server level. Answer B is incorrect because all name resolution requests should not be forwarded to DNS02. Only those requests for hostnames in the nwtraders.com domain should be forwarded to this server.

13. The correct answer is Enable Round Robin. By selecting this option, the DNS server will be able to distribute queries across the web servers. It does so by rotating the list of web servers so a different web server is returned to a client.

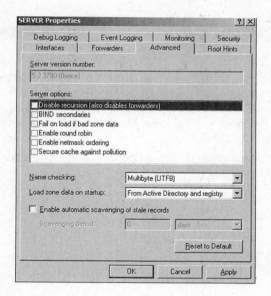

14. **B.** You should enable the BIND secondaries option on DNS-01. When this option is enabled, the Windows Server 2003 DNS server will not perform fast zone transfers because it is not supported by versions of BIND older than 4.9.4. Answer A is incorrect. This feature is disabled by default. Answers C and D are incorrect because this feature must be enabled on the Windows Server 2003 DNS server, not on the BIND DNS server.

15. **C.** You should update the SRV record. The SRV record identifies services that are running on a host, the port used by the service, and the protocol. You should not update the Host (A) record. This record identifies the IP address assigned to a host. Answer B is incorrect because an Alias (CNAME) record specifies another DNS domain name for a name that is already referenced in another resource record. Answer D is incorrect because a Well Known Service (WKS) record identifies services running on a host by the service name, not the port number.

16. **D.** To allow hosts on other subnets to resolve the NetBIOS names of the UNIX servers, static mapping must be configured because the UNIX servers are unable to register their NetBIOS records dynamically. Answers A and C are incorrect because performing these tasks does not allow hosts to resolve the NetBIOS names of the UNIX servers. Answer B is incorrect because if the clients can already resolve the names of hosts on other subnets, replication is already configured between the WINS servers.

17. **B.** To allow B-Node broadcasts to be resolved across the network, a WINS proxy agent must be configured. The WINS proxy listens for B-Node broadcasts and contacts the WINS servers on the other subnets to resolve the name resolution request on behalf of the non-WINS client. Therefore, answers A, C, and D are incorrect.

# Need to Know More?

Search the online version of TechNet and the Windows Server 2003 Resource Kit using keywords such as "DNS," "Zones," and "Dynamic Updates."

Habraken, Joe. *Sams Teach Yourself Microsoft Windows Server 2003 in 24 Hours.* Sams, 2003. ISBN: 0672324946.

Abbate, Andrew; Kovach, Eric; Morimoto, Rand; Roberts, Ed. *Microsoft Windows Server 2003 Insider Solutions.* Sams, 2003. ISBN: 0672326094.

Williams, Robert; Walla, Mark *The Ultimate Windows Server 2003 System Administrator's Guide.* Addison-Wesley Professional 2003. ISBN: 0201791064.

CHAPTER FOUR

# Maintaining Network Security

---

## Terms you'll need to understand:

✓ IP Security Monitor
✓ Automatic Updates Services
✓ Software Updates Services
✓ Event Viewer
✓ Network Monitor
✓ IPSec
✓ Secure baseline
✓ Security configuration and analysis
✓ Security templates

---

## Techniques you'll need to master:

✓ Implementing security baseline settings
✓ Auditing security settings using security templates
✓ Installing and configuring Software Updates Services
✓ Monitoring network protocol security
✓ Troubleshooting network protocol security

Although the current configuration of a server might be secure, performing day-to-day administrative tasks or failing to update the server with new patches can leave a server vulnerable. It's extremely important that organizations implement and follow standard network administration procedures to ensure that the required level of security is met and maintained. This chapter looks at some of the common network administration procedures that should be followed to ensure that security is maintained.

# Implementing Security Baseline Settings

One of the first steps you need to take to implement standard network administration procedures is to establish a baseline. What exactly is a secure baseline? The idea or concept behind a secure baseline or secure build is to implement a common standard security configuration that is used throughout an organization for installing any operating system, whether it is for a client or server platform. The baseline establishes a set of rules or recommendations that outline the minimum acceptable security configuration for new installations. Certainly no common baseline can be implemented across all organizations—needs undoubtedly vary from organization to organization. Each organization must assess its own needs and security requirements when establishing a secure baseline.

A secure baseline or build involves installing the operating system, applying service packs and hot fixes, and configuring various operating system settings, as well as documenting each step of the process so that it can be repeated. You must determine what procedures need to be performed on the computer and then establish documentation outlining the secure baseline and how to manage deployment. Remember, the purpose here is to increase security. The secure baseline therefore needs to be implemented consistently throughout an organization.

The first step in adding a new server to the network is to install the base operating system. Because the initial installation of an operating system is often vulnerable to attacks, precautions must be taken after installation to ensure that the system is not compromised. Service packs and hot fixes exist that eliminate many of the known security issues associated with the base installation of an operating system. Until those updates are installed, the server might be left vulnerable to attacks.

To perform a secure baseline installation of an operating system, it is recommended that the server be disconnected from the network until the necessary service packs and hot fixes have been added. Keep in mind that because the server will not be connected to the network, you must have the service packs and hot fixes available on CD, external drive, or even DVD.

# Preparing the Development and Test Environment

One of the steps that should be taken to ensure server security during installation is to disconnect the server from the production network until the service packs and hot fixes have been applied. Ideally, an organization will have a development and test environment that is separate from the production network where installations can be performed securely.

The goal of a development and test environment is to provide a way for administrators to securely test server installations and configurations (as well as the installation of different services and applications). The test and development environment should mirror the actual production environment as closely as possible.

# Applying Service Packs and Hot Fixes

Soon after an operating system is released, Microsoft normally releases a service pack. Service packs allow a vendor to easily distribute updates to an operating system. Users can simply access the vendor's website and download the service pack for installation. In terms of security and monitoring the updates that are installed, you can use a technology called Software Update Services, which is discussed later in the chapter. Service packs are intended to fix known issues with an operating system, keep the product up-to-date, and introduce new features. Service packs can include any of the following:

- ▶ Updates to the operating system
- ▶ New administrative tools
- ▶ Drivers
- ▶ Additional components

It is not uncommon for several service packs to be released over time for a single operating system. Keep in mind when using service packs that they are cumulative, so any new service packs contain all the fixes in the previous service packs, along with new updates.

Most organizations opt to keep up-to-date and install the latest service packs on their servers after they have been assessed in a test environment. Because service packs often contain fixes for known security issues for an operating system, applying the latest service pack is an important step in creating a secure baseline installation for servers.

Between the releases of service packs, Microsoft releases hot fixes, which are used to temporarily patch a specific problem with an operating system. One of the issues associated with installing hot fixes is that they are developed and released rather quickly and, therefore, are not tested thoroughly. So, installing the hot fix can, in turn, have a negative impact. It is important to evaluate the hot fixes released by Microsoft to determine whether they are necessary. If a particular vulnerability does not apply to your server, the patch should not be applied.

When service packs and hot fixes are deployed, they should first be deployed within a test environment so that you can evaluate the impact on the server before installing it in the production environment.

You can use the `Hfnetchk.exe` utility to determine the hot fixes that might be required for your server. When the command-line utility is run, it scans the system to determine the operating system, service packs, and programs installed. It then determines the security patches available for your system based on the components running. `Hfnetchk.exe` displays the hot fixes that should be installed to bring the system up-to-date.

You can run `HFNetChk` from Windows NT 4.0, Windows 2000, Windows XP, or Windows Server 2003 systems, and it will scan either the local system or remote systems for patches available for the following products:

▶ Windows NT 4.0, Windows 2000, Windows XP, and Windows Server 2003

▶ Internet Information Server 4.0 and 5.0

▶ SQL Server 7.0 and 2000 (including Microsoft Data Engine)

▶ Internet Explorer 5.01 and later

The system requirements to run the utility include the following:

▶ Windows NT 4.0, Windows 2000, Windows XP, or Windows Server 2003

▶ Internet Explorer 5.0 or later (an XML parser is required and one is included with Internet Explorer 5.0)

# Securing the Operating System

After the operating system has been installed and the necessary service packs and hot fixes have been added, a number of configuration changes can be made to the operating system to make it more secure. This is often referred to as operating system *hardening*. Again, the changes that are made to harden the server should be documented and made standard for all servers throughout an organization. Some of the steps that should be included with securing the operating system are as follows:

▶ Install antivirus software. All servers (and workstations) should run antivirus software.

▶ During the installation of Windows Server 2003, you must select the type of file system to use. If you did not choose NTFS during the installation, you should convert any partitions from FAT to NTFS. You can do so using the convert command without losing any data. Because NTFS offers security features that FAT does not, such as file-level security, ensure that this is the file system being used on network servers.

▶ Configure a strong password for the Administrator account. During the installation of Windows Server 2003, you are prompted to create a password for the Administrator account. Keep in mind that Windows Server 2003 does not allow you to create noncomplex passwords. Passwords must be at least six characters and they cannot contain the words "Administrator" or "Admin." Passwords must contain characters from three of the following categories: lowercase letters, uppercase letters, numbers, and non-alphanumeric characters.

▶ Disable unnecessary services. In Windows Server 2003, many of the services enabled in previous versions are now disabled by default. You can use the Services applet within the Control Panel to further restrict which services will be running.

▶ Remove or disable any unnecessary protocols, such as IPX/SPX. By default, when Windows Server 2003 is installed, the only protocol added is TCP/IP (unless you perform a custom network setup). If any other protocols are inadvertently installed and are not required, they should be removed.

▶ Any unnecessary user accounts should be disabled or deleted. Accounts that are considered inactive should be disabled, and those that are no longer needed should be removed entirely.

▶ Configure the various security settings within the local or domain security policy. This includes a password policy, an account lockout policy, a Kerberos policy, and an audit policy. You can use the *Windows Server 2003 Security Guide*, published by Microsoft, as a basis for configuring security settings for various server roles. You can find a copy of the guide at http://www.microsoft.com/technet/security/prodtech/windowsserver2003/w2003hg/sgch00.mspx.

# Keeping the System Secure

When your organization has a secure baseline installation that is followed by all administrators when installing new servers and workstations, what happens after the installation? What about after the service packs and updates have been applied? Or after you've taken the time to harden the operating system? To ensure that the level of security is maintained, some standardized methods must be put in place outlining how to maintain the security of servers. There is no point in taking the time to perform a secure baseline installation if the security configuration is not documented and maintained afterward. To ensure that the required level of security is maintained, follow these guidelines:

> ▶ Check for operating system updates on a regular basis. Because software updates are often released quite frequently, you should check for updates on a regular basis to determine whether any are applicable to your server configuration. You can also automate this process by using the Windows Update feature. Again, before deploying updates, you should test them within a controlled environment.

> ▶ Keep antivirus signature files updated. Again, many vendors have an automatic update option, so this can be done automatically.

> ▶ View the information in the audit logs on a regular basis.

> ▶ Use the Security Baseline Analyzer to ensure that the minimum security requirements continue to be met. The Security Baseline Analyzer enables you to analyze the current security settings on a computer and compare them to those within a database to find discrepancies that might occur over time.

# Implementing the Principle of Least Privilege

Implementing the principle of least privilege adds another level of security to your network. The principle of least privilege is based on the idea that a user who is logged on should have only the minimum privileges required to perform a task. This minimizes the amount of damage that can occur if the user becomes compromised. This means that even network administrators should be logged on with user accounts that have restrictive permissions when performing routine tasks. These users can perform administrative tasks under the context of another user account with additional privileges either by logging off and logging on under that account or by using the Runas command.

# Auditing Security Settings Using Security Templates

Windows Server 2003 makes it simple to deploy security configurations. A security template holds a number of security settings that Microsoft considers to be appropriate for a server, domain controller, or workstation. Windows Server 2003 comes with several predefined sample security templates. Each of the templates contains security settings for different levels of security based on the type of server to which the template is applied. For example, you can apply the high- secdc.inf template to all domain controllers in an environment requiring a high level of security. The templates can be used as-is or can be customized to meet the specific security needs of an organization. Security templates can be used to configure the following settings within a local security policy or a group policy:

- ▶ Account policies
- ▶ Local policies
- ▶ Event log
- ▶ Restricted groups
- ▶ System services
- ▶ Registry
- ▶ File system

## Using the Default Security Templates

The predefined security templates included with Windows Server 2003 can be viewed using the Security Templates snap-in. To view the default security templates, perform the following steps:

1. Click Start, Run and type MMC. Press Enter.
2. From the File menu, click Add/Remove Snap-In. From the Add/Remove Snap-In window, click Add.
3. Scroll through the list of available snap-ins. Select Security Templates and click Add (see Figure 4.1). Click Close.

**FIGURE 4.1** Adding the Security Templates snap-in.

4. Click OK.

5. Within the management console, expand Security Templates and click the default container. The preconfigured security templates are listed in the right pane, as shown in Figure 4.2.

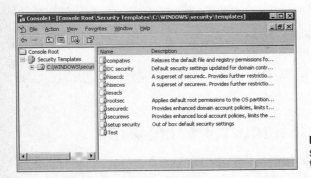

**FIGURE 4.2** Viewing the default security templates included with Windows Server 2003.

By default, the following security templates are stored within the `%system-root%\security\templates` directory:

▶ *Setup Security*—This template is created during the installation of Windows Server 2003 and contains the default security settings applied during the installation of the operating system. You should not change the settings within this template because it can be used to reapply default security settings.

▶ *Compatible (`compatws inf`)*—This template relaxes security so members of the Users group can run applications that are not a part of the Designed

Qvick books

for Windows Logo Program. The default permission allows only members of this group to run applications that are part of the Windows Logo group. Instead of adding members to the Power Users group, permissions can be relaxed so that members of this group can run the necessary applications.

▶ *Secure (secure\*.inf)*—This template modifies security settings that affect the operating system and network protocols such as the password policy, account policy, and various Registry settings. It also removes all members from the Power Users group.

▶ *Highly Secure (hisec\*.inf)*—This template increases the security of the parameters defined within the secure template. This template also removes all members from the Power Users group.

# Analyzing Security with the Security Configuration and Analysis Tool

Windows Server 2003 includes a tool known as the Security Configuration and Analysis tool. Using this tool, you can analyze the current security state of a server or workstation by comparing the existing settings against a standard template provided with the operating system. By performing a security analysis on a regular basis, administrators can ensure that a server or workstation continues to meet the security requirements of an organization. Over time, discrepancies can occur in the security configuration of a server or workstation. The analysis pinpoints any discrepancies, allowing an administrator to resolve any security conflicts that exist. After an analysis is run, the results are displayed for review.

To analyze the existing security configuration, perform the following steps:

1. Click Start, Run, and type MMC. Press Enter.

2. From the File menu, click Add/Remove Snap-In. From the Add/Remove Snap-In window, click Add.

3. Scroll through the list of available snap-ins. Select Security Configuration and Analysis, and click Add. Click Close and then click OK.

4. Within the management console, right-click Security Configuration and Analysis, and click Open Database.

5. Type a new filename to create a new database, or select an existing database.

6. If you are creating a new database, select an existing template and click Open.

7. Within the Details pane, right-click Security Configuration and Analysis, and click Analyze Computer Now.

8. Specify the path for the error log, or use the default location. Click OK.

9. After the security settings have been analyzed, double-click Security Configuration and Analysis within the Details pane. Any security settings that do not match those within the security template are marked with an X, as shown in Figure 4.3. As you can see in the figure, the values configured on the computer for Minimum Password Age and Minimum Password Length do not match the values defined within the database.

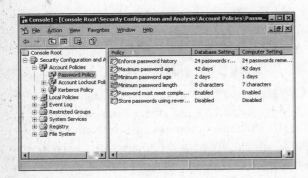

**FIGURE 4.3** Viewing the results of a security analysis.

# Applying Security Templates

A security template can be applied in two ways: locally or through a group policy. To apply a security template to a local policy, perform the following steps:

1. Within the Security Configuration and Analysis console, right-click Security Configuration and Analysis, and click Open Database.

2. Type a name for the database and click Open.

3. From the Import Template window, select a template and click Open (see Figure 4.4).

4. Right-click Security Configuration and Analysis, and click Configure Computer Now. The security settings are immediately applied to the local computer.

**FIGURE 4.4** Importing a security template into a local policy.

To import a security template for a domain or Organizational Unit, perform the following steps:

1. Click Start, Administrative Tools, and select Active Directory Users and Computers.

2. Right-click the domain or Organizational Unit for which you want the security settings applied, and click Properties.

3. From the Properties window, select the Group Policy tab (see Figure 4.5).

4. Click Edit to edit an existing group policy, or click New to create a new group policy.

**FIGURE 4.5** Using the Group Policy tab to import a security template.

5. In the Group Policy console, under Computer Configuration, expand Windows Settings and right-click Security Settings. Click Import Policy.

6. Select the security template that you want to import and click Open.

**EXAM ALERT**

Security settings on a domain controller are automatically refreshed every five minutes. Security settings on a workstation or server are automatically refreshed every 90 minutes.

After you make changes to any security settings, you can force an immediate refresh using the gpupdate command. When the command is used on its own, it automatically refreshes any user and computer settings that have changed. Using the command with the /target switch enables you to specify whether computer or user settings are refreshed. Using the /force switch means that all settings are refreshed, regardless of whether they were changed. The gpupdate command replaces the /refreshpolicy option of the secedit command in Windows 2000.

# Creating Custom Templates

The predefined security templates can be applied as-is. However, they can also serve as a starting point for configuring security. Any of the predefined templates can be customized to meet the specific security requirements of an organization.

To customize an existing template, perform the following steps:

1. Open the Security Templates snap-in. Expand the Security Templates container.

2. Click the default path folder. In the right pane, right-click the security template that you want to modify and click Save As.

3. Type a new name for the security template and click Save (see Figure 4.6).

The newly created template appears within the right pane. To modify the security settings, double-click the new template. Any of the settings contained within the template can be modified by right-clicking an attribute and selecting Properties. For example, to configure a password history, right-click the Enforce Password History option from within the Password Policies container for a security template, and click Properties. Select the option to Define This Policy Setting in the template and configure a value.

**FIGURE 4.6** Customizing a predefined security template.

If you do not want to customize one of the existing security templates and would rather define an entirely new template, you can do so again using the Security Templates snap-in. To do so, right-click the default path location within the Security Templates snap-in and click New Template. Type in a name and description for the template, and click OK. The new template is displayed within the right pane, from which you can begin configuring the security settings.

# Installing and Configuring a Software Update Infrastructure

One of the challenges most network administrators face is the need to distribute software updates to servers and workstations. In small environments, visiting each computer to perform the installation of an update might take only a few hours. However, in medium to large networks, administrators need a secure, reliable, and efficient way of distributing updates as they are released.

One of the options available for distributing updates is Software Updates Services (SUS). SUS consists of two components: the server and the client. The server (which can be running Windows 2000 or Windows Server 2003) downloads updates from Microsoft and stores them locally. As soon as the updates are posted to the Windows Update site, they are downloaded and the network administrator is notified that they are available. The clients can then download the updates from the server instead of retrieving them from the Windows Update site. One of the benefits of using SUS is that updates can be tested before being deployed. This eliminates the possibility that clients will download updates before they have been tested and approved by the network administrator.

**NOTE**

Microsoft has recently updated SUS and it is now replaced by Windows Server Update Services (WSUS). You can read more about this product on the Windows Server Update Services website (http://www.microsoft.com/windowsserversystem/updateservices/default.mspx). The information in the following section pertains to both SUS and WSUS.

# Installing and Configuring Software Update Services

Software Update Services (SUS) are installed on a server to centralize the distribution of software updates. Before you install SUS, make sure that the computer meets the hardware and software requirements outlined in the following lists:

▶ Pentium III 700MHZ

▶ 512MB of RAM

▶ 6GB free space to store updates

**NOTE**

A computer running SUS with the minimum hardware requirements listed here is capable of supporting up to 15,000 clients.

The software requirements to run SUS are as follows:

▶ Windows 2000 SP2 or higher, or Windows Server 2003

▶ IIS 5.0 or higher

▶ Internet Explorer 5.5 or higher

Also keep in mind that SUS must be installed on an NTFS partition. The system partition of the SUS host must also be formatted with NTFS. If the computer does not meet the software requirements just outlined, the SUS setup program will not permit you to install the software.

## Installing Software Update Services

After you have determined that your computer meets all the requirements, you are ready to begin the installation of SUS. The software can be downloaded for free from Microsoft's website.

After SUS has been downloaded, you can run setup using the following steps:

1. Double-click the executable called `Sus10sp1.exe`. This launches the setup program for Software Update Services with Service Pack 1. Click Next.

2. Accept the licensing agreement and click Next.

3. Select the type of installation. Performing a typical installation installs SUS with the default settings. Click Next.

4. The next window displays the URL that clients will use to connect to the SUS server. Click Install.

5. Click Finish. The SUS administration website opens, from which you can configure your SUS server.

## Configuring Software Update Services

If you choose a typical installation, the SUS server is automatically configured with specific default settings:

► The SUS server is configured to retrieve software updates from the Microsoft Windows Update servers.

► The proxy server configuration is set to automatically detect settings.

► Content that is downloaded is stored locally.

► All packages are available in all supported languages.

► Any approved packages that are later updated are not automatically approved.

► Clients locate the server using its NetBIOS name.

If the default settings are sufficient, you do not need to reconfigure the SUS server. If you need to make configuration changes, an SUS server can be configured using the SUS web administration tools. You can access the administration tools in two ways. You can access the administration site using the following URL: `http:///SUSAdmin`. You can also access the web page by clicking Start, Administrative Tools, and selecting Microsoft Software Update Services (see Figure 4.7). To begin configuring the SUS server, click the Set Options link.

From the Set Options page shown in Figure 4.8, you can configure three different options. Under Select a Proxy Server Configuration, you can specify how the SUS server accesses the Internet.

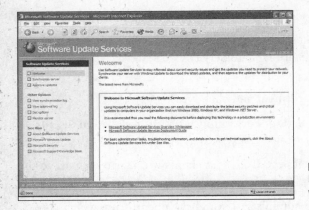

**FIGURE 4.7** Microsoft Software Update Services Administration website.

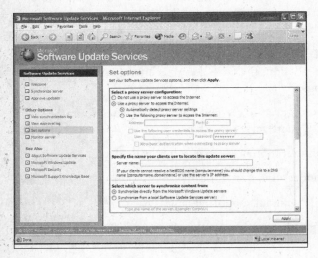

**FIGURE 4.8** The Set Options page.

Choose one of the following options based on your network configuration:

► *Do Not Use a Proxy Server to Access the Internet*—Select this option if the SUS server does not use a proxy server to connect to the Internet.

► *Use a Proxy Server to Access the Internet*—Select this option if the SUS server accesses the Internet through a proxy server.

► *Automatically Detect Proxy Server Settings*—Select this option if your network supports automatic discovery of proxy server settings.

► *Use the Following Proxy Server to Access the Internet*—Select this option if the network does not support automatic configuration of proxy settings. Specify the address or port number of the proxy server. You can also specify the user account and password that the SUS server should use if credentials are required.

The next section enables you to specify the name that clients will use to locate the SUS server. You can specify the NetBIOS name of the SUS server, or, if clients on the network do not support NetBIOS, you can specify the DNS name or the IP address.

The final section on the Set Options window enables you to configure the location from which the SUS server will get software updates. An SUS server can retrieve software updates directly from Microsoft, or it can retrieve them from another SUS server. To have the SUS server retrieve updates from Microsoft, select Synchronize Directly from the Microsoft Windows Update Servers. To have the SUS server retrieve updates from another SUS server, select Synchronize from a Local Software Update Services Server and specify the name of the server.

An administrator can also change how the SUS server handles updated content. This enables you to specify what the SUS server should do when software packages that are previously approved are updated. You can select from two options:

▶ Automatically Approve New Versions of Previously Approved Updates.

▶ Do Not Automatically Approve New Versions of Previously Approved Updates. I Will Manually Approve These Later.

If you want to test an update before it is downloaded and installed by clients, you should select the second option (Do Not Automatically Approve New Versions of Previously Approved Updates. I Will Manually Approve These Later). This means that any software packages that you previously approved but that have been updated by Microsoft require approval again by the administrator before clients can install them.

When an SUS server connects to the Microsoft Windows Update site, it can download two types of content. First, it downloads a file that describes the list of packages (Aucatalog1.cab). Second, it downloads the actual software packages.

As an administrator, you can choose whether the SUS server should download the packages or just the catalog file. If the SUS server downloads only the catalog file, any clients that are configured for Automatic Updates first check the list of approved packages from the local SUS server and then connect to the Windows Update servers to download the approved packages. You can also choose to download the packages and store them locally on the SUS server. If the updates are stored locally on the SUS server, any clients configured for Automatic Updates will download the approved software packages directly from the local SUS server. On this screen, you can also specify the locales that will be downloaded by selecting each language that you need to support on the network.

# Installing and Configuring Automatic Client Update Settings

For SUS to work, clients need to install a special version of Automatic Update software. When the updated version of Automatic Update is installed, clients can download updates from a server running SUS, and the updates can be installed at a preconfigured interval. The updated version of Automatic Update can run on Windows 2000 and later platforms.

## Installing Automatic Client Update

The Automatic Update client can be installed in a number of ways. You can run the setup locally on each client computer, or you can choose to perform a centralized deployment. Installing the client locally is a very simple process. Simply download the client from Microsoft's website and run the WUAU22.msi file. To install the client automatically using Active Directory, perform the following steps:

1. Click Start, point to Administrative Tools, and click Active Directory Users and Computers.

2. Right-click the appropriate Organizational Unit and click Properties.

3. From the Group Policy tab, click Edit to use an existing group policy object, or click New to create a new one.

4. Under Computer Configuration, select Software Settings.

5. Right-click Software Installation, point to New, and click Package.

6. Locate the WUAU22.msi file and click Open.

7. The Deploy Software window appears. Click Assigned and click OK.

## Configuring Automatic Client Update Settings

After you've installed the Automatic Updates software, you can configure the settings using the software interface on the client or through a Group Policy Object.

A few steps must be completed before you can configure Automatic Updates via a Group Policy Object. First, you must load the Automatic Update policy settings template. To do so, open the appropriate Group Policy Object. Under either Computer Settings or User Settings, right-click Administrative Templates and click Add. Type in the name for the Automatic Updates ADM file (WUAU.adm) located in the Windows\inf directory and click Open.

After you have completed these steps, you can begin configuring the Automatic Updates Group Policy Object settings for clients on the network. Table 4.1 summarizes the settings that are available (see Figure 4.9).

**FIGURE 4.9** Automatic Update group policy settings.

## TABLE 4.1  Automatic Update Settings

| Group Policy Setting | Description |
| --- | --- |
| Configure Automatic Updates | Three options are available: |
| | Notify for Download and Notify for Install—An administrative user (member of the Local Administrators group) is notified before the download and installation of any updates. This means that an administrator must approve any new updates before they are downloaded and installed. |
| | Auto Download and Notify for Install—Updates are automatically downloaded, and an administrative user is notified before installation. |
| | Auto Download and Schedule the Install—Updates are automatically downloaded and scheduled for installation. |
| Specify Intranet Microsoft Update Service Location | With this option, administrators can define the SUS server from which clients will retrieve updates. You can also specify which server clients will send statistics to, such as the successful installation of an update. |
| Reschedule Automatic Updates Scheduled Installation | If automatic updates are configured to install at a particular time and the scheduled time passes, an administrator can use this option to configure when the installation will occur next. |
| No Autorestart for Scheduled Automatic Updates Installation | This option can be used to prevent Automatic Updates from restarting a computer when a user is logged on. |

If an environment does not employ Active Directory, Automatic Update settings can be configured only by instituting various Registry entries to make the needed changes.

To define which SUS server clients you should use to retrieve updates and send status information to, add the following entries under `HKEY_LOCAL_MACHINE\Software\Policies\Microsoft\Windows\WindowsUpdate`:

▶ `WUServer`—This specifies the location of the server from which updates will be downloaded. The SUS server is identified by HTTP name, such as http://SUSserver.

▶ `WUStatusServer`—This specifies the location of the server to which the client will send status information. Again, the server is identified by HTTP name.

To configure other settings, such as the day and time that updates should occur, add the following entries under `HKEY_LOCAL_MACHINE\Software\Policies\Microsoft\Windows\WindowsUpdate\AU`:

▶ `UseWUServer`—This specifies that the client must use an SUS server to obtain updates. Set the value to 1 for clients for Automatic Updates to use an SUS server.

▶ `AUOptions`—Use this option to configure whether the local administrator should be notified of downloads and installations, as well as whether updates should be installed on a defined schedule. The possible values are 2 (notify of download and installation), 3 (automatically download and notify of installation), or 4 (automatic download and schedule installation).

▶ `ScheduledInstallDay`—This defines the day that updates should be installed. The values range from 0 to 7, where 0 indicates every day and 1–7 indicate specific days of the week (1 = Sunday and 7 = Saturday).

▶ `ScheduledInstallTime`—This defines the time of day that updates should be installed. The value is specified in 24-hour format.

▶ `RescheduleWaitTime`—This defines when updates should occur when the predefined scheduled time has passed. The value is specified in minutes (1–60).

▶ `NoAutoRebootWithLoggedOnUsers`—This defines whether Automatic Updates can reboot a computer when a user is logged on. Set this value to 1 to enable the logged-on user to choose whether to reboot the computer.

▶ `NoAutoUpdate`—This enables or disables automatic updates.

# Monitoring Network Protocol Security

Organizations want to ensure that communications remain secure. Therefore, it's important for network administrators to monitor network communications to ensure that communications are indeed trustworthy. A number of tools included with Windows Server 2003 can be used to monitor network protocol security. The following sections introduce you to some of these tools and how they can be used.

## Using the IP Security MMC Snap-In

Internet Protocol Security (IPSec) is a protocol used to secure communications between two hosts. (The IPSec protocol is covered in more detail in Chapter 5, "Routing and Remote Access.") As part of managing and maintaining network security, administrators can use the IP Security Monitor tool to validate that communications between hosts are indeed secure. It provides information such as which IPSec policy is active and whether a secure communication channel is being established between computers.

You can use the IP Security Monitor MMC to monitor IPSec on a computer running Windows Server 2003. Some of the functionality of the tool includes the following:

▶ Administrators have the capability to monitor IPSec on the local computer or on a remote system.

▶ It provides information such as the name and description of active IPSec policies.

▶ Administrators can view main mode and quick mode statistics. Main mode and quick mode are the two phases of IKE negotiations.

▶ The refresh rates can be customized.

▶ Administrators can search for filters based on a source or destination IP address.

To open the IP Security Monitor snap-in, perform the following steps:

1. Click Start and click Run.

2. Type MMC and click OK.

3. In the Microsoft Management Console, click File and then click Add/Remove Snap-in.

4. From the Add/Remove Snap-in window, click Add.

5. From the list of available snap-ins, select IP Security Monitor and click the Add button (see Figure 4.10). Click Close.

6. Click OK.

**FIGURE 4.10** Adding the IP Security Monitor snap-in.

You can use the IP Security Monitor console, shown in Figure 4.11, to view IPSec information locally or on a remote computer. To add another computer to the console, right-click the IP Security Monitor container within the console and click Add Computer. Type the name of the computer that you want to connect to, or click the Browse button to search for it.

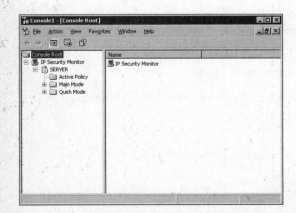

**FIGURE 4.11** The IP Security Monitor snap-in.

**EXAM ALERT**

IP Security Monitor can only be used to monitor computers running Windows XP and Windows Server 2003. The version of IP Security Monitor included with Windows Server 2003 cannot be used to monitor a computer running Windows 2000.

Expanding the IP Security Monitor container displays the name of the local computer or any remote computer that you are connected to. By expanding the computer, you will see three containers: Active Policy, Main Mode, and Quick Mode.

As noted previously, IP Security Monitor can be used to view the active IPSec policies on a computer. Clicking the Active Policy container within the console displays the following information:

▶ *Policy Name*—Lists the name of the active IPSec policy.

▶ *Policy Description*—Lists an optional description of the policy outlining the purpose of the policy.

▶ *Policy Last Modified*—Indicates when the policy was last modified. This option is applicable only to policies applied to a local computer.

▶ *Policy Store*—Specifies the storage location for the active IPSec policy.

▶ *Policy Path*—Specifies the Lightweight Directory Access Protocol path to the IPSec policy.

▶ *Organizational Unit*—Specifies the Organizational Unit to which the group policy is applied.

▶ *Group Policy Object Name*—Specifies the name of the group policy object to which the IPSec policy is applied.

You'll notice two other containers listed under your server within the IP Security Monitor console: Main Mode and Quick Mode. Clicking on either of these containers displays a number of other containers (see Figure 4.12). In any case, you can use these different options to monitor communications between hosts. A multitude of statistics can be used to monitor IPSec.

**FIGURE 4.12**  Viewing main mode statistics.

# Using the Support Tools

Windows Server 2003 also includes a number of other tools that can be used to monitor network protocol security. These tools are not installed by default. To install the support tools, perform the following steps:

1. Insert the Windows Server 2003 CD.

2. From the Welcome screen, click Browse This CD.

3. Locate the Support\Tools directory on the CD.

4. Double-click suptools.msi and follow the instructions to complete the installation.

Some of the tools that you might find useful for monitoring network protocol security include the following:

▶ *Netdiag*—Netdiag can be used to obtain basic network information. One thing to note is that the version of Netdiag included with Windows Server 2003 does not display any IPSec-specific statistics.

▶ *Netsh*—This command-line utility can be used to view or modify the network configuration of a computer.

# Troubleshooting Network Protocol Security

Monitoring network protocol security is an important aspect of maintaining overall security. By regularly monitoring network communications, you can more easily identify problems that might be occurring. This is another important aspect of an administrator's job: troubleshooting problems and resolving them as quickly and as efficiently as possible. When it comes to troubleshooting network protocol security, a number of different tools are available for determining the cause of the problem.

# Using the IP Security Monitor MMC Snap-In

As previously mentioned, IP Security Monitor can be used to monitor and fine-tune IPSec performance. However, it is also a very useful tool for troubleshooting. The IP Security snap-in can be used to determine which IPSec policy is being assigned. For example, if IPSec communication is not functioning as it should, you can use IP Security Monitor to verify which IPSec policy is currently in effect on the computer.

IP Security Monitor can also be used to view IPSec statistics, which can provide useful information for troubleshooting. For example, if you are experiencing a large number of failures when attempting IP-secured communications, you can use IP Security Monitor to view related statistics.

> **NOTE**
>
> IPSec is covered in more detail in Chapter 5 under the section titled "Implementing Secure Access Between Private Networks."

# Event Viewer

One of the most useful tools for troubleshooting is the Event Viewer. Using this tool, you can view events that are recorded in the event logs. By default, a computer running Windows Server 2003 typically has three logs listed within the Event Viewer: the application, system, and security logs. You might have additional logs listed, depending on the services installed. For example, a log file is created for the DNS service when it is installed. If the computer running Windows Server 2003 is configured as a domain controller, it will also contain the File Replication Service log and the Directory Service log. Each of the different logs is summarized in the following:

- ▶ *Application*—This log contains events pertaining to applications and programs running on the computer.

- ▶ *Security*—This log contains events pertaining to security as defined in the Audit policy. For example, this includes successful logons, resource access, and use of user rights. By default, security logging is enabled in Windows Server 2003.

▶ *System*—This log contains events generated by Windows system components.

▶ *Directory Service*—This log contains events generated by Active Directory. This log is available only if the computer is configured as a domain controller.

▶ *File Replication Service*—This log contains events generated by the Windows File Replication Service. For example, any errors generated while the sysvol on domain controllers is being updated are written to this log. Again, this log file is present only if the computer is configured as a domain controller.

▶ *DNS Server*—This log contains events generated by the DNS service. This log is present only if the computer is configured as a DNS server.

You can open the Event Viewer by clicking Start, pointing to Administrative Tools, and selecting the Event Viewer submenu (see Figure 4.13).

**FIGURE 4.13** Opening the Event Viewer to view system events.

With Event Viewer open, you can view the contents of a log file by selecting it. The entries contained with the log file are displayed on the Details pane (see Figure 4.14).

There is detailed information about every event that is written to one of the log files. By double-clicking a specific event, you can view the event header information (see Figure 4.15). Table 4.2 summarizes the available information.

**FIGURE 4.14** Viewing the contents of a log file.

**FIGURE 4.15** Viewing the event detail information.

**TABLE 4.2    Fields Contained in the Event Detail Pane**

| Information | Description |
|---|---|
| Date | The date when the event occurred. |
| Time | The specific time of day when the event occurred. |
| User | The name of the user under which the event occurred. |
| Computer | The name of the computer on which the event occurred. Normally, this is the local computer unless you are viewing the contents of a log file on a remote computer. |

*(continues)*

**TABLE 4.2** *Continued*

| Information | Description |
| --- | --- |
| Source | The software that logged the event. This can be a program or a system component. |
| Event | A number identifying the event that has occurred. This number can help support personnel to troubleshoot the event. |
| Type | The type of event. The system and application logs define an event as a warning, error, or information. |
| Classification | The classification of the event by the event source. |

As already noted in Table 4.2, different types of events can occur. The type of event depends on which log file you are examining. Event viewer displays five different types of events, as summarized in Table 4.3.

**TABLE 4.3   Event Types**

| Event Type | Description |
| --- | --- |
| Information | An event successfully occurred, such as the loading of a device driver. |
| Warning | An event has occurred that might lead to future problems. For example, a hard drive might be running low on disk space. |
| Alert | A significant problem has occurred, such as the failure of a service to start. |
| Success audit | A successful action has been performed that is defined in the audit policy. |
| Failure audit | An unsuccessful action has been performed that is defined in the audit policy. |

You can use the Event Viewer to perform the following actions:

▶ *Troubleshoot IKE (Internet Key Exchange) Negotiations*—If you've enabled successes and failures for Audit Logon Events, IKE negotiation successes and failures are logged in the Security log. During the IKE negotiations two computers generate a shared, secret key used to secure communications between them.

▶ *Troubleshoot IPSec Policies*—If Audit Policy Changes has been enabled, you can monitor any changes that are made to the IPSec policies. Changes made to the IPSec policy result in an event being written to the Security log.

▶ *Monitor Dropped Packets*—If packet event logging is enabled through the Registry, you can monitor dropped inbound and outbound packets using the System log.

# Network Monitor

As an organization increases in size, new services and applications are installed; as network shares are created, traffic on a network can increase greatly. Take, for example, the Dynamic Host Configuration Protocol (DHCP). Adding DHCP to a network most definitely has an affect on network traffic during the IP lease and the renewal process.

> **TIP**
>
> Remember that one of the ways in which you can optimize network traffic is to configure the bindings as well as disable unnecessary protocols and services.

Using a tool called Network Monitor, you can monitor and log network activity and then use the information to manage and optimize traffic. Another use for this tool is for troubleshooting network communications. For example, you can use Network Monitor to view and troubleshoot IPSec communication.

Network Monitor consists of the following components:

- ▶ *Network Monitor Driver*—The Network Monitor Driver is responsible for capturing the frames coming to and from a network adapter.

- ▶ *Network Monitor Tools*—These tools are used to view and analyze the data captured by the Network Monitor Driver.

## Installing Network Monitor

Network Monitor Tools are not installed with Windows Server 2003 by default, but they can be installed using the following process. Installing Network Monitor Tools automatically installs the Network Monitor Driver.

1. Select Start, Control Panel, Add or Remove Programs.

2. Click Add/Remove Windows Components.

3. Within the Windows Component Wizard, select Management and Monitoring Tools, and click the Details button.

4. Select the Network Monitor Tools check box (see Figure 4.16). Click OK.

5. Click Next. Click Finish.

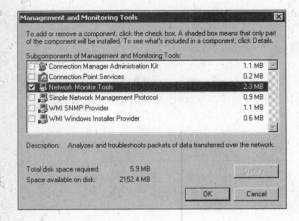

**FIGURE 4.16** Installing Network Monitor.

In some instances, you want to install only the Network Monitor Driver. For example, a computer running Network Monitor Driver can capture the information and forward it to a Systems Management Server (SMS) machine. It is also useful to capture network traffic on a subnet that is remote to where Network Monitor Tools are being run. To install the Network Monitor Driver component, perform the following steps:

1. Within the Network Connections applet, right-click the local area connection and choose Properties.

2. From the Properties window for the local area connection, click Install.

3. Click Protocol and click Add.

4. Within the Network Protocol window, click the Network Monitor Driver.

5. Click OK.

## Using Network Monitor

Network Monitor can display a large amount of information about the frames captured to and from a network adapter card. When Network Monitor is first opened, four panes are displayed within the console. The Graph pane displays the network activity in a bar chart. The Sessions Stats pane displays information about individual sessions. The Station Stats pane displays statistics about the sessions the server is participating in. The Total Stats pane displays summary statistics since the capture was started.

To view statistics about network traffic, you must first start a capture. To do so, click the Start option from the Capture menu. To view the captured data, click the Start and View option from the Capture menu. Network Monitor displays all the frames captured during the capture period with a Summary window. To view specific information about a frame, click the frame within the Summary window.

Now when you run Network Monitor, all frames going to and from the computer are captured. If you're looking for specific types of traffic, you can create a capture filter to define what types of frames should be captured. However, keep in mind that this increases the load on a server because it must examine each frame to determine whether it matches the criteria of the filter. To configure capture filters within Network Monitor, choose the Filter option from the Capture menu.

# Exam Prep Questions

1. You are the network administrator for your company. All domain controllers and member servers are running Microsoft Windows Server 2003.

   You have configured multiple IPSec policies throughout the Active Directory hierarchy. You discover that the correct IPSec policy settings are not configured on SRV01.

   You need to determine which IPSec policy is being used on SRV01.

   What should you do?

   - ○ **A.** Launch Network Monitor and capture all IPSec traffic coming to and from SRV01.

   - ○ **B.** Open the IP Security Monitor on SRV01.

   - ○ **C.** Launch the Resultant Set of Policy on SRV01.

   - ○ **D.** Open the IP Security Policy Management on SRV01.

2. You are the network administrator for your organization. All servers have been upgraded to Microsoft Windows Server 2003.

   You are trying to install Software Updates Services (SUS) on an existing server. The installation of the software continually fails. You verify that the computer meets the hardware requirements. The server is also running IIS 5.0 and Internet Explorer 6.0, and all partitions except the system partition are formatted with NTFS.

   You need to install SUS on the server.

   What could be causing the problem?

   - ○ **A.** Service pack 1 is not installed.

   - ○ **B.** The partition storing the updates is not formatted with FAT.

   - ○ **C.** IIS must be uninstalled.

   - ○ **D.** The system partition must be formatted with NTFS.

3. You are the network administrator for a small organization. Servers are running Microsoft Windows Server 2003. Client computers have been upgraded to Windows XP Professional.

   You want to configure Automatic Updates settings through a group policy. You create a new group policy object for the appropriate Organizational Unit. When you open the policy, you cannot find any Automatic Updates settings to configure.

   You need to deploy the settings through a group policy object.

What is causing the problem?

- ○ **A.** You are not permitted to edit group policy objects.
- ○ **B.** Software Update Services has not been installed.
- ○ **C.** The Automatic Updates ADM file has not been loaded.
- ○ **D.** Automatic Updates settings must be configured on each local computer.

4. You are the network administrator for your company. All domain controllers and members servers have been upgraded to Microsoft Windows Server 2003.

   You are planning to deploy Software Updates Services on an existing server. Client computers on the network are running various client operating systems.

   You need to identify which operating systems will support the updated version of Automatic Updates.

   Select the operating systems that support the updated version of Automatic Updates. (Choose all correct answers.)

   - ○ **A.** Windows 95
   - ○ **B.** Windows 98
   - ○ **C.** Windows Me
   - ○ **D.** Windows 2000
   - ○ **E.** Windows XP

5. You are the network administrator for a large accounting firm. All servers are running Microsoft Windows Server 2003.

   You discover that some of the other network administrators have made configuration changes when troubleshooting problems. You are now concerned that some of the servers on the network no longer meet the security requirements outlined by the company's security policy. You want to verify the current security settings on the servers against those in the security template applied to all new servers.

   What should you do?

   - ○ **A.** Run the Resultant Set of Policy tool. Compare the current settings to those in the security template.
   - ○ **B.** Run the Security Configuration and Analysis tool. Compare the current settings to those in the security template.
   - ○ **C.** Use the IP Security Monitor tool to determine the policy in effect. Compare the settings to those in the template.
   - ○ **D.** Use the Security Templates snap-in to compare the current settings to those in the security template.

6. You are the network administrator for a pharmaceutical company. All servers are running Microsoft Windows Server 2003.

   You are implementing a secure baseline for all new servers added to the network. You want each server to be configured with a standard set of security settings.

   You need to accomplish this with as little administrative effort as possible.

   What should you do?

   ○ **A.** Manually configure the settings on each server.

   ○ **B.** Create a security template using the Security Templates snap-in with all the required security settings and deploy it through a GPO.

   ○ **C.** Use the Security Configuration and Analysis tool to create a new template with all the required security settings. Deploy the settings through a GPO.

   ○ **D.** Use Software Updates Services to configure each new server with the required security settings.

7. You are the network administrator for your company. All servers are running Microsoft Windows Server 2003. Client computers are running Microsoft Windows XP Professional.

   You are editing the Registry to configure Automatic Updates on a client computer. You want to specify which SUS server the client computer will retrieve the updates from.

   Which of the following Registry options should you configure to specify the SUS server that the updates will be downloaded from?

   ○ **A.** UseWUServer

   ○ **B.** AUOptions

   ○ **C.** WUServer

   ○ **D.** SUSServer

8. You are the network administrator for a large insurance agency. All servers are running Microsoft Windows Server 2003.

   You have implemented an IPSec policy on several company servers. You want to specify default traffic exemptions on these servers.

   You need to accomplish this with as little administrative effort as possible.

   What should you do?

   ○ **A.** Execute the netdiag to make the necessary IPSec configuration changes.

   ○ **B.** Execute the ipsecmon command with the required parameters the make the change.

     ○  **C.**  Use the IPSec Policy Management tool to configure IPSec.

     ○  **D.**  Create a script that uses the `netsh` command to configure IPSec.

9. You are the network administrator for your company. All servers are running Microsoft Windows Server 2003.

 You discover that the IPSec policy configured for domain controllers is not behaving normally. You suspect that a configuration change was made by another administrator.

 You need to determine whether a change was made.

 What should you do?

     ○  **A.**  Open the IP Security Monitor tool and select the Active Policy container.

     ○  **B.**  Launch the Security Configuration and Analysis tool. Analyze the IPSec settings on the server.

     ○  **C.**  Open the Windows Event Viewer and view the contents of the Security log.

     ○  **D.**  Execute the `ipsecpol` command from the command prompt.

10. You are the network administrator for your organization. All servers are being migrated from Windows 2000 to Microsoft Windows Server 2003.

 IP Security Monitor will be used to monitor IPSec communications on several servers. You use the IP Security Monitor snap-in from your administrative computer to monitor the servers across the network. However, you discover that you are able to monitor only other computers running Windows Server 2003.

 What is causing the problem?

     ○  **A.**  You do not have administrative permissions on the servers running Windows 2000.

     ○  **B.**  IP Security Monitor cannot be used to monitor computers running Windows 2000.

     ○  **C.**  The Windows 2000 servers are not members of the local domain.

     ○  **D.**  The Network Monitor driver is not installed on the Windows 2000 servers.

# Answers to Exam Prep Questions

1. **B.** IP Security Monitor can be used to gather and monitor IPSec statistics. The Active Policy container will tell you which IPSec policy is currently being used. Answer A is incorrect because Network Monitor is used to capture and analyze IP packets. The results will not indicate which policy is in effect. Answer C is incorrect because

Resultant Set of Policy will not tell you which IPSec policy is currently being used. This tool can be used to identify existing policy settings. Answer D is incorrect because IP Security Policy Management is used only to create and manage IP Security policies.

2. **D.** Software Updates Services requires that the system partition be formatted with NTFS along with the partition on which the software will be installed. Answer A is incorrect because no service pack is required to install SUS. Answer B is incorrect because the partition on which SUS is installed must be NTFS as well. Answer C is incorrect because IIS 5.0 is required.

3. **C.** To deploy the Automatic Updates settings using a group policy, the ADM file must first be loaded. If it's not, the Automatic Updates settings will not be available within a group policy object. Answer A is incorrect because the scenario already states that you are an administrator. Answer B is incorrect because installing the SUS software does not automatically add the Automatic Updates settings into a group policy object. Answer D is incorrect because settings can be configured locally or through a group policy.

4. **D and E.** The updated version of the Automatic Updates software can be installed on Windows 2000 platforms and later. Therefore, the remaining answers are incorrect.

5. **B.** The Security Configuration and Analysis tool can be used to analyze the current security settings of a computer and compare them against the settings within an existing template. Answer A is incorrect because the Resultant Set of Policy tool is used for troubleshooting and planning policy settings. It cannot be used to compare existing settings to those in a security template. Answer C is incorrect because IP Security Monitor is used to monitor and troubleshoot IPSec communications. Answer D is incorrect because the Security Templates snap-in is used to configure existing templates and create new ones.

6. **B.** You can use the Security Templates snap-in to create a new template with the required security settings. The template can then be imported into a GPO. Answer A is incorrect. Although this is a viable solution, it is not the most efficient one. It requires configuring the same settings on each server. Answer C is incorrect because this tool cannot be used to create new templates. Answer D is incorrect because SUS is used to deploy software updates to clients.

7. **C.** To specify which server a client will download the updates from, you must configure the WUServer value. Answer A is incorrect because it only enabled Automatic Updates to use an SUS server. Answer B is incorrect because this option is used to specify how updates are downloaded and installed. Answer D is incorrect because there is no such option.

8. **D.** The netsh command-line utility can be used to configure IPSec. It can be used with scripting, making it easier to deploy changes to multiple servers. Answer A is incorrect because this command-line utility is no longer used to configure IPSec. Answer B is incorrect because this command is used to launch the IP Security Monitor

in Windows 2000. Answer C is incorrect because it would be easier to deploy the changes using a script instead of making the configuration change on each server. You can also not use the IPSec Policy Management console to specify default traffic exemptions.

9. **C.** As long as auditing of policy changes has been enabled, you can monitor when changes are made to an IPSec policy using the Event Viewer. Audited events are written to the Security log. Therefore answers A, B, and D are incorrect because these tools cannot be used to monitor whether an IPSec policy change was made. The `ipsecpol` command is used in Windows 2000 to configure IPSec policies, filters, and filter actions.

10. **B.** The IP Security Monitor included with Windows Server 2003 cannot be used to monitor computers running Windows 2000. Therefore answers A, C, and D are incorrect.

# Need to Know More?

Search the online version of TechNet and the Windows Server 2003 Server Resource Kit using keywords such as "IP Security Monitor," "Security," and "Security Configuration and Analysis."

Search the Windows Update site at the following URL for more information about Software Update Services: www.microsoft.com/windows2000/windowsupdate/sus/default.asp.

Windows Server 2003 Security Guide: http://www.microsoft.com/technet/security/prodtech/windowsserver2003/w2003hg/sgch00.mspx.

CHAPTER FIVE

# Routing and Remote Access

## Terms you'll need to understand:

✓ Authentication

✓ Remote Access Service (RAS)

✓ Internet Authentication Server

✓ Routing Information Protocol (RIP)

✓ Open Shortest Path First (OSPF)

✓ IP routing

✓ IPSec

## Techniques you'll need to master:

✓ Configuring a remote access server

✓ Configuring the different authentication and encryption protocols

✓ Understanding the components of a remote access policy

✓ Understanding how remote access policies are evaluated

✓ Configuring routing and remote access for Dynamic Host Configuration Protocol (DHCP) integration

✓ Configuring a virtual private network (VPN)

✓ Understanding the different routing protocols

✓ Implementing and configuring demand-dial routing

✓ Understanding the difference between dynamic and static routing

✓ Understanding and implementing IPSec

✓ Troubleshooting routing and remote access

As technology advances and enables users to be more mobile, the need for remote access is quickly increasing. Providing users with access to network resources from remote locations, such as home offices and client and business sites, is becoming a necessity. Organizations need the flexibility of providing mobile users access to network resources without a compromise in security or a drastic increase in administrative overhead.

Also, as networks continue to become interconnected, businesses are always looking for cost-effective and practical ways to implement routing. The option is always available to purchase high-end dedicated, complex routing solutions. However, with Windows Server 2003, a simple, efficient, and effective routing solution is built into the operating system.

This chapter covers important topics related to Windows Server 2003 routing and remote access. You learn how to configure a remote access server and provide access to the network without compromising security, and you learn about some of the management and monitoring tasks that go along with remote access. You also learn how to configure a virtual private network (VPN), and how to enable and configure the routing feature that is included with routing and remote access.

# Configuring Remote Access

Windows Server 2003 includes the Routing and Remote Access Service (RRAS), which enables remote clients to connect to a remote access server and use resources as though they were directly attached to the network. RRAS can be used to configure VPNs, thus expanding your LAN over the Internet.

Windows 2000 introduced routing and remote access, which replaced the remote access service of Windows NT 4.0. RRAS in Windows Server 2003 includes the following features:

► RRAS servers can be configured to use a preshared key instead of a certificate for VPN connections using the Layer 2 Tunneling Protocol (L2TP) and IP Security (IPSec).

► Network Address Translation (NAT) now supports both dynamic and static packet filtering. Dynamic filtering is implemented through the use of Basic Firewall.

► In Windows 2000, NAT did not support L2TP/IPSec connections. NAT in Windows Server 2003 can translate L2TP/IPSec VPN connections.

Windows Server 2003 remote access provides two connectivity methods:

▶ *Dial-up*—Using dial-up remote access such as an ISDN or a phone line, clients can connect to a remote access server.

▶ *VPN (virtual private network)*—Clients connect to a remote access server configured as a VPN server using an IP-based internetwork (most often the public Internet).

# Enabling Routing and Remote Access

RRAS is installed by default with Windows Server 2003. However, before you can begin using RRAS, it must first be enabled. Assuming that the server is configured with two network cards (or a network card and a modem), you can enable a server as a remote access (dial-up or VPN) server by following these steps:

1. Click Start, point to Administrative Tools, and click Routing and Remote Access.

2. Right-click the server and select Configure and Enable Routing and Remote Access. Click Next.

3. The Routing and Remote Access Server Setup Wizard opens. From the list of common configurations, select Remote Access (dial-up or VPN). The remaining options are summarized in Table 5.1. Click Next.

**TABLE 5.1  Common Remote Access Configurations**

| Configuration | Description |
|---|---|
| Remote Access (dial-up or VPN) | Enables computers to connect to the server using a dial-up or VPN connection |
| Network Address Translation (NAT) | Allows internal computers to access the Internet using a single public IP address |
| Virtual private network (VPN) access and NAT | Allows computers to access the remote access server through the Internet, and allows internal clients to access the Internet using a single public IP address |
| Secure communications between two private networks | Connects the network to a remote network |
| Custom configuration | Allows you to choose any combination of features |

4. Select the connection methods clients can use to connect to the remote access server (VPN and/or dial-up). Click Next.

5. Choose the network interface for clients to use. Click Next.

6. On the IP Address Assignment screen, select how remote access clients will receive an IP address (see Figure 5.1). IP addresses can be assigned automatically using a Dynamic Host Configuration Protocol (DHCP) server on the internal network, or you can configure a range of IP addresses on the remote access server to assign to remote access clients. If you choose the second option, the resulting wizard screen enables you to configure the range of IP addresses that are available to remote clients. Click Next.

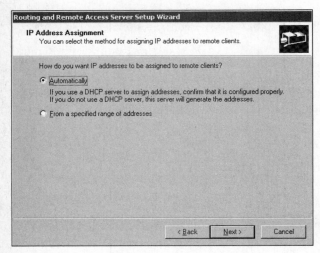

**FIGURE 5.1** You must configure IP address assignments for remote clients.

7. Specify whether to use a Remote Authentication Dial-In User Service (RADIUS) server. A RADIUS Server is used to centralize remote access authentication requests and accounting information. If you choose to use a RADIUS server, the resulting wizard screen enables you to specify the name of the primary and alternative RADIUS servers and the shared secret. Click Next.

8. Click Finish.

When you click the Finish button to exit the wizard, a warning message appears if you chose to use a DHCP server to assign IP addresses to remote clients (see Figure 5.2). The message warns you that to have DHCP messages relayed from remote clients to a DHCP server on the internal network, the remote access server must be configured as a DHCP Relay Agent. (This issue is covered in more detail in the section entitled "Configuring Routing and Remote Access for DHCP.")

**FIGURE 5.2** To complete the remote access process, you must configure a DHCP Relay Agent.

# Configuring Inbound Connections

The two main communication protocols used by dial-up remote access clients are the *Point-to-Point Protocol (PPP)* and the *Serial Line Internet Protocol (SLIP)*. PPP has become an industry-standard communications protocol because of its popularity; it provides support for multiple network protocols, including TCP/IP, IPX/SPX, and NetBEUI.

SLIP is a legacy communication protocol used primarily to connect to UNIX systems. One of the major disadvantages of SLIP is the lack of security (for example, sending passwords in clear text). Windows Server 2003 remote access supports the use of SLIP for outbound connections only. SLIP also does not support the DHCP functionality on a RAS server to assign dial-in clients an IP address.

You can configure PPP using the PPP tab in the Properties window of the remote access server (see Figure 5.3). You can enable the Multilink Connections option to allow remote access clients to aggregate multiple phone lines into a single logical connection, which increases bandwidth. For example, you can combine two B channels from an ISDN BRI connection. Although multilink enables multiple connections to act as a single logical connection, on its own it does not provide a way of dynamically adding and dropping links based on bandwidth requirements. The Bandwidth Allocation Protocol (BAP) provides this feature. BAP enables multilink connections to be added and dropped as bandwidth requirements change. For example, if the bandwidth utilization for a link goes beyond a configured level, the client who is requesting an additional link can send a BAP request message. The Bandwidth Allocation Control Protocol (BACP) works in conjunction with the Link Control Protocol (LCP) to elect a favored "peer" so that a favored peer can be identified if multiple BAP requests are received simultaneously. You can also enable or disable BAP, BACP, LCP, and software compression for PPP connections from the Properties window shown in Figure 5.3.

**FIGURE 5.3** You configure PPP via the PPP tab in the Properties window of the remote access server.

---

**NOTE**

To apply multilink at the remote access policy level, you must first enable it at the server level. This means that if multilink is not enabled through the Properties window for the remote access server, you will not be able to apply it in a remote access policy.

---

# Configuring Ports

Configuring inbound connections allows a remote access server to accept incoming connections from remote access clients. After RRAS has been enabled, a number of ports are created. Additional ports can be created, if necessary. You can configure the ports by right-clicking the Ports icon under the RAS server and selecting Properties. Select the ports that you want to configure and click the Configure button. Keep in mind that the configuration changes made apply to all ports. The configurable options are the same for PPTP and L2TP ports (see Figure 5.4). From this Properties window, you can also increase the number of ports by changing the Maximum Ports setting.

**FIGURE 5.4** You configure ports via the Ports Properties icon on the RAS server.

In the Configure Device dialog box shown in Figure 5.4, you can configure the ports for inbound use only, or for inbound and outbound use if the server is used for demand-dial routing. This is also where you can configure additional ports by setting the Maximum Ports value.

> **NOTE**
>
> Demand-dial routing enables on-demand connections using physical or virtual links. The benefits of a demand-dial connection, as opposed to a dedicated link, include reduced costs and increased security. For example, you can use demand-dial routing to enable two offices in different geographical locations to connect without incurring the cost of a dedicated link. This way, the connection is established only when necessary.

Modem and serial ports are also created for any modems that are installed on the server, and for any serial or parallel connections. These ports can also be configured in the Ports Properties dialog box.

# Configuring Routing and Remote Access User Authentication

With remote access, you are basically opening the door for remote access clients to access the internal network. With remote access arises the topic of security. You must be able to allow certain "trusted" clients to have remote access while denying access to everyone else. You also want to ensure that the data that is being sent between a remote access client and a remote access server is secure. To meet these requirements, Windows Server 2003 supports a number of authentication and encryption protocols.

# Configuring Remote Access Authentication Protocols

Windows Server 2003 supports a number of authentication protocols that can be used to authenticate dial-up clients. The supported protocols are as follows:

▶ *Password Authentication Protocol (PAP)*—PAP is the least secure of all of the authentication protocols because it sends the username and password in clear text.

▶ *Shiva Password Authentication Protocol (SPAP)*—SPAP can be used to authenticate against Shiva remote access servers and to authenticate against Windows 2003 Servers. This protocol is typically more secure than PAP but not as secure as CHAP or MS-CHAP.

▶ *Challenge Handshake Authentication Protocol (CHAP)*—CHAP does not send the username and password across the network. Instead, it uses a challenge response with a one-way hash algorithm. It is an industry-standard protocol that can be used to authenticate non[nd]Windows-based clients.

▶ *Microsoft Challenge Handshake Authentication Protocol (MS-CHAP)*—MS-CHAP is a Microsoft version of CHAP that uses mutual authentication and encryption for Windows-based clients. MS-CHAP version 2 provides strong encryption and separate encryption keys for sending and receiving data.

▶ *Extensible Authentication Protocol (EAP)*—EAP is an extension of PPP that provides support for other authentication mechanisms, such as smart cards. This authentication protocol requires the presence of a PK infrastructure.

---

**EXAM ALERT**

Knowing the features and the differences among the following authentication protocols is important for achieving success on the exam. For example, if your remote access clients use smart card authentication, you need to enable EAP on the remote access server. Or, if smart cards are not deployed, and all remote access clients are running Windows XP, you should only enable MS-CHAPv2 because it provides the most security.

---

Using the Properties dialog box for the remote access server that is shown in Figure 5.5, you can configure which authentication protocol the remote access server can use to authenticate remote clients. Clicking the Authentication

Methods button from the Security tab opens the Authentication Methods dialog box, from which you can select the authentication protocols that are available on the server.

**FIGURE 5.5**  You configure authentication methods by clicking the Authentication Methods button on the Security tab.

When you have enabled the authentication protocols at the server level, you can use the Authentication tab in the policy's Properties dialog box (see Figure 5.6) to specify which of the authentication protocols are available for each remote access policy. To do so, click the Remote Access Policies container, right-click the appropriate policy within the Details pane, and click Properties. You can access the Authentication tab by clicking the Edit Profile button.

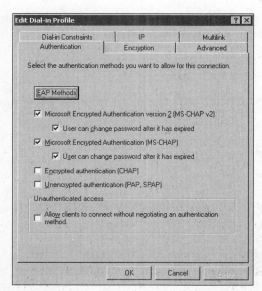

**FIGURE 5.6**  Configuring authentication methods in a remote access policy via the Authentication tab.

# Configuring Encryption Protocols

If you're sending sensitive data across the network, you might want to add another level of security by implementing some form of data encryption. The two types of encryption available are as follows:

▶ *Microsoft Point-to-Point Encryption (MPPE)*—MPPE can use 40-bit, 56-bit, and 128-bit encryption keys. MPPE encryption can be used for PPP connections, including PPTP VPN connections. MPPE is used in conjunction with EAP-TLS and MS-CHAP authentication protocols.

▶ *IP Security (IPSec)*—IPSec is used with L2TP connections. It supports the Data Encryption Standard (DES) and triple DES (3DES).

---

**NOTE**

Some older Microsoft operating systems do not support 56-bit encryption. To support these clients, you must use 40-bit encryption instead. Otherwise, you should use 56-bit encryption. Also keep in mind that 128-bit encryption is supported only in North America.

---

Encryption for a dial-up connection is configured at the policy level. Right-click the remote access policy within the Details pane for the Remote Access Policies container. Open the Properties dialog box for the remote access policy, click the Edit Profile button, and select the Encryption tab (see Figure 5.7). Select one or more of the following encryption levels:

▶ *No Encryption*—Select this option to allow remote access clients to connect without requiring a form of encryption.

▶ *Basic*—This specifies whether remote access clients can connect using MPPE 40-bit or IPSec 56-bit DES encryption.

▶ *Strong*—This specifies whether remote access clients can connect using MPPE 56-bit or IPSec 56-bit DES encryption.

▶ *Strongest*—This specifies whether remote access clients can connect using MPPE 128-bit or IPSec triple DES (3DES).

**EXAM ALERT**

For PPTP connections, 128-bit MPPE is the highest level of encryption supported by Windows 98/ME/2000/XP. For L2TP connections, 3DES is the highest level of encryption for Windows 2000/XP (Windows 2000 requires service pack 2 or later). Windows 98 requires DUN 1.4.

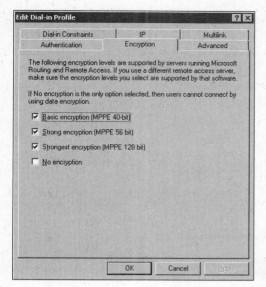

**FIGURE 5.7**  Configuring the encryption level for a profile.

# Configuring Internet Authentication Services (IAS) to Provide Authentication for Routing and Remote Access Clients

As your networks increase in size, you might need to implement multiple remote access servers. To ease the administrative overhead of managing multiple RAS servers, you can implement a RADIUS server to centralize the authentication of remote access clients and the storage of accounting information.

Windows Server 2003 can be configured for RADIUS by installing the Internet Authentication Service (IAS) through the Add or Remove programs applet in the Control Panel. With IAS, a server can be configured as a RADIUS server and a RADIUS proxy. When configured as a RADIUS server, RAS servers can forward authentication requests from RAS clients to the IAS server. IAS provides the benefit of centralizing user authentication and centralizing the storage of auditing and accounting information collected from the RAS servers. When RADIUS is implemented, the remote access server is configured as a RADIUS client. You can configure a RADIUS client when enabling routing and remote access. Any authentication requests to the remote access server are sent to the server running IAS. The server running IAS provides authentication, auditing, and accounting services for RADIUS clients.

When configured as a RADIUS proxy, an IAS server can forward authentication and accounting information to other RADIUS servers. The IAS server functions as a message router and forwards messages to another specified RADIUS server or client. Connection request[nd]processing rules are configured to tell the IAS server where to forward the authentication request messages. Keep in mind that an IAS server can function as a RADIUS server and a RADIUS proxy. Depending on the connection request[nd]processing rules configured, some connection requests can be authenticated and others can be forwarded.

## Installing IAS

IAS can be installed using the Add or Remove Programs applet within the Control Panel by performing the following steps:

1. Click Start, point to the Control Panel, and click Add or Remove Programs.

2. Click Add/Remove Windows Components.

3. From the list of Windows components, select Networking Services and click the Details button.

4. From the list of subcomponents, select Internet Authentication Service. Click OK. Click Next.

5. Click Finish.

When IAS has been installed, you can use the Internet Authentication Service MMC snap-in, which is located within the Administrative Tools menu, to configure IAS.

# Configuring Routing and Remote Access Policies to Permit or Deny Access

A *remote access policy* enables you to control which users are permitted remote access to the network and specify the characteristics of the connection. In terms of remote access, Windows 2000 introduced some major changes from Windows NT 4.0. One of these changes is the use of remote access policies. Before Windows 2000, remote access was controlled through the Properties dialog box of a user account. Windows 2000 and Windows Server 2003 use both user account properties and remote access policies to control remote access.

With remote access policies, administrators can permit or deny connection attempts based on a number of criteria (such as the time of day or group membership), giving administrators much more flexibility and granular control. When a connection has been permitted, administrators can further control the session by defining the maximum session time and encryption settings.

A remote access policy consists of the following elements, which work together to provide secure access to remote access servers:

► Conditions

► Permissions

► Profile

When remote access is enabled, two default remote access policies are created automatically: connection to Microsoft Routing and Remote Access Server and connections to other access servers. You can use the Connection to Microsoft Routing and Remote Access Server policy to grant access to remote access clients. By default, this policy is configured to deny remote access.

You can create additional policies by right-clicking the Remote Access Policies icon within the Routing and Remote Access management console and selecting the New Remote Access Policy option. The wizard prompts with the option of creating a typical policy for a common scenario using the wizard or to create a custom policy. The elements of a policy are discussed in the following section.

## Managing Remote Access Conditions

Conditions define the parameters that must match those configured on the remote access client before the server will grant remote access. These can include parameters such as the time of day and Windows group membership. Before the permissions of a remote access policy are evaluated, the connection attempt must match the conditions within a remote access policy. For example, the conditions of the policy might specify that you must be a member of the Sales group. If the user account is a member of the Sales group, the conditions have been met and the policy evaluation continues by checking the permissions of the user account. If multiple policies are configured, the first policy that matches the conditions of the connection attempt is then further evaluated for permissions and profile settings. Table 5.2 summarizes some of the commonly used conditions that can be configured for a remote access policy.

**TABLE 5.2   Conditions That Can Be Configured in a Remote Access Policy**

| Condition | Description |
| --- | --- |
| Called station ID | The number dialed by the remote access client |
| Calling station ID | The number from which the remote access client called |
| Day and time restrictions | The days of the week and time of day users are allowed remote access |
| Windows groups | The Windows groups to which the user must belong |

To configure the conditions of a remote access policy, follow these steps:

1. Open the Routing and Remote Access management console and click the Remote Access Policies container.

2. Right-click the remote access policy and click Properties.

3. From the Properties dialog box for the policy, click the Add button.

4. In the Select Attribute dialog box, select the attributes that you want to configure and click Add (see Figure 5.8).

**FIGURE 5.8** You can configure remote access conditions to further control how remote access is handled.

## Controlling Remote Access Permissions

If the connection attempt matches the conditions of a remote access policy, the permissions of that policy are then evaluated. The remote access permissions determine whether a specific user is granted or denied remote access. Windows Server 2003 uses a combination of the dial-in properties of a user account and the permissions in the remote access policy to determine whether the connection attempt is allowed. Remote access permissions can be explicitly allowed or denied through user account properties. When configuring remote access permissions using the Dial-In tab in the Properties dialog box for a user account, you have the following three options (see Figure 5.9):

▶ Allow Access

▶ Deny Access

▶ Control Access Through Remote Access Policy

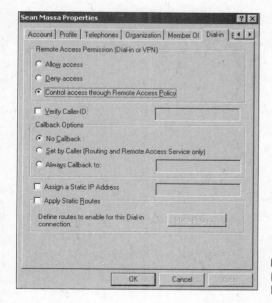

**FIGURE 5.9** Configuring remote access permissions through the user account properties.

If you explicitly allow remote access by selecting the Allow Access option, the connection attempt can still be denied if the properties configured for the user account do not match the remote access policy or if the profile settings are not met.

If you choose to have the policy control remote access permissions, you can grant or deny permission through the policy's Properties window (see Figure 5.10). If you are using the default policy, remote access permission is denied by default. You must change this setting to allow access.

From the Dial-In tab, several other settings can be configured, including caller ID, callback options, and static IP routes. Again, if you configure the settings for the user account, they must match the settings configured on the client or the connection attempt will be denied.

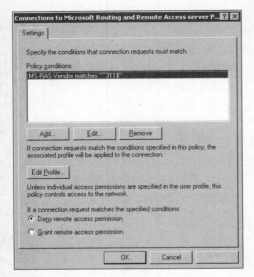

**FIGURE 5.10** Controlling access through the remote access policy.

# Configuring a Remote Access Profile

The final element of the remote access policy is the remote access profile. When the remote access client has been granted permission, the profile determines the settings of the connection. Again, the settings in the profile must match those of the connection attempt or it will be denied.

To configure the profile settings, click the Edit Profile button in the policy's Properties window. This opens the Edit Dial-In Profile dialog box, shown in Figure 5.11. Several tabs are available, as summarized in Table 5.3.

**FIGURE 5.11** You can configure a remote access profile via a remote access policy.

**TABLE 5.3    Remote Access Profile Settings**

| Property Tab | Description |
|---|---|
| Dial-In Constraints | Configure the disconnect if idle time, maximum session time, day and time restrictions, and media and number restrictions. |
| IP | Define how IP addresses are assigned to clients, and configure packet filtering for inbound and outbound connections. |
| Multilink | Enable and configure multilink and the Bandwidth Allocation Protocol. |
| Authentication | Configure the authentication methods that are available for the connections in the remote access policy. |
| Encryption | Configure the different levels of encryption for the policy. |
| Advanced | Specify additional connection parameters. |

## Evaluating Remote Access Policies

Given the many options and the complexity of remote access policy elements, it is important to have a good understanding of how policies are applied when a remote access client attempts a connection. Assuming that your domain functional level is Windows Server 2003, the following points outline the connection process:

▶ When a user attempts to establish a remote access connection, the RAS server determines whether a policy exists. The first policy in the ordered list of remote access policies is checked. If there is no policy configured (and the default policy has been deleted), the connection attempt is rejected. If a policy does exist, the evaluation process continues.

▶ The conditions of the first policy in the list are evaluated. If the connection attempt matches all the conditions, the evaluation process continues. If all conditions do not match the connection attempt, the next policy in the list is evaluated. If no more policies exist, the connection attempt is rejected.

▶ If the connection attempt matches the conditions in one of the policies, the permissions for the user are evaluated. If the user's account property is set to Deny Access, or if the permission within the policy is set to Deny Access, the connection attempt is rejected. If the policy or the account property is set to Allow Access, the process continues.

▶ The settings of the remote access profile and the properties of the user account are evaluated against the connection attempt. If the connection attempt matches both the profile and account settings, the user is granted remote access. If not, the connection attempt is rejected.

**EXAM ALERT**

Remote access policies are a popular topic on the exam. Be sure you are familiar with how remote access policies and the policy elements are evaluated. Also keep in mind that remote access policies are not stored within Active Directory; they are stored on each server.

**TIP**

If you are running in Windows 2000 native functional level, keep in mind that, unless they are set to Deny Access, the permission settings configured using the Dial-In tab for a user account override those in the policy. For example, if the account property is set to Allow Access but the profile denies it, the user is granted access and the process of evaluation continues. On the other hand, if the account property is set to Deny Access and the profile permits access, the connection attempt is rejected. By default, the Administrator and Guest accounts on a standalone remote access server or in a Windows Server 2003 functional-level domain are set to control access through the remote access policy; for a Windows 2000 native functional-level domain, they are set to Deny Access.

# Configuring Routing and Remote Access for DHCP

As you saw when enabling RRAS, you can configure the remote access server with a range of IP addresses to assign to remote access clients. (If you do, make sure the range does not conflict with the range of IP addresses configured on the DHCP server, to avoid duplicate addresses.) You can also configure the RAS server to obtain IP addresses from the DHCP server to lease to clients.

When you choose to use a DHCP server, the remote access server obtains, by default, 10 IP addresses to lease to clients. If all 10 IP addresses are in use, the remote access server obtains 10 more from the DHCP server. (Ten is the default number but can be changed through the Registry.) The benefit of using DHCP with RAS is that IP address assignment remains centralized.

For DHCP to be used with RAS, the DHCP Relay Agent must be configured on the RAS server. When you configure the DHCP Relay Agent, clients still receive IP addresses from the RAS server, but they can use DHCPInform messages to obtain optional parameters, such as the IP addresses of WINS and DNS servers, directly from the DHCP server. The relay agent component allows the RAS server to relay the DHCPInform messages between the remote access clients and the DHCP server.

To configure DHCP to work with remote access, follow these steps:

1. Within the Routing and Remote Access management console, right-click General under the IP Routing icon and select New Routing Protocol.

2. In the Select Routing Protocol window, select the DHCP Relay Agent and click OK.

3. Right-click the DHCP Relay Agent icon, listed under IP Routing, and select New Interface. Select the network connection over which DHCP messages will be routed and click OK.

4. Right-click the DHCP Relay Agent and select Properties. Type the IP addresses of the DHCP server or servers to which the RAS server should forward the DHCPInform requests (see Figure 5.12).

5. Right-click the interface to open the Properties window. From the Properties window, you can disable or enable the relaying of DHCP packets, and configure the hop count and the boot threshold.

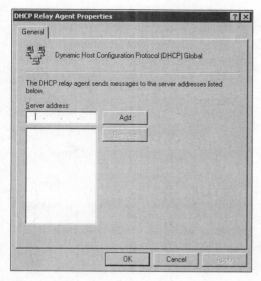

**FIGURE 5.12** You must configure the RAS server with the IP address of the DHCP server.

# Configuring a Virtual Private Network (VPN)

A virtual private network (VPN) enables you to connect to a remote server using the Internet. When a remote access client has established a connection to the Internet, a connection is created with the VPN server using a tunneling protocol (PPTP or L2TP). The tunnel provides secure communication between the user and the private network. One of the biggest advantages to implementing a VPN is the cost reduction. Remote clients can dial into a local ISP and then connect to the remote server rather than incurring possible long-distance charges.

Two types of tunneling protocols can be used to connect to a VPN server: the Point-to-Point Tunneling Protocol (PPTP) and the Layer 2 Tunneling Protocol (L2TP). Both protocols are automatically installed by default. PPTP is used over PPP connections on an IP-based network and supports the encryption and encapsulation of IP, IPX, and NetBEUI packets. L2TP can encapsulate IP traffic over a variety of networks, including Frame Relay, ATM, and X.25.

Both PPTP and L2TP encrypt data that is being transferred. PPTP has built-in encryption technologies and uses MPPE 40-bit to 128-bit encryption. L2TP uses IPSec for data encryption. IPSec uses the Data Encryption Standard (DES) to encrypt data with supported key lengths between 56-bit (DES) and 168-bit (3DES).

In terms of authentication, a user attempting to establish a VPN connection can be authenticated using EAP, MS-CHAP, CHAP, SPAP, or PAP. Computer-level and user-level authentication are provided if you are using L2TP over IPSec. The mutual authentication of computers occurs through the exchange of computer certificates; in other words, certificates must be installed on both the VPN client and the VPN server. EAP, CHAP, MS-CHAP, SPAP, and PAP can perform the user-level authentication.

Table 5.4 summarizes the differences between the two tunneling protocols.

### TABLE 5.4   Differences Between PPTP and L2TP

| PPTP | L2TP |
|------|------|
| Used only for IP-based networks | Supports any point-to-point connection, including IP, ATM, and frame relay |
| Uses PPP encryption | Encryption is handled by IPSec |
| Allows IP, IPX, and NetBEUI traffic to be encrypted | Allows IP traffic to be encrypted |
| Tunnel authentication | No tunnel authentication |

To enable a Windows Server 2003 as a VPN server, use the same process outlined when enabling a remote access server, but select the option to configure a VPN server. (Two network interfaces are required to configure VPNs.) When a VPN server is enabled, five PPTP and five L2TP ports are automatically created. If you want to allow more than five concurrent connections via each protocol, additional ports can be created and configured using the Ports container within the Routing and Remote Access console.

# Managing TCP/IP Routing

With Routing and Remote Access (RRAS), a computer running Windows Server 2003 can function as a network router, which routes IP packets between networks. This router service allows LANs and WANs to be interconnected easily. The routing technology is built into the operating system, providing small and large businesses with a cost-effective and secure way of interconnecting their networks.

## IP Routing

Routing is the process of sending a packet from the source address to the destination address. Because all IP packets have a source and destination IP address, it is possible to deliver them to the proper location. Of course, how the routing of IP packets actually occurs is much more complex.

Because each IP packet has addressing information within the header, routers can use this information to determine where a packet should be sent so that it can reach the destination host. Routers maintain information about the physical network, such as the path to a destination network and the metric associated with the route. The metric is the cost associated with using a route. Typically, this is the number of hops to the destination network. If there are multiple routes to a destination network, the route with the lowest metric is favored. For routers to know the location to which packets must be forwarded, they must also know about their neighboring routers. This information is stored within the routing table. When a router receives a packet, it checks the routing table to determine where the packet must be sent to reach the destination host. The information within a routing table can be generated statically or dynamically.

### Static Routing

With *static routing*, an administrator must manually configure the routing table by adding entries that tell the router how to reach other networks. Using the `route` command, an administrator updates the routing table by specifying the network addresses, the subnet masks, and the metric associated with each route.

When deciding whether to use static routing, keep in mind that it works best for networks that do not change on a regular basis. If the network configuration is constantly changing, the administrative overhead associated with having to update the routing tables every time something changes increases greatly because the changes must be made on each router. In such cases, it might be more beneficial to implement dynamic routing.

## Dynamic Routing

*Dynamic routing* eliminates the overhead associated with manually updating routing tables. Routers can dynamically build their own routing tables by communicating with other routers on the network.

With dynamic routing, the routing tables are built automatically through router communication. Using a routing communication protocol, routers periodically exchange messages containing location information about routes through the network. This information is used to build and update routing tables.

The major advantage of dynamic routing is that it reduces the administrative overhead associated with manually updating routing tables. For example, if a router goes down, the change is automatically propagated to all routers on the network so that they are all aware of the change in the network topology. One of the major disadvantages is the high amount of traffic it generates.

# Managing Routing Protocols

For routers to share information and dynamically update their routing tables, a routing protocol must be used. As already mentioned, the two routing protocols supported by Windows Server 2003 are Routing Information Protocol (RIP) and Open Shortest Path First (OSPF). Although both routing protocols are used for dynamic routing, there are some distinct differences between the two.

## Routing Information Protocol (RIP)

The Routing Information Protocol (RIP) is designed for small to medium-size networks. One of the main benefits in choosing RIP is that it's easy to configure and deploy. One of the major drawbacks associated with this protocol is that it is limited to a maximum hop count of 15. This means that any networks more than 15 hop counts away are considered unreachable. Also, as a network increases in size, excessive traffic can be generated from RIP announcements.

> **NOTE**
>
> As mentioned previously, all routes to a destination network are assigned a metric, which defines the distance between the source and destination. RIP uses a hop count to identify the distance between two networks. A value of 1 is added to the hop count for each router that resides between a source and destination network.

## RIPv1 and RIPv2

Windows Server 2003 supports two versions of RIP: RIP version 1 and RIP version 2. RIPv1 sends the announcements as broadcasts, whereas RIPv2 can broadcast multicast packets for the announcements. RIPv2 includes several advanced capabilities such as multicast routing update, simple password authentication, and router filtering.

If you are considering using RIPv1, keep in mind that it does not support multicasting, it does not support any type of security between routers, and it does have known issues with routing loops. Because it might take several minutes for routers to reconfigure themselves after a change in network topology—for example, when an existing router becomes unavailable—routing loops can occur in which routers send data in a circle.

Generally, you should use RIPv2, unless there are routers in the network that only support RIPv1. In such cases, you can use a combination of both RIPv1 and RIPv2 on the network. The RRAS server will have to be configured to advertise using either RIPv1 or RIPv2 broadcasts as well as accept either RIPv1 or RIPv2 announcements. Keep in mind as well that if your network supports classless interdomain routing (CIDR) or variable-length subnet masks (VLSM), RIPv1 does not provide support for them.

> **EXAM ALERT**
>
> RIPv2 supports multicasting for updating the routing tables. RIPv1 does not support this feature. RIPv1 routers cannot communicate with RIPv2 routers using multicasting for updates.

## RIPv2 Triggered Updates

When a router is first configured as an RIP router, the only entries in the routing table are for those networks to which it is physically connected. It then begins to send announcements of its availability to notify other routers of the networks it services.

When changes occur to the network topology, RIPv2 uses triggered updates to communicate the changes to other routers. With triggered updates, the change to the network topology can be propagated immediately.

## Open Shortest Path First (OSPF)

OSPF is designed for large internetworks (especially those spanning more than 15 router hops). The disadvantage of OSPF is that it's generally more complex to set up and requires a certain amount of planning.

> **EXAM ALERT**
>
> OSPF is not supported for nonpersistent, demand-dial connections.

OSPF uses the Shortest Path First (SPF) algorithm to calculate routes. The shortest path (the route with the lowest cost) is always used first. Unlike RIP, which uses announcements only to update and share routing information, OSPF maintains a map of the network known as the *link-state database*. This map is synchronized between adjacent routers, or those neighboring OSPF routers. When a change is made to the network topology, the first router to receive the change sends out a change notification. Each router then updates its copy of the link state database, and the routing table is recalculated.

> **NOTE**
>
> Poison reverse is a method by which a gateway informs its neighboring gateways that a connected gateway is no longer available. The gateway that knows about the unavailable one sets the hop count to the unconnected gateway to infinite, which means it is unreachable.

To fully understand the OSPF network topology, you need to be familiar with the concepts in the following list:

▶ *Autonomous System*—An autonomous system (AS) refers to a group of areas under the same administrative control. The different areas within an AS communicate directly using the backbone area.

▶ *Area*—An area is a section of an AS that includes contiguous subnet ranges. Routers within an area only know about their own area and the route to the backbone area.

▶ *Backbone Area*—The backbone area is the high-speed area that connects the areas in an AS together.

- *Area Border Router*—An area border router (ABR) is a system that borders and connects two or more areas.

- *Autonomous System Boundary Router*—An Autonomous System Boundary Router (ASBR) is one that connects different Autonomous Systems.

Installing and configuring RIP and OSPF is discussed further in this chapter in the section "Managing Remote Access."

# Manage Routing Tables

In some instances you need to add a static route to your Windows Server 2003 router. This, of course, has its advantages and disadvantages. Creating a static route is simple; however, the routes you configure are not shared between routers. Static routes specify the network address and subnet mask that tell the router how to reach a certain destination. The router uses the information to determine which gateway to forward the packet to so that the packet can reach the destination host.

Static routes can be configured in one of two ways. First, they can be configured using the route add command. Using the route add command, you can add static entries to the local routing table on a router. (You can also use the -p parameter to specify whether they should be persistent routes, meaning that they will remain in the routing table when the system reboots.)

The syntax for the route add command is as follows:

```
route add   mask   metric
```

The second option is to configure a static route within the RRAS management console. To configure a static route using this method, perform the following steps:

1. Within the RRAS management console, expand IP Routing.

2. Right-click Static Routes and select New Static Route. The Static Route window appears (see Figure 5.13).

3. Using the drop-down arrow, select the interface that will be used to route IP packets.

4. Type the destination IP address and subnet mask.

5. Type the IP address of the gateway for the RRAS server.

6. Click OK.

**FIGURE 5.13** Creating a new static route via the Static Route window.

# Managing Remote Access

As with most server roles, when a server has been configured, you most likely have to perform management tasks in the form of configuration changes or daily management tasks. The following section discusses some of the topics that pertain to managing a remote access server.

## Managing Packet Filters

Packet filtering enables an administrator to specify the type of inbound and outbound traffic that is allowed to pass through a Windows Server 2003 router. When configuring packet filters, you can allow all traffic except traffic prohibited by filters. Or, you can deny all traffic except traffic that is allowed by filters.

Packet filters can be created and configured through the RRAS console by performing the following steps:

1. Within the Routing and Remote Access console, expand the IP Routing container listed under your remote access server.

2. Select the General container and, within the Details pane, right-click the interface for which you want to configure packet filtering; click Properties.

3. From the General tab, select either Inbound Filters or Outbound Filters.

4. From the Inbound or Outbound Filters dialog box, click New. Specify the settings for the IP filter. Click OK.

5. Specify the action for the new packet filter. Click OK.

After a packet filter is created, it can be edited at any time by selecting the filter from the list and clicking the Edit button.

# Manage Routing and Remote Access Routing Interfaces

Two types of demand-dial connections can be created for routing: *on-demand connections* and *persistent connections*. With demand-dial connections, a connection with the remote router is established only when necessary. A connection is established to route information and is terminated when the link is not in use. The benefit of this connection is obviously the cost savings associated with not using a dedicated link. With persistent connections, the link does not need to be terminated. Even when it is not in use, it remains open. Connections between network routers can be one-way or two-way initiated, meaning that a connection can be initiated by only one router or by both the routers. With one-way initiated connections, one router is designated as the answering router and the other is designated as the calling router, which is responsible for initiating any connections.

---

**TIP**

To enable routing, right-click the remote access server and click Properties. On the General tab, select the Router option.

---

## Creating a One-Way Demand-Dial Interface

Demand-dial connections can be created within the Routing and Remote Access snap-in. How you configure the connection depends on whether you are configuring a one-way or two-way initiated connection. To create a demand-dial interface on the calling router, perform the following steps:

1. Right-click Network Interfaces within the RRAS console and click New Demand-Dial Interface. This launches the Demand-Dial Interface Wizard. Click Next.

2. Type a name for the interface. Click Next. Select the connection type. Click Next. Select the device that is used for making the connection. Click Next.

3. Type in the phone number of the remote server you are dialing. Click Next.

4. From the Protocols and Security window (see Figure 5.14), select the necessary options from the list that follows:

    ▶ Route IP Packets on This Interface

    ▶ Add a User Account So a Remote User Can Dial In

▶ Send a Plain-Text Password If That Is the Only Way to Connect

▶ Use Scripting to Complete the Connection with the Remote Router

**FIGURE 5.14** Configuring demand-dial protocols and security.

5. Configure a static route to the remote network. Click Next.

6. From the Dial Out Credentials window, specify the username and password that the dial-out router will use to connect to the remote router (see Figure 5.15). Click Next.

7. Click Finish.

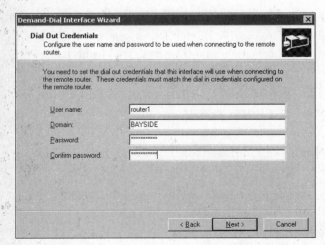

**FIGURE 5.15** Configuring dial-out credentials.

---

**TIP**

Before you attempt to create a new demand-dial interface, make sure the router is enabled for LAN and demand-dial routing instead of just a LAN router. You can enable this option by right-clicking the RRAS server and choosing Properties. From the General tab, select the LAN and demand-dial routing.

---

The answering router also needs to be configured for one-way demand-dial connections. A user account must be created on the answering router with dial-in permissions and the appropriate policy permissions. The user account is used to authenticate connections from the calling routers. A static route can then be configured on the user account. Also make sure when creating a user account that the Password Never Expires option is selected and the User Must Change Password at Next Logon option is not selected.

**EXAM ALERT**

When configuring the calling router, make sure that the dial-out credentials match the user account name configured on the answering router.

## Creating a Two-Way Demand-Dial Interface

Creating a two-way demand-dial connection is similar to configuring a one-way connection, but there are a few distinct differences. A demand-dial interface is created on each RRAS server using the process outlined previously to create a one-way demand-dial connection. You must assign a name to the interface and specify the phone number to dial, the device to be used, the protocol and security settings, and the dial-out credentials. You must also configure a user account, with the appropriate remote access permissions, on each RRAS server. Keep in mind that the user account name must be identical to the name assigned to the demand-dial interface of the calling router. Finally, you must configure a static route using the demand-dial interface.

**EXAM ALERT**

Remember when you are configuring two-way demand-dialing that the user account names on the answering router must be identical to the demand-dial interface names on the calling routers.

## Configuring a Demand-Dial Connection

When a demand-dial connection has been created, you can configure it further using the Properties window for the connection. From the Options tab (see Figure 5.16), configure the connection type: either demand dial or persistent. You can also set the dialing policy by specifying the number of times that the calling router should redial if there is no answer and by specifying the interval between redial attempts.

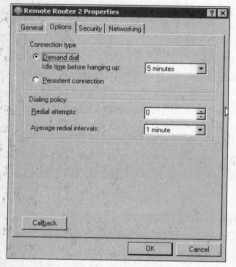

**FIGURE 5.16** Using the Options tab to configure a connection type.

The Security tab enables you to configure the security options for the dial-out connection (see Figure 5.17). This configuration includes whether unsecured passwords are permitted, whether the connection requires data encryption, and whether a script will be run after dialing.

As shown in Figure 5.18, the Networking tab is used to configure the type of dial server you use and the different network components that the connection uses.

You can make several other configurations to a demand-dial interface. Demand-dial filtering enables you to control the type of IP traffic that can initiate a connection. You can allow or deny a connection based on the type of IP traffic. For example, you might want only web and FTP traffic to initiate the demand-dial connection. Dial-out hours determine the times of day that a connection can be initiated. This enables an administrator to control when the demand-dial connection is used.

**FIGURE 5.17** Configuring security options via the Security tab.

**FIGURE 5.18** Configuring network settings for a demand-dial connection.

# Managing Routing Protocols

After the demand-dial or LAN interfaces have been created, configuring the appropriate routing protocol interfaces is the last step to configure the RRAS server as a network router. You must first add the routing protocol; you right-click the General node and choose New Routing Protocol. The window that appears lists the protocols from which you can choose (see Figure 5.19). Select RIPv2 or OSPF and click OK.

**FIGURE 5.19** Adding a new routing protocol to the General node.

After the routing protocol has been added, you must add the interfaces. To do so, right-click the appropriate routing protocol and select New Interface. After you select an interface and click OK, the Properties window for the interface appears, enabling you to configure it. The available options are discussed in the sections titled "Configuring RIP Interface Properties" and "Configuring OSPF Interface Properties."

## Configuring Routing Protocols

After RIP or OSPF has been installed, you can configure a general set of properties for each of the protocol types. Because RIP requires little configuration, the Properties window for the protocol has only two tabs, as shown in Figure 5.20.

**FIGURE 5.20** Configuring RIP properties.

From the General tab, you can configure the Maximum Delay value, which determines how long a router waits to send an update notification message to other routers on the network. The remaining options enable you to set up event logging for the protocol. The Security tab enables you to configure from which routers the local router can accept announcements.

Because OSPF is slightly more complex than RIP, it requires more detailed configuration and, as a result, has more options in its Properties window (see Figure 5.21).

**FIGURE 5.21** Configuring OSPF properties.

From the General tab, the router can be assigned an IP address that it can use to identify itself. You can also enable the router as an Autonomous System Boundary Router. By doing so, you are telling the router to advertise external routes to the rest of the OSPF network. Using the remaining options, you can enable OSPF event logging.

The Areas tab lists all the areas for the router. Using this tab, areas can be added, deleted, and edited. With OSPF, areas can be used to subdivide a network. This can be done to reduce the size of the database routers within an area by maintaining database information only for the area in which they belong. For example, as a network grows, you can create additional OSPF areas to further divide the network. By doing so, the routers within an area only contain routing information for that area, instead of having to maintain routing information for the entire network.

The Virtual Interface tab lists all the configured virtual interfaces. A virtual interface is a virtual connection between an area border router and a backbone area border router. This logical connection allows the two routers to share information.

If the Enable Autonomous System Boundary Router option is selected, you can use the External Routing tab to control which sources from which routes are accepted or ignored. The Ignore Filters button defines the specific routes that should be accepted or ignored.

## Configuring RIP Interface Properties

Every RIP interface has it own Properties window from which you can configure a number of options. Within the RRAS console, expand IP Routing, RIP; and then right-click one of the available interfaces and click Properties.

The General tab enables you to configure the operation mode. You can select either Autostatic Update Mode or Periodic Update Mode. With *autostatic update*, RIP announcements are sent when other routers request updates. Any routes learned while in autostatic update mode are marked as static and remain in the routing table until the administrator manually deletes them. In *periodic update mode*, announcements are sent out periodically. (The Periodic Announcement Interval determines how often.) These routes are automatically deleted when the router is stopped and restarted. The outgoing and incoming packet protocol enables you to configure the type of packets, such as RIPv1 or RIPv2, the router sends and accepts.

The Activate Authentication and Password options enable you to maintain an added level of security. If authentication is enabled, all outgoing and incoming packets must contain the password specified in the password field. When using authentication, make sure that all neighboring routers are configured with an identical password.

From the Security tab, an administrator can configure RIP route filters. The router can be configured to send and accept all routes, send and accept only routes from the ranges specified, or accept and send all routes except for those specified.

The Neighbors tab is used to configure how the router will interact with other RIP routers. The Advanced tab has several configurable options, which are summarized in Table 5.5.

**TABLE 5.5   Advanced RIP Options**

| Option | Description |
|---|---|
| Periodic Announcement Interval | Controls the interval at which periodic update announcements are made. |
| Time Before Route Expires | Determines how long a route remains in the routing table before it expires. |
| Time Before Route Is Removed | Determines how long an expired route remains in the routing table before being removed. |
| Enable Split Horizon Processing | Ensures that routing loops do not occur because the routes learned from a router are not rebroadcast to that network. |
| Enable Triggered Updates | Controls whether changes in the routing table are sent out immediately. |
| Send Clean-Up Updates when Stopped | Controls whether the router sends an announcement when it is stopped to notify other routers that the routes for which it was responsible are no longer available. |
| Process Host Routes in Received Announcements | Controls whether host routes received in RIP announcements are accepted or denied. |
| Include Host Routes in Send Announcements | Controls whether host routes are included in RIP announcements. |
| Process Default Routes in Received Announcements | Controls whether default routes received in RIP announcements are accepted or denied. |
| Process Default Routes in Send Announcements | Controls whether default routes are included in RIP announcements. |
| Disable Subnet Summarization | This option is available only for RIPv2. It controls whether subnets are advertised to routers on different subnets. |

**EXAM ALERT**

When a routing loop occurs, packets bounce back and forth between routers. By enabling split horizon processing, routes are not advertised back to the router from which they are learned. For example, if RouterB receives advertised routes from RouterA, RouterB will not advertise these routes back to RouterA. When Split Horizon with poison reverse is enabled, routes are advertised back to the router from which they were learned with a hop count of infinity.

## Configuring OSPF Interface Properties

If OSPF has been installed, each of the OSPF interfaces can be configured using its Properties window, just as RIP interfaces can be configured. An OSPF interface can be added the same way as a RIP interface. Simply right-click OSPF under the General node and click New Interface. Select the interface that the protocol will run on and click OK. Figure 5.22 shows the OSPF Properties window that appears.

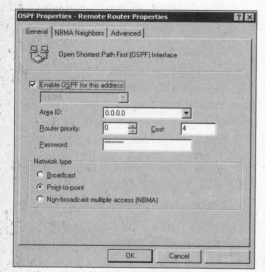

**FIGURE 5.22** Configuring an OSPF interface via the Properties window.

From the General tab, you can enable OSPF and configure the area ID, router priority, cost, and password. The Network Type options enable you to configure whether the OSPF is a broadcast interface, a point-to-point interface, or a non-broadcast multiple access interface. For normal local area networks you would select Broadcast. If the interface is a demand dial interface, select Point-to-point. Select non-broadcast multiple access (NBMA) for frame relay and X.25 networks.

The NBMA Neighbors tab is only used by X.25, ATM, and Frame Relay network. It enables you to manually specify the IP address of neighboring routers in these types of networks and associate a priority with the neighbor.

Table 5.6 summarizes the options available from the Advanced tab.

> **NOTE**
>
> If you are on a nonbroadcast multiple access (NBMA) network—a Frame Relay network that does not support broadcasts—the NBMA option on the General tab must be selected. You must also configure the IP addresses of OSPF neighbors using the NBMA Neighbors tab.

**TABLE 5.6   Advanced OSPF Options**

| Option | Description |
|---|---|
| Transit Delay | An estimation of the number of seconds for a link-state update to be transmitted over the network |
| Retransmit Interval | The number of seconds between link-state advertisement retransmissions |
| Hello Interval | How often hello packets are sent out to discover other routers |
| Dead Interval | The number of seconds until a neighboring router determines this router to be down |
| Poll Interval | The number of seconds between poll intervals sent to a dead neighbor |
| Maximum Transmission Unit (MTU) Size (Bytes) | The maximum byte size of an OSPF IP packet |

# Managing Devices and Ports

Devices and ports can be managed through the RRAS console. For example, if you are configuring a Windows Server 2003 as a dial-up remote access server, you have to configure a dial-in port to access inbound remote access connections.

To configure the devices and ports, right-click the Ports container under your remote access server and click Properties. Select the device you want to configure and click the Configure button. From the Configure Devices window, you can enable remote access inbound connections, demand-dial inbound and outbound connections, and demand-dial outbound connections only. You can also configure a phone number for the device and configure additional ports.

# Managing Routing and Remote Access Clients

Managing a remote access server also entails managing the clients that are connecting to it. You can use a number of tools with the Routing and Remote Access management console to manage remote access clients.

The management console provides administrators with a quick and easy way of viewing which clients are currently connected to a remote access server. To do so, click the Remote Access Clients container listed under your remote access server. The left pane displays the users currently connected. You can view status information for specific users by right-clicking their username and clicking the Status option. You can also disconnect a specific user by right-clicking the username and selecting the Disconnect option.

You also have the option of sending a message to a single user or all users connected to a remote access server. For example, if the server is going offline for maintenance, you can send a message to all connected users informing them of this. To send a message to a specific user, right-click the username and select Send Message. To send a message to all users currently connected to the server, right-click the Remote Access Clients container and select Send to All.

# Implementing Secure Access Between Private Networks

As networks throughout the world become more interconnected, network administrators are challenged with ensuring that data transferred across a network is secure. This is where the IP Security (IPSec) protocol comes into play and allows for authentication of hosts, data integrity, and data encryption.

IPSec is used to protect data that is sent between hosts on a network, which can be remote access, VPN, LAN, or WAN. IPSec ensures that data cannot be viewed or modified by unauthorized users while being sent to its destination. Before data is sent between two hosts, the source computer encrypts the information. It is decrypted at the destination computer. IPSec provides the following benefits:

- ▶ Secure end-to-end communication between hosts
- ▶ Secure connections for remote access clients using the Layer 2 Tunneling Protocol (L2TP)
- ▶ Secure router-to-router connections

As you will see when you begin to configure IPSec, different levels of security can be implemented to meet varying needs. IPSec is implemented through IPSec policies. The policies are created and assigned to individual computers or groups of computers (or groups of users). The policies determine the level of security that will be used.

IPSec consists of three components that work together to provide secure communications between hosts:

- ▶ *IPSec Policy Agent*—This component is responsible for retrieving policy information from the local computer or Active Directory.
- ▶ *ISAKMP/Oakley Key Management Service*—This component is responsible for establishing a secure channel between hosts and creating the

shared key that is used to encrypt the data. It also establishes a security association between hosts before data is transferred. The security association determines the mechanisms that are used to secure data.

▶ *IPSec Driver*—On the sending computer, this component monitors IP packets. Packets matching a configured filter are secured using the security association and shared key. The IPSec driver on the receiving computer decrypts the data.

The following steps outline how the different components work together to provide secure communications:

1. When Computer1 starts, the IPSec policy agent retrieves policy information from the local computer or Active Directory.

2. When Computer1 attempts to send data to Computer2, the IPSec driver examines the IP packets to determine whether they match the configured filters. If a match is determined, the IPSec driver notifies the ISAKMP/Oakley.

3. The ISAKMP/Oakley service on the two computers is used to establish a security association and a shared key.

4. The IPSec driver on Computer1 uses the key and security association to encrypt the data.

5. The IPSec driver on Computer2 decrypts the information and passes it to the requesting application.

In summary, before any data is transferred between two hosts, the security level must be negotiated. This negotiation includes agreeing on an authentication method, a hashing method, and an encryption method.

# Configuring IPSec

You can enable IPSec using the Local Security Policy snap-in. The following list describes the three default policies. You can enable any policy for the local computer by right-clicking the policy and choosing the Assign option.

▶ *Client (Respond Only)*—This is used for computers that should not secure communications most of the time, but if requested to set up a secure communication, they can respond.

▶ *Server Secure (Require Security)*—When this option is selected, the server requires all communications to be secure. If a client is not IPSec-aware, the session will not be allowed.

▶ *Server (Request Security)*—This is used for computers that should secure communications most of the time. In this policy, the computer accepts unsecured traffic but always attempts to secure additional communications by requesting security from the original sender.

If you are running Active Directory, you can create an IPSec policy that is stored within Active Directory. To view the policies, open the Group Policy snap-in, shown in Figure 5.23.

**FIGURE 5.23** IPSec policies within the Group Policy snap-in.

The three policies that exist by default are Client, Server Secure, and Server. (The process of creating new IPSec policies is outlined in the following section.) To assign an IPSec policy to Group Policy, right-click the policy and click the Assign option.

# Configuring IPSec for Transport Mode

IPSec can be used in one of two modes: transport mode or tunnel mode. *Tunnel mode* is used for server-to-server or server-to-gateway configurations. The tunnel is the path a packet takes from the source computer to the destination computer. This way, any IP packets sent between the two hosts or between the two subnets, depending on the configuration, are secured. *Transport mode* is used for host-to-host communication such as between a client and a server. This mode is normally used to secure end-to-end communications, for example, between a client and a server on the same network.

Two formats can be used with tunneling mode: ESP tunnel mode and AH tunnel mode. With Authentication Header (AH) tunnel mode, the data itself is not encrypted. It provides authentication and integrity, and it protects the data from modification, but it is still readable. With Encapsulating Security Payload (ESP) tunnel mode, authentication, integrity, and data encryption are provided.

> **EXAM ALERT**
>
> Tunnel mode is not used for remote access VPNs. IPSec/L2TP or PPTP (Point-to-Point Tunneling Protocol) is used for VPN connections. Tunnel mode is used for systems that cannot use IPSec/L2TP or PPTP VPNs.

To create a new IPSec policy, perform the following steps:

1.  Click Start and click the Run command. Type **mmc** and click OK.

2.  Click File and select Add/Remove snap-in. Click Add.

3.  From the List of available snap-ins, select IP Security Policy Management. Click Add. Click Finish. Click Close.

4.  Click OK.

5.  To create a new policy, right-click IP Security Policies on Local Computer and select Create IP Security Policy. Click Next.

6.  Type a name for the new policy. Click Next.

7.  From the Requests for Secure Communications window, leave the default option of Activate the Default Response Rule selected to have the computer respond to those that request security. Click Next.

8.  Select the authentication method. You can choose Kerberos, certificates, or a preshared key. You can edit the policy afterward to add multiple authentication methods. Click Next.

9.  Click Finish.

To configure an IPSec tunnel, perform the following steps:

1.  From the Properties window of the IPSec policy that you want to manage, select the rule you want to edit and click the Edit button.

2.  Select the Tunnel Setting tab.

3.  Select the tunnel endpoint that is specified by this IP address option and type the IP address of the tunnel endpoint.

4.  After the tunnel endpoint has been specified, you can configure the tunneling mode using the Filter Actions tab. For ESP tunnel mode, select High. For AH tunnel mode, select Medium.

# Customizing IPSec Policies and Rules

An IPSec policy tells a server what actions to perform on network traffic when using IPSec. The components of an IPSec policy define what type of IP traffic is covered by the policy, the type of authentication mechanism that should be used, and what happens to the traffic when it does or does not meet the criteria of a policy.

Each of the policies can be edited using the policy's Properties window. IPSec policies consist of several components, including the following:

▶ *Rules*—IPSec rules determine how and when communication is secured.

▶ *Filter lists*—Filter lists determine what type of IP packets trigger security negotiations.

▶ *IPSec security methods*—The security methods determine the security requirements of the rule.

▶ *IPSec authentication methods*—Authentication methods determine the ways in which hosts can identify themselves.

▶ *IPSec connection types*—This determines the types of connections, such as remote access or local area connections, to which the rule applies.

Let's take a look at an example. You can create an IPSec policy that blocks all PING traffic to and from a computer. To do so, you would need to complete the following steps:

1. Configure an IP Filter List that includes ICMP Traffic.

2. Create a Filter Action that will block the designated traffic.

3. Create a new IPSec policy.

4. Add the IP Filter List and Filter Action you created to the IPSec policy.

5. Assign the IPSec policy.

To begin configuring an IPSec policy, right-click the policy and click Properties. From the General tab of an IPSec policy's Properties window, you can change the name and description for the policy and configure the interval at which the computer will check for policy updates. Using the Advanced button, you can configure the Key Exchange Settings.

**TIP**

When configuring the Key Exchange Settings, you can select the Master Key Perfect Forward Secrecy option. This ensures that no previously used keying material is used to generate new master keys. You can also specify the interval at which authentication and key generation must take place.

The Rules tab lists all of the rules that are configured for the policy. Other rules can be added by clicking the Add button; you can edit the existing rules using the Edit button. Clicking the Edit button opens the Edit Rule Properties window (see Figure 5.24).

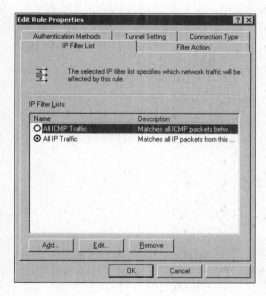

**FIGURE 5.24**   Editing IPSec rules.

The IP Filter List tab defines the type of traffic to which the rule will apply. The Filter Action tab defines whether the rule negotiates for secure traffic and how the traffic will be secured. Configuring the filter actions enables you to define the different security methods that can be negotiated. The security algorithms supported by IPSec include MD5 and SHA1. The encryption algorithms supported include DES and 3DES.

The Authentication Methods tab enables you to configure the method used to establish trust between the two computers (see Figure 5.25). If multiple authentication methods are configured for a rule, you can change the order in which they are used. The authentication methods available include these:

▶ *Kerberos*—Kerberos 5 is the default authentication method in a Windows Server 2003 domain. Users running the Kerberos protocol within a trusted domain can authenticate using this method.

▶ *Certificates*—If a trusted certificate authority is available, certificates can be used for authentication.

▶ *Preshared key*—For non–Windows Server 2003 computers or those not running Kerberos, a preshared key can be used for authentication.

**FIGURE 5.25** Configuring IPSec authentication methods.

The Connection Type tab enables you to define the types of connections to which the rule applies. This enables you to define different rules for different types of connections. Rules can be applied to local area connections, remote access connections, or all network connections.

The Tunnel Setting tab enables you to specify a tunnel endpoint where communication will take place between two specific computers.

You can edit the existing policies, or you can create and assign a new policy through the Group Policy snap-in. To create a new policy, right-click IP Security Policies on Active Directory within a Group Policy Object and select Create IP Security Policy. A wizard walks you through the process of creating the initial policy, which you can configure further using the Properties window for the new policy.

**EXAM ALERT**

In Windows 2000, the `secedit /refreshpolicy machine_policy` command was used to refresh policy settings. Windows Server 2003 uses the `gpupdate` command to refresh policy settings. When the command is used on its own, both the computer and user settings are applied. Using the command with the `/target` switch, you can specify that only the computer or user settings are applied. The `/force` switch causes all policy settings to be reapplied, regardless of whether they have changed.

One of the first steps to try when a client and server cannot communicate is to disable the IPSec policy. Matching policies must exist on both computers before communication can take place.

# Troubleshooting User Access to Remote Access Services

Troubleshooting is a major part of an administrator's job. Issues can arise related to connection problems or accessing resources beyond the remote access server. If your remote access server is configured as a router, you might encounter problems related to demand-dialing. The following section outlines some of the more common problems that you might encounter with a remote access server.

## Diagnosing and Resolving Remote Access Connection Issues

One of the most common problems you might find yourself troubleshooting is related to establishing a remote access connection with a server. If a problem like this occurs, use the following points as a starting place for troubleshooting the connection problems:

▶ Verify that the modem is working and correctly configured.

▶ Verify that the remote access service is enabled and started on the server.

▶ Verify the availability of ports. If necessary, disconnect any idle sessions, or increase the number of available ports.

▶ Verify that the remote access policy is not prohibiting the connection.

# Diagnosing and Resolving User Access to Resources Beyond the Remote Access Server

Remote access clients go through a remote access server to access network resources. The advantage of this is that clients can remotely access resources as though they were physically connected to the LAN. If clients are experiencing problems accessing resources beyond the RAS server, verify that IP routing has been enabled on the remote access server (using the IP tab from the server's Properties window), and also verify that any IP packet filters are not blocking the flow of traffic.

# Troubleshooting Demand-Dial Routing

If on-demand connections are not being established automatically, check any of the following conditions to troubleshoot the problem:

▶ Verify that IP routing is enabled. This can be done using the IP tab from the remote access server's Properties window.

▶ Verify that you have correctly configured the static routes to the remote networks.

▶ Verify that the dial-out hours have been properly configured for the interface.

▶ Verify that any filters are not preventing the connection.

# Netsh

Netsh is a command-line utility that allows you to modify the network configuration of the local computer or a remote computer. For example, using the Netsh command, you can enable the Windows Firewall on a remote computer. It also supports a scripting feature that allows you to include a group of commands in a script and run them on the local or a remote computer.

The Netsh command supports multiple contexts. These contexts allow you to manage and configure various services. For example, once you start Netsh from the command prompt, you can type dhcp to switch to the DHCP context. Netsh supports the following contexts:

▶ AAAA

▶ DHCP

▶ Network diagnostics (diag)

▶ Interface

▶ Interface IP

▶ Interface IPv6

▶ Interface Portproxy

▶ Internet Protocol security (ipsec)

▶ Network Bridge (bridge)

▶ Remote Access (ras)

▶ Routing

▶ RPC Helper (rpc)

▶ WINS

Netsh in Windows Server 2003 includes a set of diagnostic commands that can be used for troubleshooting. You can access this context by typing `netsh diag` at the command prompt.

# Exam Prep Questions

1. You are the network administrator for your company. All servers have been upgraded to Microsoft Windows Server 2003. Client computers are running Microsoft Windows XP Professional.

   Some of the employees within the company work from home offices. These users require access to network resources through the company's remote access server.

   For security purposes, you want to limit the dial-in hours from 8 a.m. to 6 p.m.

   What should you do?

   - ○ **A.** Configure the properties of each user account.
   - ○ **B.** Configure the properties of the remote access server.
   - ○ **C.** Configure the conditions of the remote access policy.
   - ○ **D.** Configure the port properties.

2. You are the network administrator for your company. All servers have been upgraded to Microsoft Windows Server 2003.

   You have configured Routing and Remote Access on an existing server. The remote access server is configured with the default settings.

   You are still using WINS on the internal network because you are still in the process of upgrading workstations. Clients report that they can successfully connect but cannot access network resources using a UNC path. Network resources are accessible to clients connected to the LAN.

   Remote access clients need to be able to access network resources.

   What should you do?

   - ○ **A.** Configure a range of IP addresses on the RAS server, as well as assign any optional IP parameters to clients.
   - ○ **B.** Manually configure the IP settings on the remote access clients.
   - ○ **C.** Configure the DHCP server to assign DHCP clients the IP address of the WINS server.
   - ○ **D.** Install the DHCP Relay Agent on the RAS server.

3. You are the network administrator for your organization. All servers have been upgraded to Microsoft Windows Server 2003.

   The network maintains multiple remote access servers. Some of the RAS servers are located in branch offices.

You want to centralize the authentication of remote access clients and accounting information.

What should you do?

- ○ **A.** Install IAS on a server. Configure the RAS servers to send authentication requests and accounting information to this server.

- ○ **B.** Install ISA on a server. Configure the RAS servers as RADIUS clients.

- ○ **C.** Install RADIUS on a server. Configure the RAS servers as RADIUS clients.

- ○ **D.** Replace all the existing remote access servers with a RADIUS server.

4. You are the network administrator for an investment company. All servers have been upgraded to Microsoft Windows Server 2003. Client computers are running Microsoft Windows XP Professional.

Some of the company employees require remote access to the network. The company's new security policy now requires all remote access users to use smart cards.

You need to configure the remote access server to use the correct authentication protocol.

Which of the following protocols should you enable?

- ○ **A.** PAP

- ○ **B.** EAP

- ○ **C.** MS-CHAP

- ○ **D.** SPAP

5. You are the network administrator for your company. All servers are running Microsoft Windows Server 2003.

You have configured routing and remote access on two servers. One server is in the head office and the other is located in a branch office. You need to create a two-way demand-dial connection between the two servers.

You need to create the user account on the answering router.

What should you do?

- ○ **A.** Create a new user account using any account name.

- ○ **B.** Create a new user account using an account name that matches the demand-dial interface name of the answering router.

- ○ **C.** Create a new user account name using an account name that matches the demand-dial interface name of the calling router.

- ○ **D.** Create a new user account using an account name that matches the computer name of the answering router.

6. Your internetwork consists of seven subnets. All subnets are connected using Windows Server 2000 RRAS servers. Nonpersistent demand-dial connections have been configured. You do not want to be burdened with updating the routing tables, and you want any changes to the network topology to be propagated immediately. Which of the following routing options should you implement?

   ○  **A.** Static routes

   ○  **B.** ICMP

   ○  **C.** OSPF

   ○  **D.** RIPv2

7. You are the network administrator for your company. All servers are running Microsoft Windows Server 2003.

   You need to add a new static route to the routing table. The new route is to the network ID 192.168.126.0 with a subnet mask of 255.255.255.0 using the default gateway of 192.168.125.1.

   You need to execute the correct command.

   Which command should you use?

   ○  **A.** `route -p 192.168.126.0 mask 255.255.255.0 192.168.125.1 metric 2`

   ○  **B.** `route add 192.168.126.0 mask 255.255.255.0 192.168.125.1 metric 2`

   ○  **C.** `route add 192.168.126.0 255.255.255.0 192.168.125.1 metric 2`

   ○  **D.** `route add 192.168.126.0 mask 255.255.255.0 gateway 192.168.125.1 metric 2`

8. You are the network administrator for a consulting company. All servers have been upgraded to Microsoft Windows Server 2003.

   You are configuring IP security for your network. You want all data to be encrypted, but you still want clients that do not support IPSec to be capable of authenticating with the server.

   You want to accomplish this with the least amount of administrative effort.

   What should you do?

   ○  **A.** Assign the Secure Server (Require Security) policy.

   ○  **B.** Assign the Client (Respond Only) policy.

   ○  **C.** Create and assign a new IPSec policy.

   ○  **D.** Assign the Server (Request Security) policy.

9. You are the network administrator for your company. All servers are running Microsoft Windows Server 2003.

   You are configuring IPSec between two servers in a workgroup. You assign Client (Respond Only) to each of the servers, but you notice that IP packets being sent between the two servers are not being secured.

   What is causing the problem?

   ○ **A.** Both are configured with the Client (Respond Only) policy.

   ○ **B.** IPSec can be used only with Active Directory.

   ○ **C.** One of the servers must be configured as an IPSec client.

   ○ **D.** The servers cannot be members of the same workgroup.

10. You are the network administrator for your company. Servers have been upgraded to Microsoft Windows Server 2003.

    You have just updated the IPSec policy settings and want to apply changes immediately.

    What should you do?

    ○ **A.** Execute the `secedit /target:machine` command.

    ○ **B.** Execute the `gpupdate /target:machine` command.

    ○ **C.** Execute the `secedit /target:user` command.

    ○ **D.** Execute the `gpupdate /target:user` command.

11. You are the network administrator for your company. All servers are running Microsoft Windows Server 2003. Client computers are running Microsoft Windows XP Professional.

    Several of the servers are configured as routers with RIP enabled. You want to eliminate any routing loops from occurring.

    You open the properties window for the RIP protocol and select the Advanced tab.

    Which of the following options will meet these requirements?

    ○ **A.** Enable split-horizon processing

    ○ **B.** Enable triggered updates

    ○ **C.** Process host routes in received announcements

    ○ **D.** Disable subnet summarization

# Answers to Exam Prep Questions

1. **C.** You can set day and time restrictions for remote users by configuring the conditions of the remote access policy. Answer A is incorrect because day and time restrictions are no longer configured through the properties of a user account as they were in Windows NT 4.0. You cannot configure day and time restrictions by configuring the properties of the remote access server or the ports; therefore, answers B and D are incorrect.

2. **D.** The clients need to be configured with the IP address of the WINS server. To do this, the DHCP Relay Agent must be installed on the RAS server so that it can forward DHCPInform messages between the clients and the DHCP server. Answer A is incorrect because optional parameters cannot be configured on the RAS server. Clients can be configured with the IP address of the WINS server; however, it's easier from a management perspective to centralize IP address assignment and use a relay agent instead. Therefore, answer B is incorrect. Answer C is incorrect. The DHCP server is already assigning the IP address of the WINS server to DHCP clients because the scenario indicates this problem is not affecting clients connected to the LAN.

3. **A.** To centralize the authentication of remote access clients and accounting information, the Internet Authentication Service (IAS) should be installed. RAS servers can then be configured as RADIUS clients. By doing so, they will forward authentication requests and accounting information to the IAS server. Answer B is incorrect because ISA, also known as Internet Security and Acceleration service, is an application layer firewall. Answers C and D are incorrect because RADIUS is the protocol used by IAS to provide authentication and accounting services.

4. **B.** The Extensible Authentication Protocol is required to support smart card authentication. Answers A, C, and D are incorrect because they do not support smart card authentication.

5. **C.** When creating demand-dial connections, the name of the user account created on the answering router must match the demand-dial interface name on the calling router. Therefore, answers A, B, and D are incorrect.

6. **D.** To have changes propagated throughout the network when changes occur and to reduce the administrative overhead associated with updating the routing tables, a routing protocol is required. Because OSPF cannot be used with nonpersistent connections, RIPv2 must be used (or RIPv1). Therefore, answers A and C are incorrect. Answer B is incorrect because ICMP is not a routing protocol.

7. **B.** The correct syntax when adding new static routes using the `route` command is `route add mask metric`. Answers A, C, and D are incorrect because they do not use the proper syntax.

8. **D.** By assigning the Server (Request Security) policy, the server will always attempt secure communications. Unsecured communications will still be allowed if the client is not IPSec-aware. Answer A is incorrect because communications will not be allowed if

the client is not IPSec-aware. Answer B is incorrect because assigning Client (Respond Only) means that the server will respond only to requests for secure communications but will not attempt to secure all communications. Answer C is incorrect because it would require less administrative effort to assign an existing policy than to create a new one.

9. **A.** If both servers are configured with the Client (Respond Only) policy, they will respond only to requests for secure communications. One of the servers must be configured with Server (Request Security). Answer B is incorrect because IPSec can be configured through Active Directory or on the local computer. Answer C is incorrect because computers are not configured as IPSec clients. Answer D is incorrect because the workgroup membership has no impact on how servers respond to security.

10. **B.** To refresh policy settings, you can use the `gpupdate` command. Because the IPSec policy is configured under the computer policy, you must refresh the computer policy settings. This is done by using the `/target:machine` option. Answers A and C are incorrect because this was the command used in Windows 2000. Answer D is incorrect because you need to refresh the computer policy settings, not the user policy settings.

11. **A.** The correct answer is enable split-horizon processing. You must select this option to ensure that any routes learned from a network are not sent as RIP announcements on the network. With this option enabled, a router cannot advertise a route on the same connection from which it was learned.

# Need to Know More?

Search the online version of TechNet and the Windows Server 2003 Server Resource Kit using keywords such as "remote access," "routing," and "VPN."

Williams, Robert and Mark Walla. *The Ultimate Windows Server 2003 Administrator's Guide.* Addison-Wesley Professional, 2003. ISBN: 0201791064.

Habraken, Joe. *Sams Teach Yourself Microsoft Windows Server 2003 in 24 Hours.* Sams, 2003. ISBN: 0672324946.

Abbate, Andrew; Kovach, Eric; Morimoto, Rand; Roberts, Ed. *Microsoft Windows Server 2003 Insider Solutions.* Sams, 2003. ISBN: 0672326094.

CHAPTER SIX

# Maintaining a Network Infrastructure

---

## Terms you'll need to understand:

✓ Network Monitor
✓ Display filter
✓ Capture filter
✓ System Monitor
✓ Performance object
✓ Performance counter
✓ Device Manager
✓ Network Diagnostics

---

## Techniques you'll need to master:

✓ Monitoring network traffic using Network Monitor
✓ Monitoring system performance using System Monitor
✓ Troubleshooting Internet connectivity problems
✓ Troubleshooting service dependencies
✓ Configuring service recovery options

Numerous tasks are involved in maintaining a network, from maintaining the physical network and servers to ensure performance, to troubleshooting various problems as they arise.

This chapter looks at topics pertaining to network maintenance, including monitoring network traffic, troubleshooting Internet connectivity, and managing network services. You also are introduced to the tools included with Windows Server 2003 that can be used to perform these various tasks.

# Monitoring Network Traffic

As network-related services become more prevalent (because new services and applications are installed and network shares are created), traffic on a network can increase greatly. For example, a recent growth in web-based training in many large companies to keep travel costs down would have a huge impact on network bandwidth use.

Network administrators must ensure that the network performs efficiently and reliably. By monitoring network performance, you can gather information that can be used for capacity planning, establishing a baseline that can help pinpoint changes in performance over time, and putting together performance-level reports. Two tools included with Windows Server 2003 can be used to monitor network traffic: Network Monitor and System Monitor.

## Network Monitor

*Network Monitor*, which is included with Windows Server 2003, enables you to monitor and log network activity and then use the information to manage and optimize traffic. You can use the information you gather to identify unnecessary protocols and misconfigured workstations, and to detect problems with network applications and services. Some of the features of Network Monitor include the following:

▶ *Display filters*—Enable you to locate specific information within a capture

▶ *Capture filters*—Enable you to specify the type of information that is captured

▶ *Triggers*—Enable certain actions to be performed based on a packet's content

Network Monitor consists of the following two components:

► *Network Monitor Driver*—The Network Monitor Driver is responsible for capturing the frames coming to and from a network adapter.

► *Network Monitor tools*—The Network Monitor tools are used to view and analyze the data captured by the Network Monitor Driver.

## Installing Network Monitor

Network Monitor is not installed with Windows Server 2003 by default, but it can be installed using the following process (installing Network Monitor automatically installs the Network Monitor Driver):

1. Click Start, point to the Control Panel, and click Add or Remove Programs.

2. Click Add/Remove Windows Components.

3. Within the Windows Component Wizard, select Management and Monitoring Tools, and click the Details button.

4. Select the Network Monitor Tools check box. Click OK.

5. Click Next. Click Finish.

In some instances you want to install only the Network Monitor Driver—for example, if you want to capture traffic for multiple servers and view the captured data from your workstation. Installing the driver enables you to capture traffic on a network interface. You then need to use software such as Systems Management Server (SMS) to view the captured data. This is useful for capturing data from a number of different servers and viewing it from a central location. For example, a computer running Network Monitor Driver can capture the information and forward it to SMS. To install only the Network Monitor Driver component, perform the following steps:

1. Within the Network Connections applet, right-click Local Area Connection and choose Properties from the pop-up menu.

2. From the properties window for the local area connection, click the Install button.

3. In the list, click Protocol and then click the Add button.

4. Within the Network Protocol window, click the Network Monitor Driver.

5. Click OK.

# Using Network Monitor

After Network Monitor is installed, it is added to the Administrative Tools menu. To launch the console, click Start, point to Administrative Tools, and click Network Monitor (see Figure 6.1).

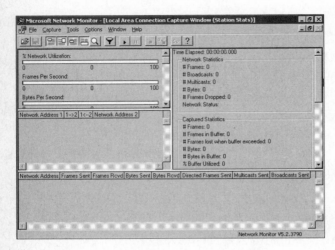

**FIGURE 6.1** The Network Monitor console.

Network Monitor can display a large amount of information about the frames captured to and from a network adapter card. When you first open Network Monitor, four panes are displayed within the console. The Graph pane, located in the top right of the window, displays the network activity in the form of a bar chart. As you can see from Figure 6.1, it includes statistics such as %Network Utilization, Frames Per Second, and Bytes Per Second.

Below the Graph pane is the Session Statistics pane. The Session Statistics pane displays information about individual sessions, including statistics about the sessions in which the server is participating. The Station Statistics pane at the bottom of the window displays information about the frames sent and received, bytes sent and received, multicasts sent, and broadcasts sent. The Total Statistics pane along the left side of the window displays the summary statistics since the capture was started.

To view statistics about network traffic, you must first start a capture to gather network traffic. To do so, click the Start option from the Capture menu. To view the captured data, click the Stop and View option from the Capture menu. Network Monitor displays all of the frames captured during the capture period with a Summary window. To view specific information about a frame, click the frame within the Summary window (see Figure 6.2).

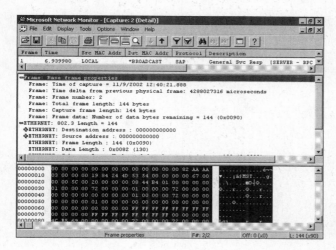

**FIGURE 6.2** Viewing captured data within Network Monitor.

**EXAM ALERT**

You should be aware of the buffer size and the frame size. Both of these can be set by selecting the Buffer Settings option from the Capture menu. The default buffer size is 1MB. After Network Monitor has captured 1MB of data, it will begin to overwrite the trace. By altering this setting, Network Monitor can be configured to only capture the headers, instead of the entire frame.

## Using Capture Filters

Now when you run Network Monitor, all frames going to and from a computer are captured. During a capture, a large number of frames might be captured. If you're looking for specific types of traffic, you can create a capture filter to define which types of frames should be captured. To configure capture filters within Network Monitor, choose the Filter option from the Capture menu (see Figure 6.3).

From the Capture Filter window, you can create filters based on the following criteria:

▶ *Protocol*—Enables you to specify the protocols or the specific protocol properties that you want to capture

▶ *Address Pairs*—Specifies the computer addresses from which frames should be captured

▶ *Pattern Matches*—Enables you to configure different variables that captured frames should meet

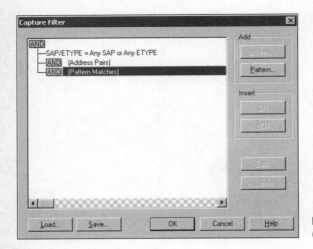

**FIGURE 6.3** Configuring a capture filter.

**NOTE**

The Network Monitor supplied with Windows Server 2003 does not run in Promiscuous mode. This means that it intercepts only packets that are intended either to or from your computer. To get the full version of Network Monitor, which includes Promiscuous mode, you need SMS.

## Using Display Filters

When you capture network traffic, a large number of packets can be displayed when you view the captured data, making it difficult to look for specific information.

Network Monitor enables you to configure display filters so that only specific types of traffic are displayed. To configure a display filter, select the Filter option from the Capture menu after you have run Network Monitor and captured the network traffic.

## Configuring Triggers

By configuring triggers, you can perform certain actions when specific conditions are met. When Network Monitor is capturing data, it examines the contents of the packets. Any packets that meet the defined conditions trigger a specific action to be taken. To configure a trigger, click the Capture menu and click Trigger (see Figure 6.4). When the trigger criteria are met, you can configure any of the following actions to occur:

▸ The computer will beep.

▸ Network Monitor will stop capturing frames.

▸ A command-line program will be executed.

**FIGURE 6.4**  Configuring a trigger.

# System Monitor

System Monitor can be used to monitor the real-time performance of the local computer or another computer on the network. System Monitor enables you to do the following:

▶ Collect real-time performance data on various aspects of system performance

▶ Control which users can view performance data locally or across the network by using the Performance Monitor Users and the Performance Log Users groups

▶ View real-time data or save data in a log file for later analysis

▶ Display captured data in various forms such as a graph or histogram

▶ Create monitoring configurations that can be used on other computers

**EXAM ALERT**

You can control which users can capture and view data using the Performance Monitor Users and Performance Log Users groups. Be prepared to encounter exam questions pertaining to this topic. By adding a user account to the Performance Monitor Users group, he or she will be capable of viewing performance counter data within System Monitor locally or from across the network. Adding a user account to the Performance Log Users group will give the user permission to manage logs and alerts as well as view counter data.

System Monitor enables you to monitor the performance of various server components, including hardware, services, and applications. System Monitor enables you to define the following:

▶ *The type of data you want to collect*—Performance objects enable you to select the various components you want to monitor. Each performance object has its own set of performance counters that determines what aspects of a particular counter you want to monitor. If multiple instances of an object exist (such as two network interfaces), you can select the counter instance you want to monitor.

▶ *Where you will collect the data from*—System Monitor enables you to collect data from the local computer or from another computer on the network.

▶ *How you will collect the data*—The sampling parameters enable you to define manual sampling, on-demand sampling, or automatic sampling.

## Using System Monitor

System Monitor is a tool that is installed with Windows Server 2003 by default. To open the Performance console, click Start, point to Administrative Tools, and click Performance. You will find the System Monitor utility within this console (see Figure 6.5). When System Monitor is initially opened, the following three counters are displayed by default:

▶ *Memory*—Pages/Sec

▶ *Physical Disk*—Avg. Disk Queue Length

▶ *Processor*—%Processor Time

**FIGURE 6.5** The Performance console.

More than likely, you will also want to monitor other components and will need to add other counters—for example, if you want to monitor the performance of a service that has recently been installed. To add a counter to System Monitor, follow these steps:

1. Click Start, point to Administrative Tools, and click Performance.

2. Right-click the System Monitor Details pane and click Add Counter (see Figure 6.6), or click the Add button on the toolbar (represented by a plus sign).

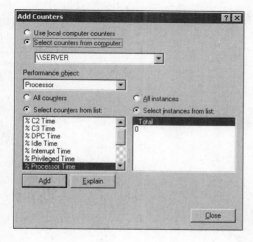

**FIGURE 6.6** Adding counters to System Monitor.

3. To monitor the local computer, select Use Local Computer Counters. To monitor another computer on the network, click Select Counters from Computer and specify the computer name or IP address.

4. Use the Performance Object box to select the specific object you want to monitor. After you select an object, the related counters are displayed.

5. Select All Counters to monitor all counters that are related to the performance object. To select specific counters, click Select Counters from List. Click each counter you want to monitor and click Add. You will also notice an Explain button that provides information about the various counters.

6. To monitor all instances associated with a counter, select All Instances. Otherwise, click Select Instances from List and select the instance to monitor.

7. Click Close.

---

**NOTE**

Before you can add a counter to a System Monitor, either you must be a member of the Administrators group, the Performance Logs Users group, or the Performance Monitor Users group, or you must be delegated the necessary permissions.

---

Using the System Monitor properties window (see Figure 6.7), you can further customize the settings. To do so, click the Properties button located on the toolbar.

**FIGURE 6.7** Configuring System Monitor property settings.

You can use the General tab to configure such things as the view (graph, histogram, or report), the display elements, and the counter values for a report or histogram. By configuring the Sample Automatically Every option, you can define the sampling interval (the default value is every one second).

Using the settings available on the Source tab, you can specify the data source that will be displayed (see Figure 6.8). You have three options: display values for the current activity, display data from an existing log file, or display data stored in an SQL database. The remaining tabs can be used to customize the display of information within System Monitor.

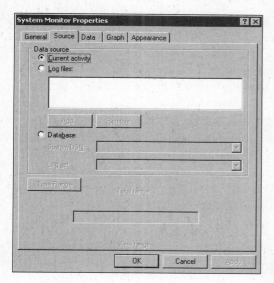

**FIGURE 6.8** Configuring the source of data displayed within System Monitor.

## Using System Monitor to Monitor Network Traffic

If TCP/IP is installed (it is installed by default), the Network Interface performance object is added to System Monitor. You can use this object to monitor data that is sent to and from a computer. When you select the performance object, you will notice that a number of counters are available. Some of the more useful counters for determining problems with a network card include these:

▶ *Packet Outbound Errors*—The number of outbound packets that could not be transmitted because of errors.

▶ *Packet Received Errors*—The number of received packets that contained errors, preventing them from being delivered to a higher-level protocol.

▶ *Packets Outbound Discarded*—The number of packets that have been discarded even though they did not contain errors. A possible cause for this scenario would be to free up buffer space.

▶ *Packets Received Discarded*—The number of received packets that were discarded even though no errors were detected.

You can also use System Monitor to monitor TCP/IP performance. Counters are available for IP, TCP, UDP, and ICMP. You can use the TCP Segments/Sec counter to monitor the number of TCP segments that the computer sent and the Segments Retransmitted/Sec counter to monitor the number of segments that the computer must resend because of errors. The IP Datagrams/Sec counter can be used to monitor the amount of TCP/IP traffic on the network. A number of other counters are available for the various protocols in the TCP/IP suite.

If your computer is functioning as a domain controller, you can use System Monitor to monitor the performance of the server service. In terms of network traffic, you should monitor the Logon Total and Logons/Sec counters, which determine the total number of logon requests the server has received since it was last restarted and the number of logon requests received per second.

## Using System Monitor to Establish a Baseline

Before you even delve into System Monitor, it's a good idea to become secure in the concept of *baselining*. A baseline is simply a set of data that depicts the norm for a particular object, event, or status. For example, the data contained within a baseline can tell you how your CPU behaves under normal circumstances. You can then compare future performance data against that of the baseline to help identify when bottlenecks may be occurring.

The objects that you would normally generate your baseline from are outlined in the following list:

▶ *Memory*—Memory is RAM. Memory is used in several different ways, and counters exist for this object that can tell you how efficiently your RAM is working for you. The two important memory counters are the Pages/sec and the Available Bytes.

▶ *Processor*—The processor object has the capability to monitor the health and welfare of a server's CPUs. As with any of these other objects, counters exist that will monitor things such as how many calculations are being performed, how many errors are being generated, and even how long the line of requests is for processes waiting to for CPU attention. You should monitor the % Total Processor Time counter. A continuously high value may indicate a bottleneck. You should also monitor the Processor Queue Length counter.

▶ *Disk*—Disk monitoring is divided into two sections: physical disk and logical disk. The physical hard disk is another object that should be monitored occasionally for obvious reasons: a bad hard disk will generate errors. An overloaded hard disk will also have problems and could very well slow down the overall server productivity—especially if the paging file is being heavily used. The two important physical disk counters are Physical Disk: Avg. Read Queue Length and Physical Disk: Avg. Write Queue Length. The values for both counters should be lower than 2. The Logical Disk counters are used to monitor specific volumes and partitions. This counter might indeed be more important than the physical disk because it can point to issues, corruptions, and performance issues that may be able to better allow you to isolate an offending application or piece of hardware. You should monitor the Logical Disk: %Free

Space and the Logical Disk: %Disk Time counters. The %Disk Time value should be less than 50%.

▶ *Network*—This particular object will give you statistics on how many network packets are being sent and received by the NIC. It will also give you statistics about bad packets and data that are being sent and received by the same NIC. The important counters include Network Interface: Output Queue Length and %Network Utilization.

## System Monitor Alerts

Alerts are counter-based, and are generated once a set threshold has been met. After this threshold (or event) has been met, the system has some pretty powerful capabilities. First, it can generate an event in the Event Viewer. It can also send a network message to someone (usually an administrator), or run a program (any program actually) that will page or email someone with information.

The true value in the Alerts option lies in the fact that once a threshold has been met, it has the ability to start a Counter Log that has already been saved and configured to handle further monitoring after the event has occurred. As an example, let's say that page faults are running high, and an alert has been created based upon your preexisting knowledge of what the norm is, and what you would perceive to be high based upon the specific system. Page faults can be due to disk problems or memory problems. Following the road toward the process of elimination, you can set up an alert to subsequently trigger a counter log that monitors both disk and memory performance. The result is that with little or no intervention from you, you can then view the counter log and determine where the offender is, and take the appropriate actions.

You can set up an alert by completing the following steps:

1. Click Start and click Run.

2. Type `perfmon.msc` and click OK.

3. Expand Performance Logs and Alerts.

4. Right-click Alerts and click New Alert Settings.

5. Type in a name for the new alert and click OK.

6. The properties dialog box for the new alert will appear. Click the Add button to specify the counters you want monitored in the alert.

7. Click Close.

8. Highlight each counter in the list and specify the value that will trigger an administrative alert.

9. Use the Sample Data Every field to configure the sampling interval.

10. Use the Run As field to specify a different user account under which the monitoring will occur.

11. Click the Action tab.

12. Choose the actions you want to occur when the alert is triggered.

13. Use the Schedule tab to specify when to begin monitoring the counters and how long to monitor them.

# Troubleshooting Internet Connectivity

You can establish Internet connectivity in a number of ways. You can use a remote access server, Internet Connections Sharing (ICS), Network Address Translation (NAT), or a direct connection using a network card, a modem, or another device. Because many organizations now rely heavily on the Internet for day-to-day operations, it is important that you have some understanding of how to troubleshoot Internet connectivity issues as they arise and the tools available to assist you.

> **NOTE**
>
> Refer to Chapter 5, "Routing and Remote Access," for specific information about troubleshooting remote access.

If you are troubleshooting Internet Connectivity, the following are some of the common steps you can take initially:

▶ If you are using a dial-up connection, verify the number and credentials being used.

▶ Verify that the hardware being used is connected.

▶ Ensure that the hardware being used to connect to the Internet (such as a modem) is functioning.

▶ Use the IPCONFIG command to check the local host's TCP/IP configuration.

▶ If you access the Internet through a gateway, verify that the gateway is operational. This can be done by pinging the gateway's IP address.

▶ For name-resolution errors, make sure that DNS is properly configured and the DNS servers are online.

▶ If Internet access is through a proxy server, verify that the outgoing traffic is permitted.

The following section examines some of the tools and utilities included with Windows Server 2003 that can be used to assist you in troubleshooting Internet connectivity.

# Hardware

Whether you have a direct connection to the Internet or have access through another computer, some form of hardware is used. If you experience hardware problems, whether with a modem, a network adapter, or another device, you can use Device Manager to attempt to troubleshoot and diagnose the problem.

You can access Device Manager by right-clicking My Computer and choosing Properties. Select the Hardware tab and click the Device Manager button. As you can see from Figure 6.9, Device Manager lists all the hardware that is currently installed on the computer.

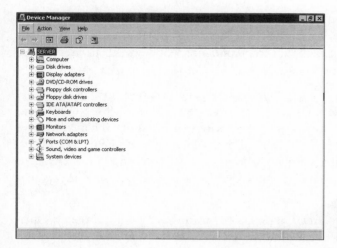

**FIGURE 6.9** Using Device Manager to troubleshoot hardware problems.

By opening the properties window for a device, such as the network interface card, you can verify its status. If there are problems with the device, click the Troubleshoot button, which gives you some basic suggestions for troubleshooting the issue at hand. If you are troubleshooting a modem problem, you can also use the Diagnostics tab, which is found on the properties window for the modem within the Phone and Modem applet.

## Driver Signing

Microsoft recommends you only install drivers that have been tested for compatibility with Windows Server 2003. Drivers that have met the Designed for Microsoft Windows logo requirements are digitally signed and safe to install on your computer.

Windows Server 2003 includes three different options for driver signing. The option you select will tell Windows what to do when it detects an unsigned driver (this is a driver that has not been tested with Windows). You can configure the driver signing options from the System Properties dialog box. The different options include the following:

▶ *Ignore—Install the Software Anyway and Don't Ask for My Approval.* Selecting this option means that any unsigned drivers will be installed on your computer and could cause instability.

▶ *Warn—Prompt Me Each Time to Choose an Action.* If this option is selected, Windows will present a warning when you attempt to install an unsigned driver.

▶ *Block—Never Install Unsigned Driver Software.* By selecting this option, no unsigned drivers will be installed on the computer.

In some cases, unsigned drivers might not cause any problems on a computer. However, you can never be sure because they have not been tested. If you want to err on the side of caution, you can configure Windows XP to prevent the installation of unsigned drivers.

To accomplish this, open the System applet within the Control Panel. From the Hardware tab, select the Driver Signing button. Select the Block—Never Install Unsigned Driver Software option. Also verify that the Make This Action the System Default option at the bottom of the dialog box is selected. Click OK to close the Driver Signing Options dialog box. Click OK to close the System Properties dialog box. Users will no longer be permitted to install drivers that have not been signed.

You can also configure Driver Signing options through the local policy. Open the Group Policy Editor (click Start, click Run, and type gpedit.msc). Expand Computer Configuration, Windows Settings, Security Settings, Local Policies, Security Options. In the details pane, double-click Devices: Unsigned Driver Installation Behavior. Use the drop-down arrow to make your selection and click OK.

## Driver Rollback

The driver Roll Back feature can be used if you encounter problems after updating a driver. For example, such problems include error messages when you access the device, faulty behavior of the device, or even the inability to start Windows.

To use the Roll Back feature in Windows Server 2003, open the Device Manager and follow these steps:

1. Right-click the device for which you want to reinstall the previous version of the driver and click Properties.

2. Click the Drivers tab.

3. Click the Roll Back Driver button.

# Troubleshooting Utilities

Aside from Device Manager, which can be used to troubleshoot hardware problems, a number of other utilities available can assist in diagnosing Internet connectivity problems. The following sections outline some of the tools that are included with Windows Server 2003.

## Network Diagnostics

Network Diagnostics is a tool that gathers information about the hardware, software, and network connections on a local computer and displays the results. It can be used to verify network connectivity and determine whether network-related services are running. The result of the network diagnostics analysis can then be used to identify connectivity problems.

---

**TIP**

You can also configure the scanning option for Network Diagnostics and specify what actions to take and what categories to include in the scan.

---

To use Network Diagnostics, perform the following tasks:

1. Click Start and click Help and Support.

2. From the list of Support Tasks, click Tools.

3. Select Help and Support Center Tools.

4. Select Network Diagnostics (see Figure 6.10).

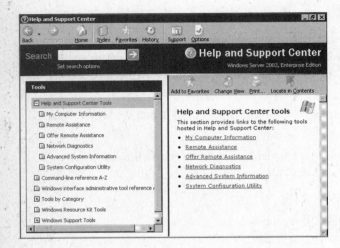

**FIGURE 6.10** Help and Support Center tools.

5. Click Scan Your System. Network Diagnostics gathers information about hardware, software, and network connections on the local computer and displays the results (see Figure 6.11).

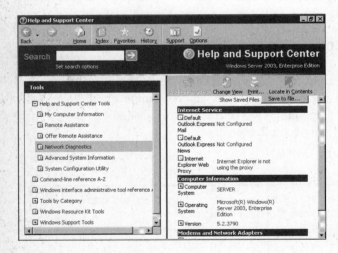

**FIGURE 6.11** Network Diagnostics results.

# The Netdiag Command

After the Windows Server 2003 Support Tools are installed, you can use the Netdiag.exe command-line utility to troubleshoot networking and connectivity problems. Netdiag performs a series of tests to determine the status of the network client. The information can be used by administrators and support personnel to isolate and troubleshoot network problems.

> **NOTE**
>
> To install the Windows Server 2003 Support Tools, open the Support\Tools directory located on the Windows Server 2003 CD-ROM and double-click the suptools.msi file.

## Netsh Command

Netsh is a command-line utility that enables you to modify the network configuration of the local computer or a remote computer. Netsh in Windows Server 2003 introduced a set of diagnostic commands that can be used for troubleshooting. Table 6.1 summarizes some of the context commands that can be useful when troubleshooting Internet connectivity.

**TABLE 6.1   Netsh diag Command Contexts**

| Command Context | Description |
| --- | --- |
| Connect ieproxy | Establishes, verifies, and drops a connection with the proxy listed in the properties of Internet Explorer. |
| Connect iphost | Establishes, verifies, and drops a connection with a specified host using a specified port. |
| Connect mail | Establishes, verifies, and drops a connection with the host specified as the mail server within Outlook Express. |
| PING | Verifies connectivity with the remote host specified. |
| PING *adapter* | Verifies connectivity through a specified adapter. If used without parameters, it tests connectivity through all installed adapters. |
| PING gateway | Verifies connectivity with the default gateways listed in the TCP/IP properties for the specified adapter. If no adapter is specified, connectivity is verified through all installed adapters. |
| PING DNS | Verifies connectivity with DNS servers listed in the TCP/IP properties for the specified adapter. If no adapter is specified, connectivity to DNS servers is tested through all installed adapters. |
| PING ieproxy | Verifies connectivity with the proxy server listed in the properties of Internet Explorer. |
| PING iphost | Verifies connectivity with a local or remote host. |
| PING mail | Verifies connectivity with the mail server configured in Outlook Express. |
| Show *modem* | Lists information about the specified modem. |
| Show gateway | Lists all Internet gateways for the specified adapter. |
| Show ieproxy | Lists all Internet Explorer proxy servers for the specified adapters. |
| Show mail | Shows the Outlook Express mail server configured on the local computer. |

## IPCONFIG

If you are experiencing network connectivity problems, one of the first actions you should perform is to verify the IP configuration on the client or server that is reporting the error. By doing so, you can verify that incorrect IP parameters configured on the computer are not causing the problem. You can use the IPCON-FIG utility from the command prompt to verify a computer's IP configuration. You can view detailed IP configuration information for all interfaces, including modems (see Figure 6.12). Table 6.2 summarizes the available switches.

**FIGURE 6.12** Using the IPCONFIG /ALL command.

**TABLE 6.2   IPCONFIG Command-Line Switches**

| Switch | Description |
| --- | --- |
| /all | Displays full configuration information |
| /release | Releases the IP address assigned to the specified adapter |
| /renew | Renews the IP address for the specified adapter |
| /flushdns | Purges the DNS resolve cache |
| /registerdns | Refreshes all DHCP leases and re-registers DNS names |

## PING

Use the PING command to verify connectivity with other hosts on a TCP/IP network or on the Internet. Connectivity is verified by sending Internet Control Message Protocol (ICMP) echo requests and replies. When the PING command is issued, the source computer sends echo request messages to another TCP/IP host. If reachable, the remote host then responds with four echo replies. The PING command is also issued at the command prompt, along with the TCP/IP address or domain name of the other TCP/IP host, as follows:

```
C:> PING 124.120.105.110
C:> PING www.bayside.net
```

> **TIP**
>
> To determine whether TCP/IP is initialized on the local computer, issue the PING command and specify the loopback address of 127.0.0.1.

The general steps for troubleshooting TCP/IP using the PING command are as follows:

1. PING the loopback address of 127.0.0.1 to ensure that TCP/IP is initialized on the local computer.

2. If successful, PING the IP address assigned to the local computer.

3. Next, PING the default gateway's IP address. If this fails, verify that the default gateway's IP address is correct and that the gateway is operational.

4. Next, PING the IP address of a host on a remote network. If this is unsuccessful, verify that the remote host is operational, verify the IP address of the remote host, and verify that all routers and gateways between the local computer and remote computer are operational.

> **TIP**
>
> A quick way to verify TCP/IP connectivity is to complete step 4 in the preceding steps first. If you can successfully PING the IP address of a remote host, steps 1 through 3 will be successful.

### TRACERT and PATHPING

Two other utilities that can be used for TCP/IP troubleshooting are TRACERT and PATHPING. The TRACERT command determines the route that is taken to a specific destination. You might want to use the TRACERT command if you cannot successfully PING the IP address of a remote host. The results of the TRACERT command indicate whether there is a problem with a router or gateway between the local computer and the remote destination.

The PATHPING command is basically a combination of the PING and TRACERT commands. When the command is issued, packets are sent to each router between the local computer and a remote computer. The output can display the degree of packet loss at each router, and the results determine which routers and gateways might be causing problems on the network.

# Troubleshooting Server Services

A *service* is an application that runs on a computer providing an operating system feature, such as event logging or error reporting.

## Diagnose and Resolve Issues Related to Service Dependency

Service dependencies can be very complex. Some services have no dependencies, meaning that you can start and stop them without worrying whether it will affect other services. However, many services have dependencies, so starting them depends on whether other specific services are first running, and stopping them might cause other services to fail. For example, consider the Clipbook service shown in Figure 6.13. The Clipbook service does not have any other services that depend upon it. However, it depends on another service that must be running before it can be started.

**FIGURE 6.13** Dependencies of the IPSec service.

## Service Dependency

Services that run on a computer might depend on other services. In other words, one service might not be capable of starting unless another service is running. Windows Server 2003 provides administrators with a quick way of determining those services upon which another is dependent, or vice versa. In other words, you can view services that the service depends on and services that depend on it to start. You can verify a service's dependencies using the Services console using the following steps:

1. Click Start, point to Administrative Tools, and click Services. This opens the Services console (see Figure 6.14).

**FIGURE 6.14** The Services console.

2. Right-click the appropriate service and click Properties.

3. From the service's properties window click the Dependencies tab (see Figure 6.15). The Dependencies tab lists those services upon which the service depends and the services that depend upon it.

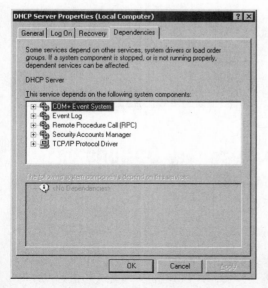

**FIGURE 6.15** Using a service's Dependencies tab.

> **NOTE**
>
> Before you attempt to stop a service, it is a good idea to verify which services depend upon it, to determine whether any other services will be affected.

# Use Service Recovery Options to Diagnose and Resolve Service-Related Issues

Windows 2000 introduced service recovery options. They enable you to specify what actions should be taken when a service fails. For example, if a service fails upon restart or while the server is running, you can attempt to have the service automatically restarted.

Four different recovery options are available. The default is not to take action when a service fails to start. You can also choose from one of the following three recovery actions. Now if a service fails, action can be taken to restart the service without direct administrative intervention.

▶ Restart the service.

▶ Run a program.

▶ Restart the computer.

You can also specify when you want these actions to occur. A recovery action can be performed when the service initially fails, when it fails for a second time, and for any subsequent failures.

> **TIP**
>
> Service recovery options are available only on computers running Windows 2000, Windows XP, and Windows Server 2003.

# Configuring Service Recovery Options

To configure recovery options, perform the following steps:

1. Click Start, point to Administrative Tools, and click Services.

2. Right-click the service for which you want to configure recovery options and click Properties.

3. From the properties window, click the Recovery tab (see Figure 6.16).

**FIGURE 6.16** Configuring service recovery options.

4. To configure a recovery action, click the arrow beside First Failure. Select one of the available options. If you select to run a program, specify the program to run, as well as any command-line parameters.

5. Repeat step 4 to configure recovery actions for second and subsequent failures.

6. Click OK.

# Other Troubleshooting Tools

Windows Server 2003 includes a number of other tools that can be used to diagnose and troubleshoot problems as they arise. Some of these tools include

▶ Task Manager

▶ System Information

▶ Event Viewer

▶ Shutdown Event Tracker

## Task Manager

Task Manager can be used to view a variety of information about the local computer. You can launch the tool by right-clicking the taskbar and selecting the

Task Manager option (see Figure 6.17). Using Task Manager, you can view the following information:

- ▶ Programs currently running
- ▶ Processes currently running
- ▶ Dynamic performance of the local computer
- ▶ Network status
- ▶ Users currently connected to the computer

**FIGURE 6.17**  Using Task Manager.

Table 6.3 summarizes the available tabs.

**TABLE 6.3   Tabs Available Through Windows Task Manager**

| Tab | Description |
| --- | --- |
| Applications | Lists all the applications currently running on the computer |
| Processes | Lists all the processes currently running on the computer |
| Performance | Displays real-time performance information |
| Networking | Displays real-time performance information for the local area connection |
| Users | Lists the users currently connected to the local computer |

## System Information

The System Information tool provides configuration information about the local computer or a remote computer. You can use the tool to quickly locate configuration information for a computer. You can open the System Information tool by selecting Start, All Programs, Accessories, System Tools, System Information. The tool provides the following information:

▶ *Hardware Resources*—Provides information about resource usage

▶ *Components*—Provides information about the components installed on the computer

▶ *Software Environment*—Provides system configuration information

▶ *Internet Settings*—Provides information about the Internet settings configured on the computer

## Event Viewer

You can use Event Viewer to view the contents of the Windows Server 2003 event log files. Every computer running Windows Server 2003 has three log files: Application, Security, and System. Additional log files might be present depending on the configuration of the computer. For example, a computer running DNS will have a DNS server log. The contents of the log files can be used to track events and troubleshoot problems as they arise.

## Shutdown Event Tracker

The Shutdown Event Tracker option enables an administrator to monitor why users shut down or restart their computers. This feature is enabled by default on all computers running Windows Server 2003 and is disabled on Windows XP Professional workstations. When Shutdown Event Tracker is enabled, users are prompted to provide a reason as to why they are shutting down or restarting a computer. The information is then recorded in the system log.

# Exam Prep Questions

1. You are the network administrator for an accounting firm. All servers have been upgraded to Microsoft Windows Server 2003.

   You have been running Network Monitor to capture traffic to and from one of the company's servers. You need to limit the information displayed in the captured data. You only want traffic containing the SMB protocol displayed.

   What should you do?

   - ○  **A.** Configure a trigger.
   - ○  **B.** Configure a capture filter.
   - ○  **C.** Configure a display filter.
   - ○  **D.** Configure a packet filter.

2. You are the network administrator for your organization. Domain controllers and member servers have been upgraded to Microsoft Windows Server 2003. Client computers are running Microsoft Windows XP Professional.

   You need to give another user permission to view real-time data as it is captured using System Monitor. The user must be able to perform this task from the server or from his workstation.

   You need to give the user the appropriate permission while following the principle of least privilege.

   What should you do?

   - ○  **A.** Add the user's account to the Performance Log Users group.
   - ○  **B.** Add the user's account to the Administrators group.
   - ○  **C.** Add the user's account to the Performance Monitor Users group.
   - ○  **D.** Add the user's account to the Domain Admins group.

3. You are the network administrator for your company. Servers on the network are running Microsoft Windows Server 2003.

   You have been running Network Monitor to analyze specific types of network traffic coming to and from one of the network servers. You want to configure Network Monitor to only capture specific types of traffic.

   What should you do?

   - ○  **A.** Configure a display filter.
   - ○  **B.** Configure a capture filter.
   - ○  **C.** Configure a packet filter.
   - ○  **D.** Configure an alert.

4. You are the network administrator for a consulting firm. Network servers are running Microsoft Windows Server 2003.

   The network hosts an SQL 2005 server. Your manager has requested that you gather specific performance data for this server.

   You need to gather statistics about the total amount of TCP/IP traffic on the local computer.

   What should you do?

   - ○ **A.** Monitor the Packet Outbound Errors counter.
   - ○ **B.** Monitor the TCP Segments/Sec counter.
   - ○ **C.** Monitor the IP Datagrams/Sec counter.
   - ○ **D.** Monitor the Logons/Sec counter.

5. You are the network administrator for your company. Servers are running Microsoft Windows Server 2003. Client computers are running Microsoft Windows 2000 Professional.

   One of the servers has a dial-up connection to a local ISP. You are having trouble connecting to the ISP using the dialup connection.

   You need to verify the TCP/IP configuration on the server.

   What command should you use?

   - ○ **A.** IPCONFIG
   - ○ **B.** PING
   - ○ **C.** TRACERT
   - ○ **D.** PATHPING

6. You are the network administrator for your company. You have installed Microsoft Windows Server 2003 on a computer.

   The computer connects to the Internet through a DSL connection. You are having problems establishing a connection and want to verify that the network card is working. Which of the following utilities can you use to verify the status of the network card?

   - ○ **A.** System Monitor
   - ○ **B.** Network Monitor
   - ○ **C.** PING
   - ○ **D.** Device Manager

7. You are the network administrator for a small insurance company. You have recently upgraded the two company servers to Microsoft Windows Server 2003.

You want to gather network performance statistics for the company domain controller. You specifically want to determine the number of logons the domain controller has received since the last time it was restarted.

Which counter should you monitor?

○ **A.** Total Logons Received

○ **B.** Logon Total

○ **C.** Logons Received/Sec

○ **D.** Logons/Sec

8. You are the network administrator for your company. All servers are running Microsoft Windows Server 2003. Client computers are running Microsoft Windows XP Professional.

Clients on the network cannot obtain an IP address from the DHCP server on the network. You soon discover that the DHCP service on the server has failed to start. You reboot the server, and the service still does not start.

What should you do?

○ **A.** Continue to reboot the server until the service starts.

○ **B.** Verify that any services DHCP is dependent on are started using the Services console.

○ **C.** Use the DHCP console to start the service.

○ **D.** Reinstall the DHCP service.

9. You are the network administrator for your organization. Network servers are running Microsoft Windows Server 2003.

You are configuring the service recovery options for the server service on a Windows Server 2003 domain controller.

If a service fails to start, which of the following actions can be performed? (Choose all correct answers.)

○ **A.** The computer can attempt to restart the service.

○ **B.** The computer can be rebooted.

○ **C.** The services that it is dependent upon can be restarted.

○ **D.** An email message can be sent to the network administrator.

10. You are the network administrator for your company. All servers have been upgraded to Microsoft Windows Server 2003.

A new network service has been installed on one of the existing servers. You want to determine how much more traffic has been generated since its installation.

Which of the following tools can be used to capture and analyze network traffic?

- ○ **A.** Task Manager
- ○ **B.** Network Diagnostics
- ○ **C.** Network Monitor
- ○ **D.** Event Viewer

11. You are the network administrator for your company. All servers are running Microsoft Windows Server 2003. Client computers are running Microsoft Windows XP Professional.

    One of the servers is running a business critical application. Users report that this server is slow to respond. You need to monitor network traffic on the server.

    You want to use Network Monitor to capture network traffic. However, you do not need to capture entire frames and you do need to reduce the chance of captured data being overwritten.

    What should you do? (Choose two. Each answer represents part of the solution.)

    - ○ **A.** Increase the buffer size.
    - ○ **B.** Decrease the frame size.
    - ○ **C.** Decrease the buffer size.
    - ○ **D.** Decrease the frame size.

12. You are the network administrator for your company. All servers are running Microsoft Windows Server 2003. Client computers are running Microsoft Windows XP Professional.

    You are configuring the IPSec policies for your company. You need to meet the following requirements:

    - ▶ All communication between SRV01 and SRV02 must be secured.
    - ▶ All communication between SRV02 and network clients must be secured.
    - ▶ All communication between SRV02 and network clients should be secured.
    - ▶ You need to implement the correct IPSec policies.
    - ▶ From the list on the right, select an IPSec policy and place it beneath the appropriate computer.

    Server (Request Security)

    Secure Server (Require Security)

    Client (Respond Only)

SRV-01

SRV-02

Windows XP
computers

You must assign the Server (Request Security) IPSev policy to SRV01. This means the server will always attempt to use IPSec but does not require it. Any clients that do not support IPSec will still be able to communicate with the server.

You must assign SRV02 with the Secure Server (Require Security IPSec policy. This way all communications between SRV01 and SRV02 will be secured and all communications between SRV01 and network clients will be secured. Any clients that do not support IPSec will not be able to communicate with the server.

# Answers to Exam Prep Questions

1. **C.** By configuring a display filter within Network Monitor, you can filter captured data to display only specific types of information. Answer A is incorrect because triggers enable actions to be performed based on a set of conditions that must first be met. Answer B is incorrect because capture filters are configured to specify the type of information that is captured. Answer D is incorrect because packet filters are configured to specify the type of inbound and outbound traffic a computer can accept.

2. **C.** By adding a user account to the Performance Monitor Users group, he will be capable of viewing performance counter data within System Monitor locally or from across the network. Answer A is incorrect because adding the user's account to the Performance Log Users group will give him permission to manage logs and alerts as well. Answers B and D are incorrect because they would give the user administrative permissions to the server. This goes against the principle of least privilege.

3. **B.** Configuring a capture filter instructs Network Monitor to capture only data that meets the criteria you specify. Answer A is incorrect because display filters are used to filter data that has already been captured. Answer C is incorrect because packet filters are configured to control inbound and outbound traffic. Answer D is incorrect because alerts are used to notify an administrator when certain events occur.

4. **C.** By monitoring IP Datagrams/Sec, you can monitor the total number of IP datagrams sent and received by the computer per second. Answer A is incorrect because this is the number of outbound packets that could not be transmitted because of errors. Answer B is incorrect because this counter monitors only the number of TCP segments sent per second. Answer D is incorrect because this counter monitors the number of logon requests received per second by the computer.

5. **A.** The IPCONFIG command can be used to verify the TCP/IP configuration of a computer. Answer B is incorrect because the PING command is used to verify connectivity with a remote host. Answer C is incorrect because TRACERT is used to trace the route a packet takes to reach a remote host. Answer D is incorrect because PATHPING is a combination of PING and TRACERT used to determine which routers and gateways between two hosts might not be functioning.

6. **D.** Device Manager can be used to verify that a hardware device is functioning properly. Answer A is incorrect because System Monitor is used to monitor the performance. Answer B is incorrect because Network Monitor is used to capture and analyze network traffic. Answer C is incorrect because PING is a command-line utility used to verify network connectivity.

7. **B.** The Logon Total counter determines the number of logon requests that the domain controller has received since the last time it was restarted. Answers A and C are incorrect because there are no such counters within System Monitor. Answer D is incorrect because this counter determines the number of logon requests received per second.

8. **B.** If the service will not start, use the Services console to verify that any services that DHCP is dependent upon are also started. Therefore, answer A is incorrect. Answer C is incorrect because if the service fails to start, attempting to start it within the DHCP console will make no difference. Answer D is incorrect because this should be a last resort in terms of troubleshooting.

9. **A and B.** If a service fails to start, you can configure the computer to automatically attempt to restart the service, or you can have the computer automatically reboot. The third option is to have a specific program run. Answers C and D are incorrect because recovery actions do not include the capability to automatically restart the failed service's dependencies or to send an email to the network administrator.

10. **C.** Network Monitor can be used to capture and analyze network traffic. Answer A is incorrect because Task Manager is used to view the programs and processes running on a computer, as well as the performance statistics. Answer B is incorrect because Network Diagnostics is used to gather information about the hardware, software, and services running on a local computer. Answer D is incorrect because Event Viewer is used to view the contents of the various event logs.

11. **A and D.** To reduce the chance that captured data will be overwritten, you should increase the size of the buffer. This will allow Network Monitor to store more data. By decreasing the frame size, you can capture only header information instead of entire frames. Therefore, answers B and C are incorrect.

12. You must assign the Client (Respond Only) IPSec policy to the client computers. Clients will always respond to requests to secure communications.

# Need to Know More?

Search the online version of TechNet and the Windows 2000 Server resource kit using keywords such as "System Monitor," "Network Monitor," and "Service Dependencies."

Morimoto, Rand, et al. *Microsoft Windows Server 2003 Unleashed, R2 Edition.* Indianapolis, IN: Sams Publishing, 2006. ISBN: 0-672-32898-4

# 7

# Practice Exam #1

Do not read Chapters 7–10 until you have learned and practiced all the material presented in the preceding chapters of this book. These chapters serve a special purpose; they are designed to test whether you are ready to take Exam 70-291, "Implementing, Managing, and Maintaining a Microsoft Windows Server 2003 Network Infrastructure." In these chapters, you will find two self-tests. Each self-test is followed by an answer key and a brief explanation of the correct answers, along with an explanation of why the other answers are incorrect. Reading these chapters before the other chapters is like reading the climax of a story and then going back to find out how the story arrived at that ending. You don't want to spoil the excitement, do you?

# How to Take the Practice Tests

Each self-test in this book consists of 60 questions; you should complete each test within 120 minutes. The number of questions and the time duration in the actual exam might vary but should be close to this number.

After you have studied the material presented in the preceding chapters of this book, you should take Practice Exam #1 to check how well you are prepared. After the self-test is complete, evaluate yourself using the answer key in Chapter 8, "Answer Key for Practice Exam #1." When you evaluate yourself, note which questions you answered incorrectly, identify the corresponding chapters in the book, and then read and understand that material before taking Practice Exam #2. After taking the second exam, evaluate yourself again and reread the material corresponding to any incorrect answers. Finally, take both tests again until you have correctly answered all of the questions. The information presented in the following sections should help you prepare for the exams.

# Exam-Taking Tips

I strongly suggest that when you take these practice exams, you treat them just as you would treat the actual exam at the test center. Use the following tips to get maximum benefit from the exams:

▶ Before you start, create a quiet, secluded environment where you are not disturbed for the duration of the exam.

▶ Provide yourself with a few empty sheets of paper before you start. Use some of these sheets to write your answers, and use the others to organize your thoughts. At the end of the exam, use your answer sheet to evaluate your exam with the help of the answer key that follows the sample exam.

▶ Don't use any reference material during the exam.

▶ Some of the questions might be vague and require you to make deductions to come up with the best possible answer from the choices given. Others might be verbose, requiring you to read and process a lot of information before you reach the actual question.

▶ As you progress, keep track of the elapsed time and make sure that you'll be able to answer all the questions in the given time limit.

# Practice Exam

1. You are the network administrator for your company. All servers are running Microsoft Windows Server 2003.

   You have been using Network Monitor to capture and analyze DHCP-related traffic. You notice a large amount of traffic from IP address lease requests, and the frequency of the requests is high.

   You verify that there are more IP addresses in the scope than DHCP clients on the network.

   You want to reduce network traffic.

   What should you do?

   ○ **A.** Configure half of the clients with static IP addresses.

   ○ **B.** Increase the lease duration for the scope.

   ○ **C.** Configure another DHCP server on the network.

   ○ **D.** Add a DHCP Relay Agent to the network.

2. You are the network administrator for your company. All servers are running Microsoft Windows Server 2003. The network is divided into three different subnets.

   You need to implement an IP addressing solution. You add a DHCP server to each of the subnets. Each DHCP server is configured with a scope for the local subnet.

   Users on Subnet1 soon report that they cannot access any resources outside of their local subnet. You discover that all clients are leasing IP addresses but no clients can access resources on other subnets.

   You need to resolve the problem.

   What should you do?

   ○ **A.** Activate the scopes on all servers.

   ○ **B.** Configure the properties of TCP/IP on each workstation, and configure the IP address of the gateway.

   ○ **C.** Authorize the DHCP servers within Active Directory.

   ○ **D.** Configure the 003 router option on each DHCP server.

3. You are the network administrator for your organization. All servers are running Microsoft Windows Server 2003.

   You have assigned a junior administrator the task of installing a DHCP server in a test environment. He successfully installs the DHCP service on a member server and adds a scope. However, he soon discovers that the service is constantly being shut down.

What is causing the problem?

○ **A.** The junior administrator did not activate the scope.

○ **B.** The junior administrator must install the DHCP service on a domain controller.

○ **C.** The junior administrator did not authorize the DHCP server.

○ **D.** The junior administrator configured the server with incorrect scope information.

4. You are the network administrator of a Windows Server 2003 network. You are in charge of implementing an IP addressing solution.

   You install the DHCP service on an existing server. Three servers on the network are running applications that require the servers to have static IP addresses.

   You need to ensure that these servers are always using the same IP addresses.

   What should you do?

   ○ **A.** Manually assign the servers IP addresses. Exclude the IP addresses that will be used for the servers from the scope.

   ○ **B.** Create three client reservations. Exclude the IP addresses from the scope. Configure the servers as DHCP clients.

   ○ **C.** Configure a client reservation for each of the servers. Configure the three servers as DHCP clients.

   ○ **D.** Configure a superscope and add to it the IP addresses that will be assigned to the servers. Configure the three servers as DHCP clients.

5. DHCP is deployed on the network, and all clients are configured to automatically obtain an IP address. If the DHCP server is unavailable, clients will use an IP address from which of the following address ranges?

   ○ **A.** 192.168.0.1 to 192.168.255.254.

   ○ **B.** 192.168.0.1 to 192.168.0.254

   ○ **C.** 127.0.0.1 to 127.255.255.154

   ○ **D.** 169.254.0.0 to 169.254.255.255

6. You are the network administrator for your company. All servers are running Microsoft Windows Server 2003.

   You are responsible for implementing DHCP on the network. The network consists of multiple subnets. A single DHCP server is installed on Subnet A. DHCP Relay Agents are enabled on the remaining subnets. The configuration is tested, and all clients are successfully leasing IP addresses.

You soon discover that only users on subnet B can communicate outside of their local subnet.

What is causing the problem?

- ○ **A.** The DHCP server is configured with a single scope.
- ○ **B.** The DHCP Relay Agents are not configured with the correct IP address for the DHCP server.
- ○ **C.** The scopes on the DHCP server have not been activated.
- ○ **D.** The 003 router option has been configured at the server level.

7. You are one of the network administrators for your company. All servers are running Microsoft Windows Server 2003. They are all members of the same Active Directory domain.

You need to deploy DHCP on the network. You install and configure the service on an existing server. You configure and activate a scope.

When you attempt to authorize the DHCP server, you receive an access denied error message.

What is causing the problem?

- ○ **A.** You must be a member of the DNSUpdateProxy group to authorize a DHCP server.
- ○ **B.** You must be a member of the Enterprise Admins group to authorize a DHCP server.
- ○ **C.** You must be a member of the Domain Admins group to authorize a DHCP server.
- ○ **D.** You must be a member of the Administrators group to authorize a DHCP server.

8. You are a network administrator for your company. All servers are running Microsoft Windows Server 2003.

You are in the process of deploying dynamic IP addressing on the network. You need to configure a DHCP server to lease IP addresses to client computers on multiple subnets.

All clients must be assigned to the IP address of their local default gateway. The 003 router option must be configured at the correct level.

From the following list, place the scope options in the order that they are applied.

Class

Scope

Server

Client

9. You are the network administrator for your company. All servers are running Microsoft Windows Server 2003.

Three servers on the network are configured with the following static IP addresses: 192.168.0.10, 192.168.0.11, and 192.168.0.12.

You install a DHCP server on the network and configure a scope with a range of IP addresses from 192.168.0.1 to 192.168.0.254.

You want to make sure that the IP addresses assigned to the server are not leased to any DHCP clients.

What should you do?

- ○ **A.** Configure client reservations for the three servers.
- ○ **B.** Exclude the three IP addresses from the scope.
- ○ **C.** Enable conflict detection on the DHCP server.
- ○ **D.** Create a superscope for the three static IP addresses.

10. You are the network administrator for your company. All servers on the network are running Microsoft Windows Server 2003. Client computers are running Microsoft Windows XP Professional.

The network consists of two subnets connected by a BOOTP-enabled router. You have placed a DHCP server on each subnet.

You want to ensure that users can access all network resources should the DHCP server on their local subnets be unavailable. You want to accomplish this with the least amount of administrative effort.

What should you do?

- ○ **A.** Enable automatic IP addressing on the client computers.
- ○ **B.** Configure each DHCP server with a scope for each subnet.
- ○ **C.** Enable a DHCP relay agent on each subnet.
- ○ **D.** Configure the alternate configuration option on the client computers.

11. You are the network administrator for a medium-size company. The company is in the process of upgrading the existing network infrastructure. Servers are now running Microsoft Windows Server 2003. Client computers are still running Microsoft Windows 95 and configured with static IP addresses.

   You have been instructed to implement dynamic IP addressing. You install Dynamic Host Configuration Protocol on a Windows Server 2003 server. The server is authorized and a scope is created and activated. Most of the client computers are configured for dynamic IP addressing.

   You soon receive reports from a few users that there are IP address conflicts on the network. You do not know the specific IP addresses within the scope range that are still used for static IP addressing. You need to resolve the problem as quickly as possible.

   What should you do?

   - ○ **A.** Increase the number of conflict detection attempts.

   - ○ **B.** Exclude the IP addresses from the DHCP scope.

   - ○ **C.** Create client reservations for the client computers with static IP addresses.

   - ○ **D.** Change the start and end IP addresses for the scope.

12. You are the network administrator for your company. All servers are running Microsoft Windows Server 2003.

   You have just installed the DHCP service on an existing server. The scope has been configured, and the server now needs to be authorized.

   Which administrative console should you open to perform this task?

   - ○ **A.** DHCP console

   - ○ **B.** Active Directory Sites and Services

   - ○ **C.** Active Directory Users and Computers

   - ○ **D.** Active Directory Domains and Trusts

13. You are the network administrator for your company. All servers are running Microsoft Windows Server 2003.

   There is a DHCP server and a DNS server on the network. Workstations are running a variety of different platforms. You want to identify which client computers on the network will be able to update their own host records with the DNS server.

Select the operating systems from the list on the right that can update their host records with the DNS server. Place these operating systems in the list on the left.

> Windows 95
>
> Windows Me
>
> Windows 2000
>
> Windows XP
>
> Windows 98

14. You are the network administrator for your company. All servers have been upgraded to Microsoft Windows Server 2003. Client computers are running Microsoft Windows XP Professional.

    A user reports that she is unable to connect to any other computers on the network. You want to verify that the workstation is receiving an IP address from a DHCP server.

    What should you do?

    - ○ **A.** Execute the `nslookup` command on the client computer.

    - ○ **B.** Ping the IP address of the DHCP server.

    - ○ **C.** Execute the `IPCONFIG /ALL` command on the client computer.

    - ○ **D.** Use the properties of `TCP/IP` to verify the client computer is configured to obtain an IP address automatically.

15. You are the network administrator for your company. All servers are running Microsoft Windows Server 2003.

    One of the client computers on the network still uses NetBIOS. You are configuring an LMHOSTS file that will be used by the client to resolve NetBIOS names to IP addresses.

    You want certain entries in the LMHOSTS file placed in the NetBIOS name cache each time the computer is restarted.

    What should you do?

    - ○ **A.** Add the `#pre` directive to the entries.

    - ○ **B.** Add the `#include` directive to the entries.

    - ○ **C.** Add the `#mh` directive to the entries.

    - ○ **D.** Add the `#DOM: domain_name` directive to the entries.

16. You are the network administrator for your company. All servers are running Microsoft Windows Server 2003.

    You are planning the implementation of DHCP for a network that consists of a single subnet. Your manager is concerned that clients will not be able to access the company database server if the DHCP server is unavailable. All clients and servers are configured as DHCP clients. The workstations are running a number of different platforms. You inform your manager that the computers will use private IP addressing if a DHCP server is unavailable.

Which of the following platforms will support automatic private IP addressing? (Choose all correct answers.)

- ○ **A.** Windows 95
- ○ **B.** Windows 98
- ○ **C.** Windows Me
- ○ **D.** Windows XP
- ○ **E.** Windows NT 4.0

17. You are the network administrator for your company. All servers are running Microsoft Windows Server 2003. Client computers are running Microsoft Windows XP Professional.

Client computers are configured to use dynamic IP addressing. The DHCP server is configured to perform DNS updates on behalf of DHCP clients. The zone is configured for secure updates only.

You must ensure that the DHCP server can still perform updates to the zone file.

What should you do?

- ○ **A.** Authorize the DHCP server.
- ○ **B.** Add the DHCP server to the DnsUpdateProxy group.
- ○ **C.** Configure the dynamic update credentials.
- ○ **D.** Configure static IP addresses for all clients.

18. You are the network administrator for your company. All servers have been upgraded to Microsoft Windows Server 2003.

The network hosts a DHCP server and a DNS server. The zone is configured for dynamic updates. The DHCP server is configured with the default settings.

Client computers are running Windows 95, Windows 2000 Professional, and Windows XP Professional.

Which of the following statements are true regarding dynamic updates? (Select two.)

- ○ **A.** All clients will update their own PTR records and A records.
- ○ **B.** The DHCP server will update PTR records for Windows 2000 and Windows XP clients.

○ **C.** The DHCP server will update A records and PTR records on behalf of all clients.

○ **D.** Windows 2000 and Windows XP clients will update their own A records.

○ **E.** The DHCP server will update A and PTR records on behalf of Windows 95 clients.

19. You are the network administrator of a Microsoft Windows Server 2003 network. All computers are members of a single Active Directory domain.

The DNS service is installed on two member servers. You upgrade both of these servers to domain controllers.

SRV01 is configured as the primary DNS server. SRV02 is configured as a secondary DNS server. You want to use the Active Directory replication topology for updating the zone file on SRV02.

What should you do?

○ **A.** From the properties window for the DNS server, select the General tab and click the Change button beside the Zone Type option. Select the option to store the zone in Active Directory.

○ **B.** From the properties window for the zone, select the Security tab and click the Change button. Select the option to store the zone in Active Directory.

○ **C.** From the properties window for the DNS server, select the Security tab and click the Change button. Select the option to store the zone in Active Directory.

○ **D.** From the properties window for the zone, select the General tab and click the Change button beside the Zone Type option. Select the option to store the zone in Active Directory.

20. You are the network administrator for your company. All domain controllers are running Microsoft Windows Server 2003. The company maintains a UNIX DNS server.

A mail server has just been added to the network. You soon discover that mail is not getting delivered properly. You suspect that the mail is not getting routed to the proper server because its name might be unknown to the UNIX DNS server.

You need to ensure that mail is properly delivered to the proper server.

What should you do?

○ **A.** Verify that the appropriate MX record exists.

○ **B.** Verify that the UNIX server is configured for dynamic updates.

○ **C.** Verify that clients have been configured with the IP of the mail server through the properties of TCP/IP.

○ **D.** Verify that a CNAME record exists for the mail server.

**21.** You are the network administrator for an insurance company. All servers are running Microsoft Windows Server 2003. The company uses a single Active Directory domain.

You have installed and configured the DNS service on an existing member server. The server hosts the zone file for the domain.

You are concerned about fault tolerance. You want users to be able to resolve host names if the existing DNS server is unavailable.

You want to install the DNS service on a second member server.

What should you do?

- ○ **A.** Configure the server as caching-only.
- ○ **B.** Configure the server as a second primary DNS server for the zone.
- ○ **C.** Configure the server as a secondary DNS server for the zone.
- ○ **D.** Configure the server to host an Active Directory–integrated copy of the zone.

**22.** You are the network administrator for your company. All servers are running Microsoft Windows Server 2003. The company has a head office and several branch offices. The branch offices connect back to the head office via slow links.

The company has two DNS servers placed in the head office. Users in the branch offices report that name-resolution response time is slow. The budget allows you to place a DNS server within each location. However, you do not want any zone transfer traffic on the slow links.

What should you do?

- ○ **A.** Configure each of the new DNS servers as primary DNS servers for the zone.
- ○ **B.** Configure each of the new DNS servers as secondary DNS servers for the zone.
- ○ **C.** Configure each of the new DNS server as a caching-only server.
- ○ **D.** Configure each of the new DNS servers as a master name server for the zone.

**23.** You are the network administrator for your company. All servers have been upgraded to Microsoft Windows Server 2003.

You are using the `nslookup` command to determine the hostname associated with the IP address of 192.168.0.35. You can successfully resolve other IP addresses to host-names using the command. However, you are unable to resolve the IP address of 192.168.0.35 to a hostname.

What is causing the problem?

- ○ **A.** There is no A record for Computer1.

- ○ **B.** The DNS server is not online.

- ○ **C.** There is no MX record for Computer1.

- ○ **D.** The PTR record has not been created for Computer1.

**24.** You are the network administrator for your company. All servers are running Microsoft Windows Server 2003. Client computers are running Microsoft Windows XP Professional with the default configuration.

The network is shown in the diagram. DHCP-01 is configured with 20% of the IP addresses for Subnet 2 and Subnet 3. You have enabled a Dynamic Host Configuration Protocol (DHCP) Relay Agent on Subnet 2 and Subnet 3.

You want to verify that client computers can obtain IP addresses if DHCP-02 and DHCP-03 are offline. You stop the DHCP service on these DHCP servers. However, client computers on Subnet 2 are unable to lease IP addresses. You verify that this problem is not affecting Subnet 3.

You need to resolve the problem.

What should you do first?

○ **A.** Verify that the correct interface is added under the DHCP Relay Agent on Subnet 2.

○ **B.** Verify that the Relay DHCP packets option is selected for the DHCP Relay Agent interface on Subnet 2.

○ **C.** Verify that the DHCP Relay Agent on Subnet 2 is configured with the correct IP address for DHCP-01.

○ **D.** Verify that the scope options on DHCP-01 are correctly configured.

25. You are the network administrator for your company. The company uses a single Active Directory domain. All servers are running Microsoft Windows Server 2003.

The company's domain controller hosts the Active Directory–integrated zone for the domain. You want to increase security by specifying which users and groups can update the zone file.

What should you do?

○ **A.** From the properties window for the DNS server, select the General tab and change the Dynamic Updates option to Secure Only.

○ **B.** From the properties window for the zone, select the General tab and change the Dynamic Updates option to Secure Only.

○ **C.** From the properties window for the DNS server, select the Security tab and change the Dynamic Updates option to Secure Only.

○ **D.** From the properties window for the zone, select the Security tab and change the Dynamic Updates option to Secure Only.

26. You are the network administrator for your company. The company uses a single Active Directory Domain. There is a head office and several branch offices. Branch offices connect to the head office via slow, heavily used connections.

A primary DNS server exists within the head office of the Riverside Corporation. Each branch office hosts a secondary DNS server. Users in the branch offices must be able to resolve domain names if the local secondary DNS server goes offline. The budget allows for the purchase of additional DNS servers.

You want to place another DNS server in each branch office while minimizing the amount of traffic on the WAN connections.

What should you do?

○ **A.** Configure the existing secondary DNS servers as the master name servers for the new secondary DNS servers.

○ **B.** Configure the new DNS servers as caching-only DNS servers.

    ○   **C.**  Configure the new secondary DNS servers to receive zone transfers from the primary DNS server in the head office.

    ○   **D.**  Configure the new secondary servers as forwarders.

**27.** You are the network administrator for a medium-size network. All servers have been upgraded to Microsoft Windows Server 2003. Client computers are running Microsoft Windows XP Professional.

There are multiple subnets on the network. You need to configure a new server on Subnet 2 with a static IP address. You open the Internet Protocol (TCP/IP) Properties window on another server on the Subnet 2. The output is shown in the figure.

Based on this information, which of the following is a valid IP address to configure the new server with?

    ○   **A.**  192.168.0.25

    ○   **B.**  192.168.0.30

    ○   **C.**  192.168.0.45

    ○   **D.**  192.168.0.60

**28.** You are the network administrator for your company. All servers have been upgraded to Microsoft Windows Server 2003.

The primary and secondary DNS servers are connected by slow links that are already heavily used. You want to reduce the amount of traffic on the WAN connection.

What should you do?

    ○  **A.**  Decrease the TTL.

    ○  **B.**  Increase the refresh interval.

    ○  **C.**  Decrease the retry interval.

    ○  **D.**  Alter the serial number.

**29.** You are a network administrator for your company. Servers are running Microsoft Windows Server 2003 and Microsoft Windows 2000 Server.

SRV01 and SRV02 are running DNS on Windows Server 2003. SRV01 is the primary DNS server for the bayside.net zone. SRV02 is the secondary DNS server for the zone.

You run the Active Directory Installation Wizard (dcpromo.exe) on a server named SRV03 to create an Active Directory domain named bayside.net for the network. You also run the wizard on a computer named SRV04 to create an additional domain controller for the domain. SRV03 is located at the head office and hosts all of the operation's master roles. SRV04 is located at a branch office.

You need to prepare SRV03 to host an Active Directory–integrated zone for bayside.net. You install the DNS server service on SRV03.

What should you do next?

    ○  **A.**  Create an Active Directory application partition.

    ○  **B.**  Create a secondary zone for bayside.net on SRV03.

    ○  **C.**  Create a stub zone for bayside.net on SRV03.

    ○  **D.**  Create a primary zone for bayside.net on SRV03.

**30.** You are the network administrator for the Bayside company. All servers are running Microsoft Windows Server 2003.

A merger has just occurred between the Bayside and Riverside corporations. Each network maintains its own DNS servers. You want the DNS servers in Bayside to send all queries for hosts in the Riverside organization directly to the Riverside DNS servers.

What should you do?

    ○  **A.**  Using the Forwarders tab from the zone's properties window, configure the Bayside DNS server to forward all name-resolution requests to the Riverside DNS servers.

    ○  **B.**  Using the Forwarders tab from the DNS server's properties window, configure the Bayside DNS server to forward all name-resolution requests to the Riverside DNS servers.

○ **C.** Using the Forwarders tab from the DNS server's properties window, configure the Bayside DNS server to forward all name-resolution requests for
clients in the Riverside domain to the Riverside DNS servers.

○ **D.** Using the Forwarders tab from the zone's properties window, configure the
Bayside DNS server to forward all name-resolution requests for clients in
the Riverside domain to the Riverside DNS servers.

**31.** You are a network administrator for your company. Servers are running Microsoft
Windows Server 2003 and client computers are running Microsoft Windows XP
Professional. Computers are members of a domain called bayside.net.

You have installed DNS on two domain controllers named SRV01 and SRV02. The zone
for bayside.net is Active Directory–integrated.

Your company opens a new subsidiary in Canada that will use a separate DNS namespace. Administrators in Canada will configure SRV03 as a domain controller for an
Active Directory domain named riverside.net. They will also add three more domain
controllers running the DNS server service to the domain.

You need to ensure that SRV01 has information about all the name servers for river-
side.net, including the name servers that are added after the new zone is created. Your
solution must minimize the amount of disk space used to store DNS data on SRV01.

What should you do?

○ **A.** Create a stub zone for riverside.net on SRV01.

○ **B.** Configure conditional forwarding for riverside.net on SRV01.

○ **C.** Configure replication between SRV03 and SRV01.

○ **D.** Configure SRV01 as a secondary DNS server for canada.bayside.net.

**32.** You are the network administrator for your organization. All servers are running
Microsoft Windows Server 2003.

You have just finished installing and configuring a new DNS server for the network.
The DNS server is still in the test environment.

You want to ensure that the DNS server is functioning before placing it on the network.
You specifically want to verify that the DNS server is resolving hostname queries.

What should you do?

○ **A.** Ping the IP address of the DNS server.

○ **B.** Check the Event Viewer for any DNS-related events.

○ **C.** Use the Monitoring tab from the DNS server's properties window to test
the configuration.

○ **D.** Verify that the appropriate records exist within the zone file.

33. You are the network administrator for your company. All servers running critical network services have been upgraded to Microsoft Windows Server 2003.

    The network maintains several UNIX hosts that use only DNS. There are also legacy
    clients on the network that use NetBIOS. The UNIX hosts cannot resolve the NetBIOS
    names of the legacy clients.

    The UNIX hosts must be able to resolve NetBIOS names.

    What should you do?

    - ○ **A.** Enable DNS for WINS lookup.

    - ○ **B.** Configure replication between DNS and WINS.

    - ○ **C.** Install a WINS proxy agent on the network.

    - ○ **D.** Configure DHCP to register NetBIOS names with the DNS server.

34. You are the network administrator for your company. All servers are running Microsoft
Windows Server 2003. The network currently consists of a single subnet.

    You need to subnet the existing network to optimize network traffic. You plan to use a
    class C network ID of 192.168.0.0. The network will be subdivided into 12 different
    subnets. There may be future plans to add an additional 2 subnets.

    Which subnet mask should you choose?

    - ○ **A.** 255.255.255.224

    - ○ **B.** 255.255.255.240

    - ○ **C.** 255.255.255.248

    - ○ **D.** 255.255.255.252

35. You are the network administrator for your company. All servers have been upgraded
to Microsoft Windows Server 2003.

    Due to budget constraints, you are only able to implement a single WINS server on
    a network that consists of two subnets. You place the WINS server on the subnet
    with the most users. A computer on the other subnet will be configured as a WINS
    proxy.

    How should you proceed?

    - ○ **A.** Install the WINS proxy component using the Add/Remove programs applet.

    - ○ **B.** Install the WINS service and select the WINS proxy component during the
    installation.

   ○  **C.** Edit the `HKEY_LOCAL_MACHINE\System\CurrentControlSet\Services\Netbt\Parameters` Registry key on the local computer and change the value of the `EnableProxy` parameter to 1.

   ○  **D.** Edit the local computer Registry and change the value of the `WINSProxy` parameter to 1.

**36.** You are the administrator of a Windows Server 2003 network. The head office hosts a primary DNS server that is also used by the branch office.

You want to place a DNS server within the branch office location without increasing the network traffic on the WAN link.

What should you do?

   ○  **A.** Configure another primary DNS server in the branch office location.

   ○  **B.** Configure a secondary DNS server in the branch office location, but do not configure a master name server.

   ○  **C.** Configure a caching-only DNS server in the branch office location.

   ○  **D.** Configure a master name server in the branch office location.

**37.** You are the network administrator for your company. All servers are running Microsoft Windows Server 2003.

There are a number of DNS servers on the network. DNS01 is a primary DNS server. You want to limit which secondary servers are permitted to receive zone updates from DNS01.

What should you do?

   ○  **A.** Use the Security tab from the zone's properties window to list servers that can receive updates.

   ○  **B.** Use the Zone Transfers tab from the zone's properties window to list servers that can receive updates.

   ○  **C.** Use the Security tab from the DNS server's properties window to list servers that can receive updates.

   ○  **D.** Enable zone transfers to all servers using the Zone Transfers tab from the zone's properties window.

**38.** You are the network administrator for your company. All servers are running Microsoft Windows Server 2003. Client computers are running Microsoft Windows 95 and Microsoft Windows 2000 Professional. All computers are members of the bayside.net domain.

Your company has just acquired another company with an existing domain called riverside.net. You plan to keep the existing network infrastructure and each domain will maintain its own DNS servers. You want BAYDNS, the DNS server for bayside.net, to send DNS queries for hosts in riverside.net to RIVDNS, the DNS server for riverside.net.

What should you do?

- ○ **A.** Open the BAYDNS properties dialog box. Use the Forwarders tab to config-ure BAYDNS to forward all name resolution requests for riverside.net to RIVDNS.

- ○ **B.** Open the bayside.net zone properties dialog box. Use the Forwarders tab to configure BAYDNS to forward all name resolution requests to RIVDNS.

- ○ **C.** Open the BAYDNS properties dialog box. Use the Forwarders tab to config-ure BAYDNS to forward all name resolution requests to RIVDNS.

- ○ **D.** Open the bayside.net zone properties dialog box. Use the Forwarders tab to configure BAYDNS to forward all name resolution requests for riverside.net to RIVDNS.

**39.** You are the network administrator for your company. All servers are running Microsoft Windows Server 2003. Client computers are running Microsoft Windows XP Professional.

The company maintains a web server on the intranet. You have assigned an IPSec policy on this server.

You want to verify that all communication with the web server is being secured. You want to accomplish this with the least amount of administrative effort.

Which of the following tools should you use?

- ○ **A.** IP Security Policy management console

- ○ **B.** Network Monitor

- ○ **C.** IP Security Monitor

- ○ **D.** System Monitor

**40.** You are the network administrator for your company. Servers have been upgraded to Microsoft Windows Server 2003. Client computers are running Microsoft Windows XP Professional.

You are implementing Software Update Services to streamline the process of applying updates to computers on the network. You need to install Software Update Services on an existing server.

What software components are required on the server before installing SUS?

Select the software components from the list on the right that are required to install WSUS. Place these software components in the list on the left.

Internet Explorer 5.0 or later

IIS 5.0 or later

Active Directory

NTFS system partition

Service Pack 1

SQL Server 2005

**41.** You are the network administrator for your company. The company maintains a single Active Directory domain. All servers are running Microsoft Windows Server 2003.

You have installed SUS on a member server. You need to configure client computers to use the SUS server.

You create a new Group Policy Object (GPO) for the appropriate OU. When you open the GPO to edit the automatic update settings, they are not available.

What is causing the problem?

- ○ **A.** You do not have sufficient privileges to edit the policy settings.
- ○ **B.** SUS must be installed on a domain controller.
- ○ **C.** You must configure the settings on each workstation.
- ○ **D.** The Automatic Updates ADM file has not been loaded.

**42.** You are the network administrator of a Microsoft Windows Server 2003 network. You have just finished installing Software Update Services. The server is configured and ready to be placed on the network.

You need to install the updated version of Automatic Updates on the client computers. The computers are running a variety of platforms.

Which of the following platforms will support the updated version of Automatic updates?

Select the operating systems from the list on the right that will support SUS. Place these operating systems in the list on the left.

Windows 2000

Windows 95

Windows Me

Windows XP

Windows 98

**43.** You are the administrator of a Windows Server 2003 network. You have created a security template that is applied to all new servers on the network.

You discover that the account lockout threshold on one of the network servers has been changed. You are concerned that several other settings might have been changed.

You want to determine if any other settings on the server have been changed.

What should you do?

- ○ **A.** Open the Security log to see if additional configuration changes have been made.

- ○ **B.** Run the Resultant Set of Policy tool on the server.

- ○ **C.** Compare the existing settings against the original template using the Security Configuration and Analysis.

- ○ **D.** Open the Active Policy container with the IP Security Monitor.

**44.** You are the network administrator for your company. All servers are running Microsoft Windows Server 2003 and have been placed in the server OU. The company uses a single domain called bayside.net.

You need to configure the security settings on six member servers. You want all six servers to have the same security settings. You need to accomplish this using the least amount of administrative effort.

What should you do?

- ○ **A.** Configure the security settings on each server.

- ○ **B.** Configure a security template and import it on each server.

- ○ **C.** Configure a security template and deploy it through a GPO.

- ○ **D.** Configure a security template and deploy it using SUS.

**45.** You are the network administrator for your company. All servers are running Microsoft Windows Server 2003. Client computers are running Microsoft Windows XP Professional.

You have installed SUS on a member server. You want to enable the client computers to use an SUS server for automatic updates.

What should you do?

- ○ **A.** Set the value for the UseWUServer to 1.

- ○ **B.** Set the value for the AUOptions to 2.

- ○ **C.** Configure the value for WUServer to point to the URL of the SUS server.

- ○ **D.** Configure the value for the WUStatusServer to point to the URL of the SUS server.

**46.** You are the network administrator for your company. All servers are running Microsoft Windows Server 2003. SUS is installed on a member server.

You have enabled Automatic Updates on a Windows XP workstation to use SUS. You now want to specify the SUS server from which the workstation will download options.

Which Registry value should you configure?

- ○ **A.** UseWUServer
- ○ **B.** AUOptions
- ○ **C.** WUServer
- ○ **D.** WUStatusServer

**47.** You are the new network administrator for your company. You maintain several servers running Microsoft Windows Server 2003. Client computers are running Microsoft Windows XP Professional.

The previous administrator left no documentation about the existing servers. Managers have asked you to document server configuration. Your documentation must include the following:

- ○ Misconfigurations with the operating system
- ○ Identification of missing security updates

You need to have this information as soon as possible.

What should you do?

- ○ **A.** Install mbsacli.exe and run the program from your administrative computer.
- ○ **B.** Install HFNetHCK.exe and run the program on each server you want to document.
- ○ **C.** Open and run the Security Configuration and Analysis utility on each server.
- ○ **D.** Open the security policy on each computer and export the settings to a database.

**48.** You are the network administrator for your company. All servers have been recently upgraded from Microsoft Windows 2000 Server to Microsoft Windows Server 2003.

You have assigned IPSec policies to several network servers. You want to view IPSec statistics using the IP Security Monitor on a Windows Server 2003 server.

How can you open the IP Security Monitor utility in Windows Server 2003?

- ○ **A.** Using Administrative Tools located on the Start menu
- ○ **B.** Using the IP Security Monitor icon within the Control Panel

○ **C.** Using the run command and typing `ipsecmon.exe`

○ **D.** Using the Microsoft Management Console and adding the IP Security Monitor snap-in

**49.** You are the network administrator for your company. All servers are running Microsoft Windows Server 2003.

The internal network is using the private IP address range of 192.168.0.0/24. DHCP is being implemented. Two servers will continue to use static IP addresses.

You want to ensure that there are no address conflicts on the network.

What should you do?

○ **A.** Configure client reservations for both servers.

○ **B.** Exclude the static IP addresses from the scope.

○ **C.** Place the static IP addresses within a separate scope.

○ **D.** Configure the scope options on the DHCP server.

**50.** You are the network administrator for your company. Your organization is still in the process of migrating to Microsoft Windows Server 2003. Some of the servers are still running Microsoft Windows 2000 Server.

You have assigned IPSec policies to the servers. You want to monitor the servers to ensure that communication between servers is secured. You use the IP Security Monitor snap-in from your computer to monitor the servers across the network. However, you discover that you can monitor only computers running Windows Server 2003.

What is causing the problem?

○ **A.** You do not have administrative permissions on the servers running Windows 2000.

○ **B.** IP Security Monitor cannot be used to monitor computers running Windows 2000.

○ **C.** The Windows 2000 servers are not members of the local domain.

○ **D.** The Network Monitor driver is not installed on the Windows 2000 servers.

**51.** You are the network administrator for your company network. All servers are running Microsoft Windows Server 2003. Client computers are running Microsoft Windows XP Professional.

Your company is restructuring the network and creating 20 subnets using a Class A IP address. It plans to add an additional 8 subnets within the next year.

Which of the following subnet masks should you use?

- ○ **A.** 255.192.0.0
- ○ **B.** 255.224.0.0
- ○ **C.** 255.240.0.0
- ○ **D.** 255.248.0.0

**52.** You are trying to install Software Updates Services on a member server running Microsoft Windows Server 2003. The installation of the software continually fails. You verify that the computer meets the hardware requirements. The server is also running IIS 5.0 and Internet Explorer 6.0, and all partitions except the system partition are formatted with FAT.

What could be causing the problem?

- ○ **A.** Service Pack 1 is not installed.
- ○ **B.** The partition storing the updates is not formatted with FAT.
- ○ **C.** IIS must be uninstalled.
- ○ **D.** An NTFS partition has not been detected.

**53.** You are the network administrator for your company. All servers are running Microsoft Windows Server 2003.

The company has opened a new branch office. You are in charge of implementing dynamic IP addressing in the new branch office. There is an existing DHCP server in the head office.

Fault tolerance is a priority. Client computers in the branch office should be able to obtain an IP address if the WAN link to the head office becomes unavailable.

What should you do? (Select three.)

- ○ **A.** Place a DHCP server in the branch office location.
- ○ **B.** Configure the local DHCP server with 80% of the available IP addresses. Configure the DHCP server within the head office with the remaining 20% of the IP addresses.
- ○ **C.** Enable the DHCP Relay Agent on a server within the branch office.
- ○ **D.** Configure all clients with the IP address of both DHCP servers.

**54.** You are the network administrator for your company. All servers are running Microsoft Windows Server 2003.

Most client computers are running Microsoft Windows XP Professional. A few client computers are still running Windows 95. You have installed DNS on a member server in the domain. You notice that the Windows 95 clients are not dynamically updating their host records with the DNS server.

What should you do?

- ○ **A.** Configure DNS for dynamic updates.
- ○ **B.** Configure the properties of TCP/IP on the Windows 95 workstations, and enable them for dynamic updates.
- ○ **C.** Configure the DHCP server to perform updates for legacy clients.
- ○ **D.** Place a DHCP relay agent on the network.

55. You are the junior network administrator of a Windows Server 2003 network. The senior network administrator has requested that you install DHCP on an existing standalone server.

You install the service and configure the scope. When you attempt to authorize the DHCP server within Active Directory, the Authorize option is not available within the DHCP console.

What is causing this to occur?

- ○ **A.** You are not a member of the DHCP Administrators group.
- ○ **B.** You are a member of the Enterprise Admins group.
- ○ **C.** DHCP has been installed on a standalone server and, therefore, does not need to be authorized.
- ○ **D.** You must authorize the DHCP server using the Active Directory Users and Computers snap-in.

56. You are the network administrator for a large insurance company. All servers are running Microsoft Windows Server 2003 and are members of the bayside.net domain.

The company has recently opened a new subsidiary. The domain for the subsidiary is sales.bayside.net. You have delegated sales.bayside.net to another DNS server on the network.

You want to ensure that the name server for bayside.net is notified any time a new authoritative name server is added to the sales.bayside.net zone.

What should you do?

- ○ **A.** Using the Name Servers tab from the sales.bayside.net zone, configure the DNS server to notify the DNS server in the parent domain of any changes.
- ○ **B.** Configure a stub zone on the DNS server within the parent domain.

○ **C.** Configure a DNS server within the bayside.net zone to be a secondary server to the sales.bayside.net zone.

○ **D.** Nothing. The name server for bayside.net will be automatically notified.

**57.** You are the network administrator for your company. Servers are running Microsoft Windows Server 2003. All computers are members of the bayside.net domain.

You have installed DNS on all the domain controllers. The zone for bayside.net is Active Directory–integrated.

You want to verify that replication between DNS servers is occurring as it should.

Which tool can you use to verify this?

○ **A.** System Monitor

○ **B.** Replication Monitor

○ **C.** DNS management console

○ **D.** DNS Monitor

**58.** You are the network administrator for your company. Servers are running Microsoft Windows Server 2003.

Your company has recently moved its website to another server. Clients now report that they no longer can view the site.

Upon further examination, you discover that the DNS server is providing clients with the IP address of the old web server. You suspect a problem with the cache.

What should you do?

○ **A.** Uninstall the DNS server service.

○ **B.** Delete the cache.dns file.

○ **C.** Use the Clear Cache option from the DNS server's property window.

○ **D.** Use the Clear Cache option from the Action menu.

**59.** You are the network administrator for your company. Servers are running Microsoft Windows Server 2003. Client computers are running Microsoft Windows XP professional.

You are testing Software Update Services within a test environment on two computers before implementing the service in the production environment. You install Software Update Services on a standalone server.

You need to configure a client computer in the test environment to use the SUS server. You want to configure automatic updates so that the local administrator is notified of downloads and installations.

What should you do?

- ○ **A.** Edit the Registry and configure the UseWUServer Registry value.

- ○ **B.** Edit the Registry and configure the appropriate value for the AUOptions entry.

- ○ **C.** Install the Automatic Updates ADM file. Configure the WUServer option within a Group Policy.

- ○ **D.** Install the Automatic Updates ADM file. Configure the SUSServer option through a Group Policy.

**60.** You are the network administrator for your company. All servers are running Microsoft Windows Server 2003.

The company has recently configured a web server on the intranet. You want to monitor and log network activity coming to and going from the web server.

Which of the following tools can you use? (Select two.)

- ○ **A.** System Monitor
- ○ **B.** IP Security Monitor
- ○ **C.** Network Monitor
- ○ **D.** Event Viewer

# Answer Key for Practice Exam #1

## Answer Key

| | | |
|---|---|---|
| **1.** B | **21.** C | **41.** D |
| **2.** D | **22.** C | **42.** List |
| **3.** C | **23.** D | **43.** C |
| **4.** A | **24.** A | **44.** C |
| **5.** D | **25.** B | **45.** A |
| **6.** D | **26.** A | **46.** C |
| **7.** B | **27.** C | **47.** A |
| **8.** List | **28.** B | **48.** D |
| **9.** B | **29.** B | **49.** B |
| **10.** B | **30.** C | **50.** B |
| **11.** A | **31.** A | **51.** D |
| **12.** A | **32.** C | **52.** D |
| **13.** List | **33.** A | **53.** A, B, C |
| **14.** C | **34.** B | **54.** C |
| **15.** A | **35.** C | **55.** C |
| **16.** C, D | **36.** C | **56.** D |
| **17.** C | **37.** B | **57.** B |
| **18.** B, D | **38.** A | **58.** D |
| **19.** D | **39.** C | **59.** B |
| **20.** A | **40.** List | **60.** A, C |

## Question 1

Answer B is correct. By increasing the lease duration, clients will not have to renew their IP address leases with the DHCP server as often. Answer A is incorrect because, although this would reduce the amount of DHCP traffic, it does not really address the problem at hand and decentralizes IP address administration. Answer C is incorrect because placing a second DHCP server on the network would provide load balancing but would not address the amount of traffic being generated. Answer D is incorrect because a DHCP Relay Agent is used to forward DHCP requests from one subnet to the DHCP server located on another subnet.

## Question 2

Answer D is correct. For clients to communicate outside of their local subnet, they must be configured with the IP address of the default gateway. This can be done by configuring the 003 router option on each DHCP server. Answers A and C are incorrect because the clients can successfully lease IP addresses. This eliminates both of these options as the correct answer. Answer B is incorrect because the clients are configured for DHCP, so the gateway option can be assigned dynamically when the clients are assigned an IP address.

## Question 3

Answer C is correct. If a DHCP server is not authorized in Active Directory, the service will be shut down when it attempts to start. Answer A is incorrect because an inactive scope will not cause the service to fail. Answer B is incorrect because the DHCP service can be installed on a member server, domain controller, or a standalone server. Answer D is incorrect because misconfigured scope information would not cause the DHCP service to fail.

## Question 4

Answer A is correct. You should manually configure IP addresses for the servers and exclude those addresses from the scope. This is a better option than configuring the servers as DHCP clients because it eliminates the servers as being dependent on another server to obtain an IP address. Answer C is incorrect. By configuring a client reservation for each server, the servers can remain as DHCP clients but will always be assigned the same IP address. However, if the DHCP server is unavailable, they will not be able to obtain the IP address. Answer B is incorrect because scope options are used to configure DHCP clients with optional parameters. The 003 option also is used to assign clients the IP addresses of network routers. Answer D is incorrect because superscopes are used to organize existing scopes.

## Question 5

Answer D is correct. If a DHCP server is unavailable, clients will use Automatic Private IP Addressing and will use an IP address in the range of 169.254.0.0 to 169.254.255.255. Therefore, answers A, B, and C are incorrect.

## Question 6

Answer D is correct. For all clients to be able to communicate outside of the local subnet, the 003 router option must be configured at the scope level. Because there are multiple subnets, all client computers are not configured with the same default gateway. Answers A and C are incorrect because all clients are successfully leasing IP addresses. Answer B is incorrect because if the DHCP Relay Agents were configured with the incorrect IP address for the DHCP server, clients would not be able to lease IP addresses.

## Question 7

Answer B is correct. To authorize the DHCP servers, a user must be a member of the Enterprise Admins group. Answers A, C, and D are incorrect because these groups have insufficient privileges to perform the operation.

## Question 8

The correct order is server, scope, class, and client.

## Question 9

Answer B is correct. To ensure that there are no address conflicts on the network, you must exclude the IP addresses already assigned to the three servers from the scope. Answer A is incorrect because client reservations ensure that certain DHCP clients are always assigned the same IP address. Answer C is incorrect because conflict detection is used to ensure that a DHCP server does not lease an IP address that is currently in use on the network. Answer D is incorrect because superscopes do not prevent IP addresses from being leased to clients.

## Question 10

Answer B is correct. You should configure each DHCP server with a scope for each subnet. If the DHCP server on the local subnet is unavailable, clients can obtain an IP address from the DHCP server on the remote network. Answer A is incorrect. Automatic IP addressing provides limited ability to communicate on the network. Because APIPA does not assign a default gateway, communication outside of the local subnet is not possible. Answer C is incorrect because a DHCP Relay Agent is not required. Because the routers are BOOTP-enabled, they can forward IP address requests between subnets. Answer D is incorrect because this solution would require more administrative effort.

## Question 11

Answer A is correct. You should increase the number of conflict detection attempts. By default this value is set to zero. When this value is increased, the DHCP server will ping an IP address before leasing it to a DHCP client. If the ping is successful, the DHCP server will not lease the IP address. Answer B is incorrect because this would require more administrative effort to identify the static IP addresses and then exclude them from the scope. Answer C is incorrect because a client reservation is created when a DHCP client requires the same IP address. The DHCP server always leases the same IP addresses to the DHCP client. Answer D is incorrect because you do not know the IP addresses that are still statically configured on client computers.

## Question 12

Answer A is correct. The DHCP console is used to authorize a DHCP server within Active Directory. Therefore, answers B, C, and D are incorrect.

## Question 13

The correct answer is Windows 2000 and Windows XP. Any Windows 2000 and Windows XP clients can update their own records with the DNS server. The remaining clients do not support the dynamic update feature; in such cases, the DHCP server can be configured to update the records on their behalf.

## Question 14

Answer C is correct. The IPCONFIG /ALL command can be used to view detailed information about TCP/IP parameters on a computer, including whether the IP address is being leased from a DHCP server. Answer A is incorrect because the nslookup command is used to troubleshoot name resolution. Answer B is incorrect because the PING command is used to test connectivity, and it has already been determined that the client cannot communicate on the network. Answer D is incorrect because if the client is configured to dynamically obtain an IP address, it will not be listed in the TCP/IP properties window.

## Question 15

Answer A is correct. The #pre directive defines which entries in the LMHOSTS file should be preloaded into the local NetBIOS name cache. Answer B is incorrect because the #include directive is used to specify another LMHOSTS file from which entries should be used. Answer C is incorrect because the #mh directive is used to add multiple entries for a multihomed computer. Answer D is incorrect because the #DOM directive is used to indicate that the record is for a domain controller.

## Question 16

Answers C and D are correct. Of the platforms listed, only Windows Me and Windows XP support automatic private IP addressing. Therefore, answers A, B, and E are incorrect.

## Question 17

Answer C is correct. If the zone is configured to accept only secure updates, you must configure the dynamic update credentials on the DHCP server. This is the username and password under which the DHCP server will perform the updates to the DNS database. Answer A is incorrect because clients are already leasing IP addresses. If the DHCP server is not authorized, the service will fail to start. Answer B is incorrect because the DnsUpdateProxy group is used when there are multiple DHCP servers performing dynamic updates. It allows DNS records updated by one DHCP server to be updated by another DHCP server. Answer D is incorrect because if clients are configured with static IP addresses, dynamic updates would not be required, nor would DHCP.

## Question 18

Answers B and D are correct. By default, Windows 2000 and Windows XP clients will dynamically register their own A records. Answer A is incorrect because the DHCP server will register the PTR records for clients. Answer C is incorrect because the DHCP server will not update A records unless requested to do so. Answer E is incorrect because a DHCP server will not update any records on behalf of legacy clients unless it is configured to do so.

## Question 19

Answer D is correct. A zone type can be changed using the General tab from the zone's properties window. Select the option to store the zone in Active

Directory. Answer B is incorrect because the Security tab is used to configure permissions to the zone file. Answers A and C are incorrect because a zone type cannot be changed from the DNS server's properties window.

## Question 20

Answer A is correct. MX records are used to identify mail servers. Answer B is incorrect because some versions of UNIX support dynamic update. However, there is no mention of what version of UNIX is being used, so you can assume that dynamic updates are not updated. Answer C is incorrect because you cannot configure the IP address of a mail server through the properties of TCP/IP. Answer D is incorrect because CNAME records are used to assign alias names to an existing host.

## Question 21

Answer C is correct. A secondary DNS server maintains a copy of the zone file. If the primary DNS server goes offline, clients can still resolve hostnames using the secondary DNS server. Answer A is incorrect because caching-only DNS servers do not maintain zone information; they only cache records as they are resolved. Answer B is incorrect because a primary server already exists. There can only be one Primary DNS server for a zone. Answer D is incorrect because the DNS service must be installed on a domain controller in order to implement Active Directory–integrated zones.

## Question 22

Answer C is correct. Because caching-only servers do not maintain any zone information, no traffic is generated from zone transfers. As the server builds up, the contents of the cache response time will be decreased for DNS clients. Answers A and B are incorrect because primary and secondary DNS servers will generate zone-replication traffic. There can only be one primary DNS server for a zone. Answer D is incorrect because a master name server is the DNS server from which a secondary DNS server gets zone updates.

## Question 23

Answer D is correct. To use the nslookup command to resolve the hostname associated with an IP address, the appropriate PTR record must exist within the reverse lookup file. Answer A is incorrect because the A record is not used to resolve the hostname associated with an IP address. Answer B is incorrect because the nslookup command returns results for other queries. Answer C is incorrect because MX records are used to identify mail servers.

## Question 24

Answer A is correct. Your first step should be to verify that the correct interface is added under the DHCP Relay Agent on Subnet 2. If the incorrect interface has been added, client computers will not be able to obtain an IP address from the DHCP server on Subnet 1. Answers B and C are incorrect. After you have verified that the correct interface has been added, you should then proceed to verify that the DHCP Relay Agent is configured with the correct IP address of the DHCP server on the remote subnet. Also check that the Relay DHCP Packets option is selected. Answer D is incorrect. Incorrect scope information will not prevent client computers from leasing an IP address.

## Question 25

Answer B is correct. To specify which users and groups can update the zone file, the zone must be configured for secure updates. This can be done through the zone's properties window using the General tab. Answers A and C are incorrect because a zone cannot be configured for secure updates from the DNS server's properties window. Answer D is incorrect because the Security tab is used to configure users and groups that have permission to update the zone file.

## Question 26

Answer A is correct. By configuring the existing secondary DNS servers as the master name servers for the new secondary DNS servers, zone replication for the new servers can occur locally instead of across the slow link. Answer B is incorrect because caching-only DNS servers do not store any zone information. They only cache results. Answer C is incorrect because this will result in more replication traffic. Answer D is incorrect because forwarders are configured to tell a DNS server where to forward name-resolution requests.

## Question 27

Answer C is correct. You could use the IP address of 192.168.0.45. You can determine from the configuration on the other server that the network has been subnetted because the subnet mask is 255.255.255.240. The network address is 192.168.0.0. The following address ranges are supported by this subnet mask:

192.168.0.16–192.168.0.31

192.168.0.32–192.168.0.47

192.168.0.48–192.168.0.63

192.168.0.64–192.168.0.79

192.168.0.80–192.168.0.95

192.168.0.96–192.168.0.111

192.168.0.112–192.168.0.127

192.168.0.128–192.168.0.143

192.168.0.144–192.168.0.159

192.168.0.160–192.168.0.175

192.168.0.176–192.168.0.191

192.168.0.192–192.168.0.207

192.168.0.208–192.168.0.223

192.168.0.224–193.168.0.239

Because the existing server has been configured with an IP address of 192.168.0.42, the new server must be configured with an IP address from the same address range. Therefore, 192.168.0.45 is correct.

The server should not be configured with any of the other IP addresses listed because the server will then appear to be on a different subnet.

## Question 28

Answer B is correct. The refresh interval defines how often a secondary server will poll its master name server for updates to the zone file. By increasing this value, the secondary DNS server will not poll the master name server as often. Answer A is incorrect because the TTL defines how long records can remain within the cache before they must be purged. Answer C is incorrect because this defines how often the secondary server will continue to poll for updates if the master name server does not respond. Decreasing this value will increase traffic on the WAN connections. Answer D is incorrect because the serial number is used to determine whether the zone file has changed.

## Question 29

Answer B is correct. You should create a secondary zone for bayside.net on SRV03. You should ensure that a zone transfer is done and that all of the records for the zone replicate successfully to SRV03. You should then change the zone type to primary and select the option to store the zone in Active Directory. Answer A is incorrect. You do not need to create an Active Directory application partition for DNS to prepare DC-Main to host an Active Directory–integrated zone for bcdtrain.com. Answer C is incorrect. You should not create a stub zone to prepare the server to host an Active Directory–integrated zone for bayside.net. You use a stub zone to ensure that a DNS server for a zone has information about all name servers that host a zone for a DNS subdomain, even the name servers that are added after the subdomain is delegated. In this scenario, there is only a single DNS domain, so a stub zone is not necessary. Answer D is incorrect. You should not create a primary zone for bayside.net on SRV03 to prepare the server to host an Active Directory–integrated zone. To replicate all records from the current primary server, you must create a secondary zone on SRv03. You should convert the zone to a primary zone.

## Question 30

Answer C is correct. Using the Forwarders tab from the DNS server's properties window, configure the DNS server to forward all name-resolution requests for clients in the Riverside organization to the Riverside DNS servers. Answers A and D are incorrect because forwarders cannot be configured from the zone's properties window. Answer B is incorrect because you do not want all name-resolution requests forwarded to the Riverside DNS servers.

## Question 31

Answer A is correct. You should create a stub zone for riverside.net on SRV01. A DNS server running Windows Server 2003 that hosts a stub zone queries a master name server for the zone periodically to obtain the name server (NS) records from the zone. The server that hosts the stub zone stores the NS records, the start of authority (SOA) record, and address (A) records of the name servers in the stub zone. Answer B is incorrect because conditional forwarding is used to define the name servers to which requests should be forwarded. This list is not updated automatically as new name servers are added to a zone. Answers C and D are incorrect. Both of these solutions would use more disk storage on SRV01 than a stub zone would use.

## Question 32

Answer C is correct. Using the Monitoring tab, you can perform simple queries against the DNS server to test the configuration. Therefore, answers A, B, and D are incorrect.

## Question 33

Answer A is correct. If the UNIX hosts do not support NetBIOS, WINS lookup can be enabled on the DNS server. The DNS server can query the

WINS server if it cannot resolve the hostname. Answer B is incorrect because you cannot configure replication between DNS and WINS. Answer C is incorrect because a WINS proxy forwards NetBIOS broadcasts to a WINS server. Answer D is incorrect because a DHCP server cannot update NetBIOS names with a DNS server.

## Question 34

Answer B is correct. You should use a subnet mask of 255.255.255.240. The will allow for a total of 14 subnets. You can determine the number of subnets by using the formula of $2^x - 2$ where $x$ is the number of bits taken from the host IDs and used for the subnet mask. With a subnet mask of 255.255.255.240, 4 bits have been used and $2^4 - 2$ is equal to 14. Therefore, a total of 14 subnets can be created. Answers A, C, and D are incorrect. You should not use a subnet mask of 255.255.255.224 because it only allows you to create a maximum of 6 subnets. The remaining subnets should not be selected because they support far more subnets than will ever be required.

## Question 35

Answer C is correct. To enable a computer as a WINS proxy, change the `EnableProxy` value to 1 within the local Registry. Answers A and B are incorrect because you do not have to install additional software to enable a WINS proxy. Answer D is incorrect because there is no option called `WINSProxy` within the Registry.

## Question 36

Answer C is correct. Caching-only DNS servers do not maintain any zone information; therefore, no additional traffic would exist on the WAN link. Answer A is incorrect because a primary DNS server already exists for the zone. Answers B and D are incorrect because they maintain zone information and would result in zone transfers.

## Question 37

Answer B is correct. Using the Zone Transfers tab, you can specify which secondary servers can receive zone updates. Answer A is incorrect because the Security tab is used to configure users and groups that can perform updates. Answer C is incorrect because you must configure this at the zone level. Answer D is incorrect because you do not want all secondary DNS servers to be capable of requesting updates.

## Question 38

Answer A is correct. You should open the properties dialog box for the DNS server, which in this case will be BAYDNS. You should then select the Forwarders tab and configure the DNS server to forward any name resolution requests for hosts in the riverside.net domain, the RIVDNS. Answers B, C, and D are incorrect. You should not open the zone properties dialog box for bayside.net. Forwarding must be configured at the server level, not the zone level. You should not configure BAYDNS to forward all name resolution requests to RIVDNS. You only want name resolution requests for clients in the riverside.net domain forwarded to this specific DNS server.

## Question 39

Answer C is correct. The IP Security Monitor utility can be used to view IPSec statistics and verify traffic is being secured. Therefore, answers A, B, and D are incorrect. You could use Network Monitor. However, this would require more administrative effort to capture the network traffic and analyze it.

## Question 40

The correct answers are: Internet Explorer 5.0 (or later), IIS 5.0 (or later), and the system partition must be NTFS. The remaining answers are incorrect because they are not required to install SUS.

## Question 41

Answer D is correct. To configure Automatic Updates settings through a Group Policy Object, the Automatic Updates ADM file must be loaded. Answer A is incorrect because the user is already an administrator. Answer B is incorrect because SUS can be installed on any server as long as it meets the software requirements. Active Directory is not a software requirement. Answer C is incorrect because settings can be configured locally or through a Group Policy.

## Question 42

The correct answers are: Windows 2000 and Windows XP. There two platforms support the updated version of Automatic Updates.

## Question 43

Answer C is correct. The Security Configuration and Analysis tool enables you to compare current security settings against those in a template. Answer A is incorrect because auditing must be enabled before you can track changes made to the server. The scenario does not indicate that auditing is being used. Answer B is incorrect because Resultant Set of Policy in logging mode is used to determine the policy settings currently applied to a computer. Answer D is incorrect because IP Security Monitor is used to monitor and troubleshoot IPSec communications.

## Question 44

Answer C is correct. The simplest way to configure the same security settings on each server is to configure a security template and deploy it through a GPO. Answers A and B are incorrect because these options would require visiting each of the servers. Answer D is incorrect because SUS cannot be used to deploy security settings.

## Question 45

Answer A is correct. This parameter specifies that Automatic Updates uses an SUS server. Answer B is incorrect because this option specifies how updates are downloaded and installed. Answer C is incorrect because this option specifies which SUS server updates are downloaded from. Answer D is incorrect because this option specifies which server the client will send status information to.

## Question 46

Answer C is correct. This option specifies which SUS server updates will be downloaded from. Answer A is incorrect because this option enables only Automatic Updates to use an SUS server. Answer B is incorrect because this option specifies how updates are downloaded and installed. Answer D is incorrect because this option specifies which server the client will send status information to.

## Question 47

Answer A is correct. You must download and install the Microsoft Security Baseline Analyzer. This will scan a Windows system and identify any misconfigurations with the operating system that may affect local security. It will also identify any missing security updates. Answer B is incorrect because the HFNetChk.exe program will only identify security patches that need to be installed on a system. Answer C is incorrect because the Security Configuration and Analysis utility is used to compare existing security settings against those in a security template. However, it will not provide you with the specific information you are looking for. Answer D is incorrect because this will only be useful in identifying the security settings configured on the computer. It will not identify misconfigurations or missing security updates.

## Question 48

Answer D is correct. The IP Security Monitor utility can be opened from the Microsoft Management Console. Therefore, answers A and B are incorrect. Answer C is incorrect because this is the command used in Windows 2000 to launch IPSec Monitor.

## Question 49

Answer B is correct. The static IP addresses assigned to the servers must be excluded from the scope configured on the DHCP server. Therefore, answers C and D are incorrect. Answer A is incorrect because client reservations are created for DHCP clients that are required to lease the same IP address.

## Question 50

Answer B is correct. The IP Security Monitor included with Windows Server 2003 cannot be used to monitor computers running Windows 2000. Therefore, answers A, C, and D are incorrect.

## Question 51

Answer D is correct. You should use the subnet mask of 255.248.0.0. This subnet mask will allow for a maximum of 30 subnets, which meets the company's new addressing requirements. Answers A, B, and C are incorrect. You should not select a subnet mask of 255.192.0.0 because it will only allow for two subnets. However, the new infrastructure requires a maximum of 28. You should not select 255.224.0.0 because this subnet mask only allows for a maximum of 6 subnets, which does not meet the requirements. You should not select 255.240.0.0 because this subnet mask only allows for a maximum of 14 subnets, which does not meet the requirements.

## Question 52

Answer D is correct. Software Updates Services requires that the partition on which the software will be installed be formatted with NTFS. Answer A is incorrect because no service pack is required. Answer B is incorrect because the partition on which SUS is installed must be NTFS as well. Answer C is incorrect because IIS 5.0 is required.

## Question 53

Answers A, B, and C are correct. By placing a DHCP server within the branch office and configuring the remote server with 20% of the IP addresses, you can eliminate DHCP and the WAN link as points of failure. The DHCP Relay Agent is required for DHCP clients to lease an IP address from a DHCP server on a remote subnet. Answer D is incorrect because clients are not configured with the IP address of DHCP servers.

## Question 54

Answer C is correct. The DHCP server must be enabled to perform updates for clients that cannot update their own host records. Answer A is incorrect because DNS is already configured for dynamic updates because the Windows XP clients are successfully performing updates. Answer B is incorrect because Windows 95 clients cannot be configured to perform dynamic updates. Answer D is incorrect because a DHCP relay agent forwards IP address lease requests to a DHCP server.

## Question 55

Answer C is correct. A standalone server is not authorized in Active Directory. The Authorize option is not available on a standalone server. Therefore answers A, B, and D are incorrect.

## Question 56

Answer D is correct. You do not need to do anything. When you delegate a zone, the parent zone is always aware of the name servers in the child domain. Therefore, answers A, B, and C are incorrect. Answer B is incorrect. A stub zone is only used if there are separate DNS namespaces. However, in this case, the zone is not a separate namespace.

## Question 57

Answer B is correct. If the support tools have been installed, you can use Replication Monitor to ensure that replication between DNS servers is occurring on a regular basis. Answer A is incorrect because System Monitor is used to monitor the real-time performance of a DNS server. Answer C is incorrect because the DNS management console is used to configure and manage a DNS server but cannot be used to monitor DNS replication. Answer D is incorrect because there is no such tool as the DNS Monitor.

## Question 58

Answer D is correct. Using the Clear Cache option from the Action menu within the DNS management console allows you to delete the contents of the cache file. Although uninstalling the service would clear the contents of the cache, it's not the easiest way to perform the task; therefore, answer A is incorrect. Answer B is incorrect because deleting the file completely removes it. Answer C is incorrect because there is no Clear Cache option available from the server's property window.

## Question 59

Answer B is correct. This option enables you to configure how updates are downloaded and installed. Because Active Directory is not installed, the Automatic Updates settings must be configured through the Registry, not a Group Policy. Answer A is incorrect because this option enables Automatic Updates to use SUS. Answer C is incorrect because this option specifies the SUS server from which updates are downloaded. Answer D is incorrect because this option specifies which SUS server the client will send status information to.

## Question 60

Answers A and C are correct. Network Monitor can be used to monitor and log network activity. System Monitor can also be used to monitor various network components. Therefore, answers B and D are incorrect.

# Practice Exam #2

## Practice Exam

1. You are the network administrator for your organization. Servers are running Microsoft Windows Server 2003.

   You have enabled Routing and Remote Access on a server. Some of the users in your organization have home offices, where they work during the weekdays. They require access to network resources.

   Users currently have access 24 hours a day, 7 days a week. For security purposes, you want to limit the dial-in hours from 8 a.m. to 6 p.m.

   What should you do?

   - ○ **A.** Configure the properties of each user account.
   - ○ **B.** Configure the properties of the RAS server.
   - ○ **C.** Configure the conditions of the remote access policy.
   - ○ **D.** Configure the port properties.

2. You are the network administrator for your company. All servers have been upgraded to Microsoft Windows Server 2003. Client computers are running Microsoft Windows XP Professional.

   Your company has opened a new branch office. You are in charge of configuring a two-way demand dial connection between your head office and the new branch office. You configure the demand dial routers with the following settings:

   Branch Office Router Settings

   Interface: SRV01_Public

   User Account: SRV01

   Calling Number: 555-1212

Head Office Routing Settings

Interface: SRV02_Public

User Account: SRV02

Calling Number: 555-3434

When you go to test your configuration, neither of the routers can establish a connection.

What should you do?

- ○ **A.** Change the interface name on the router in the head office to SRV01_Public.

- ○ **B.** Change the demand dial interface name on each router to match the name of the user account on the remote answering router.

- ○ **C.** Change the interface name on the router in the branch office to SRV02_Public.

- ○ **D.** Change the names assigned to the user accounts on each router so they are identical.

**3.** You are the network administrator for your company. You are currently in the process of upgrading the server to Microsoft Windows Server 2003. You plan to decommission the WINS server once all client computers have been upgraded.

You have enabled Routing and Remote Access on a server that has been already been upgraded. The RAS server is configured with the default settings.

Remote access clients report that they can successfully connect to the RAS server. However, clients cannot access network resources using the UNC path.

What should you do?

- ○ **A.** You must configure a range of IP addresses on the RAS server, as well as assign any optional IP parameters to clients.

- ○ **B.** You must manually configure the IP settings on the remote access clients.

- ○ **C.** You must configure the RAS server with the IP address of the WINS server.

- ○ **D.** You must install the DHCP Relay Agent on the RAS server.

**4.** You are the network administrator for your company. Servers have been upgraded to Microsoft Windows Server 2003. Client computers are running Microsoft Windows XP Professional.

You have just changed several computer and user policy settings on SRV01. You want the changes to be applied immediately.

What should you do?

- ○ **A.** Execute the `secedit /refresh` command.
- ○ **B.** Execute the `gpupdate /force` command.
- ○ **C.** Execute the `gpupdate /target:computer` command.
- ○ **D.** Execute the `gpupdate /refreshpolicy` command.
- ○ **E.** Execute the `secedit /refreshpolicy` command.

**5.** You are the network administrator for your company. All servers are running Microsoft Windows Server 2003. Client computers are running Microsoft Windows XP Professional.

Several servers on the network have been configured as routers to connect multiple subnets. You have implemented OSPF routing protocol on the network.

You manage a router named Area1BR. The server is configured as an area border router. Area1BR is connected to Area 0.0.0.0 and to Area 1. For Area 1, Area1BR advertises the summarized route 172.16.0.0/18.

Which two Internet Protocol (IP) addresses define subnets that you can include in Area1? (Choose two.)

- ○ **A.** 172.31.192.0/18
- ○ **B.** 172.31.128.0/18
- ○ **C.** 172.31.96.0/18
- ○ **D.** 172.31.160.0/18
- ○ **E.** 172.31.224.0/18

**6.** You are the network administrator for an accounting company. The company has decided to implement tighter remote access security.

You have decided to implement smart cards on all remote access client computers. You have installed the smart cards and need to configure the remote access server to support the new authentication mechanism.

Which of the following protocols should be enabled?

- ○ **A.** PAP
- ○ **B.** EAP
- ○ **C.** MS-CHAP
- ○ **D.** SPAP

7. You are the network administrator of a Windows Server 2003 network. The company has just opened a new branch office.

   You are configuring demand-dial routing between a server in the head office and a server within a branch office. Both servers are running Windows Server 2003.

   You need to create the user account on the answering router.

   Which of the following statements is true?

   ○ **A.** Any user account name can be used.

   ○ **B.** The user account name should match the demand-dial interface name of the answering router.

   ○ **C.** The user account name should match the demand-dial interface name of the calling router.

   ○ **D.** The user account name must match the computer name of the answering router.

8. You are the network administrator for an insurance company. You have recently upgraded all servers to Microsoft Windows Server 2003.

   The internetwork consists of seven subnets. All subnets are connected using RRAS servers. Nonpersistent demand-dial connections have been configured.

   You want to minimize the amount of administrative effort required to maintain the routing tables. You want any changes to the network topology to be propagated immediately.

   What should you do?

   ○ **A.** Configure static routes on the servers.

   ○ **B.** Enable the RIPv1 protocol.

   ○ **C.** Enable the OSPF protocol.

   ○ **D.** Enable the RIPv2 protocol.

9. You are the network administrator for your company. All servers are running Microsoft Windows Server 2003.

   A new subnet has been added to the existing network infrastructure. You need to add a static route to the routing table to reach the new subnet. The subnet ID in use is 192.168.126.0.

   Which of the following commands would add a static route to the routing table?

   ○ **A.** `route -p 192.168.126.0 mask 255.255.255.0`
       `192.168.125.1 metric 2`

   ○ **B.** `route add 192.168.126.0 mask 255.255.255.0`
       `192.168.125.1 metric 2`

   ○  **C.** `route add 192.168.126.0 255.255.255.0 192.168.125.1`
       `metric 2`

   ○  **D.** `route add 192.168.126.0 mask 255.255.255.0 gateway`
       `192.168.125.1 metric 2`

**10.** You are the network administrator for Contoso Ltd. The company has recently upgraded all domain servers to Microsoft Windows Server 2003. You are in the process of upgrading client computers to Microsoft Windows XP Professional.

The company is implementing a new security policy. All data between SRV01 and clients should be encrypted. However, those clients that have not yet been upgraded do not support IPSec. You must ensure that these client are still capable of authenticating with the server.

You need to assign an IPSec policy to SRV01.

What should you do?

   ○  **A.** Within the IP Security Monitor snap-in, assign the Secure Server (Require Security) policy.

   ○  **B.** Configure the settings of the appropriate group policy object and assign the Client (Respond Only) policy.

   ○  **C.** Configure the Properties of TCP/IP and assign the Secure Server (Require Security) policy.

   ○  **D.** Edit the appropriate group policy object and assign the Server (Request Security) policy.

**11.** You are the network administrator for your company. All servers are running Microsoft Windows Server 2003. All server communications must be encrypted according to company security policy.

You are configuring IPSec between two servers in a workgroup. You assign the Client (Respond Only) policy to SRV01 and SRV02.

When you open the IP Security Monitor, you notice that IP packets being sent between the two servers are not being secured.

What is causing the problem?

   ○  **A.** Both are configured with the Client (Respond Only) policy.

   ○  **B.** You can use IPSec only with Active Directory.

   ○  **C.** One of the servers must be configured as an IPSec client.

   ○  **D.** The servers cannot be members of the same workgroup.

**12.** You are the network administrator for your company. All servers are running Microsoft Windows Server 2003. Client computers are running Microsoft Windows XP Professional.

You are configuring IPSec policies for two servers on the network. SRV-01 hosts the company website and SRV-02 hosts the company database. The following requirements must be met:

All communications between SRV-01 and SRV-02 must be secured.

Communications between SRV-02 and clients on the private network must always be secure.

Non–IPSec-aware client must be able to communicate with SRV-01. All other communication should be secured.

The other servers on the network are not configured with IPSec policies. Client computers on the network must be able to communicate with servers.

You need to assign the correct IPSec policies.

Select an IPSec policy from the list on the right and place it beneath the appropriate computer. You can use a policy more than once and you may not have to use them all.

Server (Request Security)

Server (Require Security)

Client (Respond Only)

**13.** You are the network administrator for your company. All servers have been upgraded to Microsoft Windows Server 2003.

You are planning a VPN solution for the company network. The branch office will connect to the head office using a VPN connection.

You need to enable the correct protocols on the remote access server.

Which of the following protocols should you use to establish a VPN tunnel with a Windows Server 2003 VPN server?

- ○ **A.** PPP
- ○ **B.** PPTP
- ○ **C.** SLIP
- ○ **D.** L2TP

14. You are the network administrator for your company. You have been instructed to set up remote access for several client computers.

    You have enabled Routing and Remote Access on a computer running Microsoft Windows Server 2003. Clients will establish a VPN connection with the server.

    You determine that there may be up to 20 clients accessing the VPN server at one time. You need to increase the number of available PPTP ports.

    How can you accomplish this task from within the Routing and Remote Access management console?

    - ○ **A.** From the Properties window for the server, select the Ports tab.
    - ○ **B.** Using the Edit Profile button within the properties window for the policy, select the Ports tab.
    - ○ **C.** Use the Properties window for the Ports option.
    - ○ **D.** Use the PPTP tab from the Ports properties window.

15. You are the network administrator for your organization. Company servers have been upgraded to Microsoft Windows Server 2003.

    You have enabled RRAS on SERVER01. All remote access clients are running Microsoft Windows XP Professional.

    You want to configure the most secure authentication protocol.

    Which of the following should you enable?

    - ○ **A.** PAP
    - ○ **B.** CHAP
    - ○ **C.** MS-CHAP version 1
    - ○ **D.** MS-CHAP version 2

**16.** You are the network administrator for an accounting firm. You have recently upgraded the servers to Microsoft Windows Server 2003.

The network consists of three subnets: Subnet A, Subnet B, and Subnet C. There is an RRAS server on Subnet C configured with a range of IP addresses to assign to remote access clients.

There are two DNS servers on the network, DNS01 and DNS02. You want remote access clients to use DNS02.

What should you do?

- ○ **A.** Configure the RRAS server to use DHCP. Install a DHCP server on Subnet C. Configure a scope on the DHCP server for the remote access clients. Configure the DHCP relay agent on the DNS server.

- ○ **B.** Install a DHCP server on the network and configure the RRAS server to use DHCP for IP address assignment. Configure a scope on the DHCP server for the remote access clients.

- ○ **C.** Install a DHCP server on the network. Configure a scope on the DHCP server for remote access clients. Configure RRAS to use DHCP. Configure the relay agent on the DHCP server.

- ○ **D.** Install a DHCP server on Subnet C. Configure a scope on the DHCP server for remote access clients. Configure RRAS to use DHCP. Configure the relay agent on the RRAS server.

**17.** You are the administrator of a Windows Server 2003 network. You have enabled Routing and Remote Access on a server running Microsoft Windows Server 2003.

Because of the security requirements of the company, you have created multiple remote access policies. User A attempts to gain remote access. The connection attempt does not meet the conditions of the first remote access policy.

Which of the following statements is true?

- ○ **A.** The connection attempt is denied.

- ○ **B.** The properties of the user's account are evaluated.

- ○ **C.** The next policy in the list is evaluated.

- ○ **D.** The profile settings are evaluated.

**18.** You are the network administrator for your company. All servers are running Microsoft Windows Server 2003.

You need to implement Routing and Remote Access to give users the ability to access resources from other locations while still maintaining a high level of security. Specifically, the company president needs to be able to access resources from his home office and other locations. Network administrators also require remote access when they are work-ing from home. You enable remote access on an existing server.

You need to configure callback for the user accounts.

What should you do?

- ○ **A.** Choose No Callback for the president's account and Set by Caller for the network administrators' accounts.

- ○ **B.** Choose Set by Caller for the president's account and No Callback for the network administrators' accounts.

- ○ **C.** Choose Always Callback To for the president's account and Set by Caller for the network administrators' accounts.

- ○ **D.** Choose Set by Caller for the president's account and Always Callback To for the network administrators' accounts.

19. You are the senior network administrator for your company. You have recently upgraded the servers to Microsoft Windows Server 2003.

You have assigned a junior network administrator the task of installing and configuring a remote access server. Certain users need to be able to dial directly into the server to access network resources.

To test the configuration, you attempt to connect to the server but are unsuccessful. When you open the Routing and Remote Access snap-in, you notice that the default remote access policy has been deleted.

What should you do?

- ○ **A.** Disable Routing and Remote Access and then re-enable the service.

- ○ **B.** Create a remote access policy.

- ○ **C.** Configure the dial-in properties of the user accounts.

- ○ **D.** Configure the remote access profile settings.

20. You are the network administrator for your company. You have enabled Routing and Remote Access on a server running Microsoft Windows Server 2003.

You have configured two remote access policies. The profile settings of Policy A are configured so that remote access is permitted only during the hours of 8 a.m. and 5 p.m. This policy is applied to the Sales group.

Policy B has no dial-in restrictions configured, and it is applied to the Managers group. Policy A is listed first.

Mike is a member of the Sales and Managers groups. He attempts to dial into the remote access server at 6 p.m.

Which of the following statements is true?

O **A.** Mike will be permitted remote access.

O **B.** Because the connection attempt does not match the profile settings of Policy A, Policy B is evaluated.

O **C.** The connection attempt is denied.

O **D.** The dial-in restrictions configured for Mike's user account determine whether he has remote access permission.

**21.** You are in the process of configuring profile settings for a remote access policy. You configure the settings as shown in the following figure. Which of the following statements are true? (Choose all correct answers.)

O **A.** Users will be disconnected after 8 hours of inactivity.

O **B.** Users will be disconnected after 30 minutes of inactivity.

O **C.** Users can remain connected as long as necessary.

O **D.** Users can dial in only between 6 p.m. and 6 a.m.

O **E.** Users can dial in only between 6 a.m. and 6 p.m.

O **F.** Users can dial any number for remote access.

22. You are the administrator of a Windows Server 2003 network. A user reports that he is unable to communicate with any hosts on a remote subnet.

    You execute the `ipconfig` command to verify that TCP/IP is properly configured on the workstation. You then execute the `ping` command to test whether TCP/IP is initialized on the local computer.

    You proceed to ping the IP address assigned to the local workstation. Both pings have successful results.

    You need to identify the cause of the problem.

    What should you do next?

    ○ **A.** Ping the IP address of a local host.

    ○ **B.** Ping the IP address of the default gateway.

    ○ **C.** Ping the IP address of a remote host.

    ○ **D.** Ping the IP address of a remote router.

23. You are the network administrator for Contoso Ltd. All servers are running Microsoft Windows Server 2003.

    You have captured a large amount of network traffic using Network Monitor. You want to limit the captured information to only display traffic containing the SMB protocol.

    What should you do?

    ○ **A.** Configure a trigger.

    ○ **B.** Configure a capture filter.

    ○ **C.** Configure a display filter.

    ○ **D.** Configure a packet filter.

24. You are the network administrator for a large company. All servers within the company domain are running Microsoft Windows Server 2003.

    You often run System Monitor on the servers to capture performance data. You want to give another user the ability to view real-time data as it is captured using System Monitor.

    He should be able to perform this task from the server or from his administrative computer.

    What should you do?

    ○ **A.** Add his user account to the Performance Log Users group.

    ○ **B.** Add his user account to the Administrators group.

○ **C.** Add his user account to the Performance Monitor Users group.

○ **D.** Add his user account to the Domain Admins group.

25. You are the network administrator for your company. Client computers are running Microsoft Windows XP Professional. Servers are running Microsoft Windows Server 2003.

    You are running Network Monitor to analyze specific types of network traffic. You want to configure Network Monitor to only gather information pertaining to specific protocols and traffic type.

    What should you do?

    ○ **A.** Configure a display filter.

    ○ **B.** Configure a capture filter.

    ○ **C.** Configure a trigger.

    ○ **D.** Configure an IP packet filter.

26. You are the network administrator for your company. The servers in the company have recently been upgraded to Microsoft Windows Server 2003.

    Your managers have asked you to put together a performance report for the web server on the intranet.

    You need to gather statistics about the total amount of TCP/IP traffic on the local computer.

    Which of the following counters should you monitor?

    ○ **A.** Packet Outbound Errors

    ○ **B.** TCP Segments/sec

    ○ **C.** IP Datagrams/sec

    ○ **D.** Logons/sec

27. You are the network administrator for a large insurance company. The network consists of 50 servers running Microsoft Windows Server 2003. There are 700 client computers running Microsoft Windows XP Professional. The company has updated its security policy and requires all network traffic to be encrypted.

    You are deploying IPSec in a test environment that has a single server and 10 client computers. You have assigned the required IPSec policies.

    You need to verify that traffic between the server and the client computers is being secured.

What should you do?

   ◯  **A.** Launch IP Security Monitor and open the Main Mode Security Associations folder.

   ◯  **B.** Launch the Event Viewer and examine the contents of the Security log.

   ◯  **C.** Run the Resultant Set of Policy in logging mode.

   ◯  **D.** Execute the `ipsecmon.exe` command.

**28.** You are the network administrator for your company. All servers are running Microsoft Windows Server 2003.

One of the servers on the network connects to the Internet through a dial-up connection. You are having problems establishing a connection and you want to verify that the modem is working.

Which of the following can you use to verify the status of the modem?

   ◯  **A.** System Monitor

   ◯  **B.** Network Monitor

   ◯  **C.** `ping`

   ◯  **D.** Device Manager

**29.** You are the network administrator for your company. All domain controllers and member servers are running Microsoft Windows Server 2003.

You need to gather network-performance statistics for DC01. You want to determine the number of logons the domain controller has received since the last time it was restarted.

Which counter should you monitor?

   ◯  **A.** Logons Received Total

   ◯  **B.** Logon Total

   ◯  **C.** Logons Received/sec

   ◯  **D.** Logons/sec

**30.** You are the network administrator for Contoso Ltd. All computers are members of the contoso.com domain. Servers are running Microsoft Windows Server 2003.

You have installed the DHCP service on SRV01. Clients report that they are unable to access network resources. You discover that they are all using APIPA.

You soon determine that the DHCP service on the server has failed to start. You reboot the server and the service still does not start.

What should you do?

  ○  **A.** Continue to reboot the server until the service starts.

  ○  **B.** Verify that any services DHCP depends on are started using the Services console.

  ○  **C.** Use the DHCP console to start the service.

  ○  **D.** Reinstall the DHCP service.

**31.** You are the network administrator for your company. Servers are running Microsoft Windows Server 2003.

You are configuring the service-recovery options for the server service on a domain controller.

If a service fails to start, which of the following actions can be performed?

From the list on the right, select the actions that a computer running Windows Server 2003 can take if a service fails to start. Place these actions in the list on the left.

        The computer can attempt to restart the service.

        The computer can automatically reboot.

        The services that the failed service depends on can be restarted.

        An email message can be sent to the network administrator.

**32.** You are the network administrator for your company. All servers are running Microsoft Windows Server 2003.

You have recently installed a new network service on one of the servers. You need to determine how much more additional traffic is generated since it was installed.

Which of the following tools can you use to capture and analyze network traffic?

  ○  **A.** Network Performance

  ○  **B.** Network Diagnostics

  ○  **C.** Network Monitor

  ○  **D.** Network Manager

**33.** You are the network administrator for a small accounting firm. All servers are running Microsoft Windows Server 2003. Client computers are running Microsoft Windows XP Professional.

The network consists of three different subnets. Dynamic routing is being implemented on three multihomed computers running Windows Server 2003 on which Routing and Remote Access has been enabled.

You open the Routing and Remote Access console on SRVRRAS-1 and configure the computer for LAN routing. You select New Routing Protocol from the General node of the IP Routing node, and you choose RIP version 2 for Internet Protocol from the New Routing Protocol dialog box.

What should you do next?

- ○ **A.** Add the IP address of the DHCP server to the properties dialog box for the DHCP Relay Agent.
- ○ **B.** Add the interface that RIP will run using the RIP node.
- ○ **C.** Use the `route` command to configure the routes to the remote subnets.
- ○ **D.** Use the `route` command to delete all static routers from the routing tables.

34. A new service pack has just been released for Windows Server 2003. You download the service pack. What should you do before installing it?

- ○ **A.** Notify users that the server will be down.
- ○ **B.** Take all production servers offline.
- ○ **C.** Install the service pack in a test environment.
- ○ **D.** You need do nothing but proceed with the installation.

35. You are the network administrator for your company. The company is in the process of migrating to Microsoft Windows Server 2003.

You have just finished installing Windows Server 2003 on a new server. You are now in the process of performing some basic steps to secure the operating system.

You need to configure your administrative access to the server while maintaining the principle of least privilege.

What should you do?

- ○ **A.** Create a new user account for yourself and add it to the local Administrators group so that you can perform administrative tasks at any time.
- ○ **B.** Nothing. You should always log on with the Administrators account.
- ○ **C.** Create a new group and add the group to the local Administrators group. Create a user account for yourself and add it to the new group.
- ○ **D.** Create two user accounts: one with restrictive permissions for performing daily tasks and the other with additional privileges for performing administrative tasks.

**36.** You are the network administrator for your company. All servers are running Microsoft Windows Server 2003.

You are concerned that the security settings on one of the servers have been changed. All servers are configured with the same security settings before they are placed on the network.

You run the Security Configuration and Analysis utility on the server. You notice that several of the results appear with a red X beside them.

What does this red X indicate?

- ○ **A.** It indicates that the system settings correspond with those in the template.

- ○ **B.** It indicates that the configured system settings do not match those in the template.

- ○ **C.** It indicates that these values do not need to be configured based on the server role.

- ○ **D.** It indicates that these settings have not been configured.

**37.** You have recently been hired as the network administrator for a medium-sized network. The network hosts several servers running Microsoft Windows Server 2003. Client computers are running Microsoft Windows XP Professional.

The previous administrator left no documentation about the existing servers. Managers have asked you to document server configuration. Your documentation must

- ► Include misconfigurations with the operating system

- ► Identify missing security updates

You need to have this information as soon as possible.

What should you do?

- ○ **A.** Run the HFNetHCK.exe program.

- ○ **B.** Use the Security Configuration and Analysis tool.

- ○ **C.** Run the Microsoft Security Baseline Analyzer.

- ○ **D.** Execute the Resultant Set of Policy tool.

**38.** You are the network administrator for your company. All servers are running Microsoft Windows Server 2003.

You are testing the impact of various security settings within a test environment. You make several changes to the security settings on a standalone server.

What is the default interval at which security settings will be automatically refreshed?

○ **A.** 24 hours

○ **B.** 12 hours

○ **C.** 120 minutes

○ **D.** 90 minutes

**39.** You are the network administrator for your company. All servers are running Microsoft Windows Server 2003.

SRV03 stores all the company's shared folders. You have enabled auditing on the server to monitor access to the shared folders and any changes that might be made to the server's configuration.

You suspect that one of the junior network administrators has made changes to some of the settings with the group policy object.

Which log file should you use to verify your suspicions?

○ **A.** Application

○ **B.** Audit

○ **C.** Security

○ **D.** System

**40.** You are the network administrator for Contoso Ltd. The company has upgraded to Microsoft Windows Server 2003.

You have been asked to implement a strategy for deploying updates. You decide to install SUS on an existing server. You need to determine whether the server meets the hardware requirements to run the software.

Which of the following are considered to be minimum hardware requirements for installing SUS?

From the list on the right, select the minimum hardware requirements for SUS. Place these requirements in the list on the left.

Pentium III 500MHz

Pentium III 700MHz

265MB RAM

512MB RAM

4GB storage space

6GB storage space

**41.** You are the network administrator for your company. All servers are running Microsoft Windows Server 2003.

You want the company to implement DHCP instead of using static IP addressing. You need to put together some documentation for your managers outlining how DHCP works.

You want to document the process that occurs when a client computer attempts to lease an IP address.

From the list on the right, select the steps that occur during the IP address lease process. Place these steps in the order that they occur in the list on the left.

> DHCPAck
>
> DHCPDiscover
>
> DHCPOffer
>
> DHCPRequest

**42.** You are the network administrator for your company. You have upgraded all servers to Microsoft Windows Server 2003. All computers are members of the same Active Directory domain.

You have just finished configuring a new DHCP server. You have installed the service as well as configured and activated a scope.

You now need to authorize the DHCP server.

Which administrative tool should you use to perform this task?

- ○ **A.** Active Directory Users and Computers
- ○ **B.** DHCP console
- ○ **C.** Active Directory Sites and Services
- ○ **D.** Service applet

**43.** You are the network administrator for your company. All servers are running Microsoft Windows Server 2003. Client computers are running Microsoft Windows XP Professional.

You have been instructed to implement a dynamic IP addressing solution. You decide to implement DHCP on an existing member server.

You need to ensure that the DHCP server can lease IP addresses to client computers.

From the list on the right, select the actions that you must perform to allow the DHCP server to function on the network. Place these actions in the list on the left.

Install DHCP.

Activate a scope.

Create a scope.

Authorize the DHCP server.

Configure the scope options.

Install Active Directory on the local server.

Enable dynamic updates.

**44.** Your DHCP server must support multicasting. When configuring a multicast scope, which IP address range can you use?

- ○ **A.** 192.160.0.1–192.168.0.255
- ○ **B.** 127.0.0.1–127.0.0.255
- ○ **C.** 169.254.0.1–169.254.255.254
- ○ **D.** 224.0.0.1–239.255.255.255

**45.** You are the network administrator for your company. Servers are running Microsoft Windows Server 2003.

The network consists of two subnets: Subnet A and Subnet B. Each has its own DHCP server. You configure the scope on DHCP1 for Subnet A.

Users are all leasing an IP address but report that they cannot access any resources outside of their own subnet.

What should you do?

- ○ **A.** Activate the scope on DHCP1.
- ○ **B.** Configure the default gateway on each workstation.
- ○ **C.** Configure the 003 router option on DHCP1.
- ○ **D.** Configure the 006 DNS server option on DHCP1.

**46.** You are the network administrator for your company. All servers are running Microsoft Windows Server 2003. Client computers have been upgraded to Microsoft Windows XP Professional.

You have installed SUS on two member servers in the company domain. The updated version of automatic updates has been deployed to all client computers.

You want to ensure that requests are balanced equally between the two servers. You also want to accomplish this with as little administrative effort as possible.

What should you do?

- ○ **A.** Remotely add the WUServer value to the registry of client computers.

- ○ **B.** Configure the Specify Microsoft Update Service Location setting through a GPO.

- ○ **C.** Manually change the UseWUServer value to 1 on each client computer.

- ○ **D.** Enable Round Robin on the company DNS server.

47. You are the network administrator for your company. You have added the DHCP service to a computer running Microsoft Windows Server 2003. Client computers are running Microsoft Windows XP Professional.

All client computers are configured to obtain an IP address automatically. Three of the member servers host print devices. These servers must always use the same IP address.

How can you ensure that these print servers lease the same IP address from the DHCP server? (Choose all correct answers.)

- ○ **A.** Exclude the IP addresses from the scope.

- ○ **B.** Create a separate scope for each of the print servers.

- ○ **C.** Create a client reservation for each print server.

- ○ **D.** Configure the DHCP options for the scope.

48. You are the network administrator for your company. All servers are running Microsoft Windows Server 2003.

Because of security needs and the different needs of dial-in clients, you have configured three separate remote access policies.

When a remote access client attempts to connect to a remote access server, which of the following statements is true regarding policy evaluation?

- ○ **A.** All policies in the list are evaluated.

- ○ **B.** The first policy to match the conditions of the connection attempt is evaluated.

- ○ **C.** Only the first policy in the list is evaluated.

- ○ **D.** The first policy that gives the user remote access is evaluated.

49. You are the network administrator for your company. All computers are members of the contoso.com domain. Servers are running Microsoft Windows Server 2003.

Your primary DNS server is located in the corporate head office. The five branch offices are all configured with secondary DNS servers. The WAN links between offices are extremely slow. You want to increase the interval at which secondary servers poll the primary server for updates to the zone file.

Which of the following settings should you change?

- ○ **A.** Retry interval
- ○ **B.** Serial number
- ○ **C.** Refresh interval
- ○ **D.** Time to Live

50. You are the network administrator for your company. You recently deployed a DHCP server to centralize the administration of all IP addresses on the network. Prior to this step, all IP addresses were statically configured.

All users are successfully leasing IP addresses but sometimes report that they cannot print to the network interface printers. The printers are not configured as DHCP clients and are still configured with static IP addresses. Upon examining the event log, you notice there are IP address conflicts.

What should you do?

- ○ **A.** Define separate scopes for each of the print devices.
- ○ **B.** Create client reservations for the print devices.
- ○ **C.** Exclude the IP addresses of the print devices from the scope.
- ○ **D.** Create client exclusions for the print devices.

51. You are the network administrator for Contoso Ltd. All computers are members of the contoso.com Active Directory domain. Servers are running Microsoft Windows Server 2003.

The primary DNS server for contoso.com is located on the corporate head office. The five branch offices are all configured with secondary DNS servers. Each branch office is now being configured with a second DNS server. You do not want any more traffic generated on the WAN links or the LAN from zone transfers.

What should you do?

- ○ **A.** Configure the new servers as secondary DNS servers with the existing secondary DNS servers as master name servers.
- ○ **B.** Configure the new DNS servers as caching-only servers.
- ○ **C.** Configure the new DNS servers as secondary DNS servers with the primary DNS server as the master name server.
- ○ **D.** Configure the new DNS servers as primary DNS servers.

**52.** You are the network administrator for your company. Members of the Sales department need to access the company network when traveling to client sites.

You are implementing a remote access solution. You enable Routing and Remote Access on a server running Microsoft Windows Server 2003.

All client computers requiring remote access are running Microsoft Windows XP Professional. You want all remote access users to authenticate using MS-CHAP version 2.

What should you do?

- ○ **A.** Enable MS-CHAP version 2 through the Properties of the remote access server.

- ○ **B.** Edit the conditions of the remote access policy and enable MS-CHAP version 2.

- ○ **C.** Configure the profile of the remote access policy and enable MS-CHAP version 2.

- ○ **D.** Enable MS-CHAP version 2 through the Properties of each user account.

**53.** You are the network administrator of a Microsoft Windows Server 2003 network. The network consists of two subnets: Subnet A and Subnet B.

Subnet A has a WINS server that is used by all clients on the network to resolve NetBIOS names to IP addresses. A Windows Server 2003 DHCP server assigns IP addresses to clients. The DHCP 044 WINS/NBNS Servers option is configured at the scope level to assign clients the IP address of WINSRV A.

You move the WINS server from Subnet A to Subnet B and configure the 044 WINS/NBNS option at the server level to assign clients the new IP address of the WINS server. You discover that clients are still being assigned the old IP address.

What is causing the problem?

- ○ **A.** Clients must use the `ipconfig /renew` command to obtain the new WINS IP address.

- ○ **B.** The IP address of the WINS server must be statically configured on client workstations.

- ○ **C.** You must configure the 046 WINS/NBT node type.

- ○ **D.** The new 044 WINS/NBNS option must be configured at the scope level.

**54.** You are the network administrator for your company. Servers are running Microsoft Windows Server 2003. Client computers are running Microsoft Windows XP Professional.

You have been advised that all communication between clients and the web server on the intranet should be secured. However, you need to ensure that non-IPSec–aware clients can authenticate to the web server.

Which of the following policies should you assign to the web server?

- ○ **A.** Client (Respond Only)
- ○ **B.** Server (Request Security)
- ○ **C.** Secure Server (Require Security)
- ○ **D.** Secure Client (Respond Only)

**55.** You are the network administrator for your company. You have been instructed to implement a remote access solution.

All users on the network require remote access. All users should have the same remote access security requirements except the Administrators group. Users in the Administrators group will have less stringent security requirements.

You need to configure the remote access server to meet the security requirements.

What should you do?

- ○ **A.** Create two groups within RRAS, one for users and one for administrators. Create two remote access policies and use the Windows Groups condition to apply each policy to the appropriate set of users.
- ○ **B.** Create two groups within Active Directory User and Computers, one for users and one for administrators. Create two remote access policies and use the Windows Groups condition to apply each policy to the appropriate set of users.
- ○ **C.** Create two groups within RRAS. Configure different settings within a single policy for each group.
- ○ **D.** Create two access policies. Using the Dial-In tab for each user account, specify which remote access policy should be applied.

**56.** You are the network administrator for Contoso Ltd. The company DNS servers are running Microsoft Windows Server 2003.

A client reports that it is unable to resolve a hostname. You verify that the DNS server is online.

You want to clear the contents of the DNS resolver cache on the client computer.

What command should you use?

- ○ **A.** ipconfig /clearcache
- ○ **B.** ipconfig /all
- ○ **C.** ipconfig /flushdns
- ○ **D.** ipconfig /cleardns

**57.** You are the network administrator for your company. All servers are running Microsoft Windows Server 2003.

You are implementing an IP security policy for your network. SRV1 requires the highest level of security because it hosts sensitive company data. SRV2 does not require this level of security but should respond to any requests for secure communication.

How should you proceed? (Choose two.)

- ○ **A.** Assign the Server (Request Security) policy on SRV1.
- ○ **B.** Assign the Secure Server (Require Security) policy on SRV1.
- ○ **C.** Assign the Client (Respond Only) policy on SRV2.
- ○ **D.** Assign the Server (Request Security) policy on SRV2.
- ○ **E.** Assign the Secure Server (Require Security) policy on SRV2.
- ○ **F.** Assign the Client (Respond Only) policy on SRV1.

**58.** You are the network administrator of a Microsoft Windows Server 2003 network. The internetwork consists of 10 subnets. All subnets are connected using Windows Server 2003 RRAS servers. You configured nonpersistent demand-dial connections. You do not want to manually update routing tables. You want to configure password authentication between routers.

Which of the following should you implement?

- ○ **A.** Static routes
- ○ **B.** ICMP
- ○ **C.** OSPF
- ○ **D.** RIPv2

**59.** You are one of the network administrators for your company. The network hosts several computers running Microsoft Windows Server 2003. Client computers are running Microsoft Windows XP Professional.

One of the servers is configured as a Domain Name System (DNS) server. This server maintains the primary forward zone and reverse lookup zone for the company domain.

You attempt to use the `Nslookup` command from your administrative workstation, Computer-01. However, you are unable to resolve the IP address of Computer-12 using the command. You can successfully use the command to resolve the IP addresses of other computers on the network.

What should you do?

- ○ **A.** Create a host (A) record for Computer-12.
- ○ **B.** Create a host (A) record for Computer-01.
- ○ **C.** Create a pointer (PTR) record for Computer-12.
- ○ **D.** Create a pointer (PTR) record for Computer-01.

**60.** You are the network administrator for your company. Domain controllers and member servers are running Microsoft Windows Server 2003.

The network consists of several subnets. The subnets are connected using Windows Server 2003 routers. You need to configure a static route on Router01 to Subnet5. The static router must not be deleted from the routing table if the computer is restarted.

Which of the following parameters should you use with the `route` command?

- ○ **A.** /f
- ○ **B.** /s
- ○ **C.** /r
- ○ **D.** /p

# 10

# Answer Key for Practice Exam #2

## Answer Key

| | | | | | |
|---|---|---|---|---|---|
| **1.** C | **21.** B, E | **41.** List |
| **2.** B | **22.** B | **42.** B |
| **3.** D | **23.** C | **43.** List |
| **4.** B | **24.** C | **44.** D |
| **5.** A, B | **25.** B | **45.** C |
| **6.** B | **26.** C | **46.** B |
| **7.** C | **27.** A | **47.** C |
| **8.** D | **28.** D | **48.** B |
| **9.** B | **29.** B | **49.** C |
| **10.** D | **30.** B | **50.** C |
| **11.** A | **31.** List | **51.** B |
| **12.** Drag/Drop | **32.** C | **52.** B |
| **13.** D | **33.** B | **53.** D |
| **14.** C | **34.** C | **54.** B |
| **15.** D | **35.** D | **55.** B |
| **16.** D | **36.** B | **56.** C |
| **17.** C | **37.** C | **57.** B, C |
| **18.** D | **38.** D | **58.** D |
| **19.** B | **39.** C | **59.** A |
| **20.** C | **40.** List | **60.** D |

## Question 1

Answer C is correct. You can set day and time restrictions for remote users by configuring the conditions of the remote access policy. Answer A is incorrect because day and time restrictions are no longer configured through the properties of a user account as they were in Windows NT 4.0. You cannot configure day and time restrictions by configuring the properties of the remote access server or the ports; therefore, answers B and D are incorrect.

## Question 2

Answer B is correct. You must change the user account names on each router to match that of the name assigned to the demand-dial interface name on the answering routing. In order for a two-way demand dial connection to work, the user account names used for authentication must be identical to the name assigned to the demand dial interface. The name of the demand dial interface on the branch office router must be changed to SRV02. The name of the demand dial interface on the head office routing must be changed to SRV01. Answer D is incorrect because the user accounts used for remote authentication between the demand dial routers do not need to be identical. Answers A and C are incorrect because the demand dial interface on the calling router must be identical to the user account name on the calling router.

## Question 3

Answer D is correct. You need to configure the clients with the IP address of the WINS server. To do so, you must install the DHCP Relay Agent on the RAS server so that it can forward DHCPInform messages between the clients and the DHCP server. Answer A is incorrect because you cannot configure optional parameters on the RAS server. You can configure clients with the IP address of the WINS server; however, it's easier from a management perspective to centralize IP address assignment and use a relay agent instead. Therefore, answer B is incorrect. Answer C is incorrect because configuring the RAS server with the IP address of the WINS server will not resolve the problem.

## Question 4

Answer B is correct. You use the gpupdate/force command to manually refresh all settings regardless of whether they have changed. Answers A and E are incorrect because secedit was the command used in Windows 2000 to refresh policy changes. Answer C is incorrect because this command refreshes only the computer settings. Answer D is incorrect because the gpupdate command does not support the /refreshpolicy switch.

## Question 5

Answers A and B are correct. You can include the subnets 172.31.128.0/18 and 172.31.192.0/18 in Area1. With the routing protocol Open Shortest Path First (OSPF), an area consists of contiguous subnets that can be represented via route summarization. The network prefix "/18" indicates that the first 18 bits represent the subnet identifiers (IDs). This includes the first two bits of the third octet. The subnets that can be defined in this octet are represented in binary notation as 00000000, 01000000, 10000000, and 11000000. In decimal notation, the value of the subnet ID in the third octet can be 0, 64, 128, or 192. Answers C, D, and E are incorrect. The address 172.31.96.0/18 represents a host on subnet 172.31.64.0. The address 172.31.160.0/18 represents a host on subnet 172.31.128.0. The address 172.31.224.0/18 represents a host on subnet 172.31.192.0.

## Question 6

Answer B is correct. The Extensible Authentication Protocol (EAP) is required to support smart card authentication. Answers A, C, and D are incorrect because they do not support smart card authentication.

## Question 7

Answer C is correct. When you create demand-dial connections, the user account name on the answering router must match the demand-dial interface name on the calling router. Therefore, answers A, B, and D are incorrect.

## Question 8

Answer D is correct. To have changes propagated throughout the network when changes occur, and to reduce the administrative overhead associated with updating the routing tables, a routing protocol is required. Because you cannot use OSPF with nonpersistent connections, you must use RIPv2 (or RIPv1). Therefore, answers A and C are incorrect. Answer B is incorrect because whenever possible you should use RIPv2 instead of RIPv1. RIPv2 supports enhanced features that are not available with RIPv1.

## Question 9

Answer B is correct. The correct syntax when adding new static routes using the route command is route add mask metric. Therefore, answers A, C, and D are incorrect.

## Question 10

Answer D is correct. If you assign the Server (Request Security) policy, the server always attempts secure communications. Unsecured communications are still allowed if the client is not IPSec-aware. Answer A is incorrect because communications are not allowed if the client is not IPSec-aware. Answer B is incorrect because Assigning Client (Respond Only) means that the server responds only to requests for secure communications but does not attempt to secure all communications. Answer C is incorrect because IPSec is not configured through the properties of TCP/IP.

## Question 11

Answer A is correct. If both servers are configured with the Client (Respond Only) policy, they respond only to requests for secure communications. You must configure both of the servers with Server (Require Security). Answer B is incorrect because you can configure IPSec through Active Directory or on the local computer. Answer C is incorrect because computers are not configured as IPSec clients. Answer D is incorrect because the workgroup membership has no impact on how servers respond to security.

## Question 12

SRV-01 should be configured with the Server (Request Security) IPSec policy. This will ensure that the server always attempts to use IPSec but does not require it. Non–IPSec-aware clients will still be able to communicate with the server. SRV-02 should be configured with the Secure Server (Require Security) IPSec policy. This will ensure that any communications between SRV-01 and SRV-02 and communications between client computers and SRV-02 are always secure. SRV-02 will require IPSec and will not be able to communicate with non–IPSec-aware clients. Client computers on the private network should be configured with the Client (Respond Only) IPSec policy. This ensures that any communications between client computers and the two servers is always secured but still allows them to communicate with non–IPSec-aware servers.

## Question 13

Answer D is correct. The two tunneling protocols supported by Windows Server 2003 are the Point-to-Point Tunneling Protocol (PPTP) and the Layer 2 Tunneling Protocol (L2TP). However, when all systems are running Windows Server 2003, PPTP should not be used. PPTP should be used only for backward compatibility. Therefore answer B is incorrect. PPP and SLIP establish dial-up connections. Therefore, answers A and C are incorrect.

## Question 14

Answer C is correct. To increase the number of available PPTP ports, open the Ports properties window within the Routing and Remote Access management console. Select PPTP and click Configure. Therefore, answers A, B, and D are incorrect.

## Question 15

Answer D is correct. Because all the remote access users are running Windows XP Professional, the authentication protocol should be MS-CHAP version 2. Answers B and C are incorrect because they are not as secure as MS-CHAP version 2. Answer A is incorrect because PAP sends credentials in cleartext and should only be used for non-Windows clients.

## Question 16

Answer D is correct. Install a DHCP server on Subnet C and configure it with a scope for remote access clients. The scope should assign the clients the IP address of the DHCP server. Configure RRAS to use DHCP and configure it as a relay agent. This step ensures that remote users are assigned the IP address of the DNS server. Therefore, answers A, B, and C are incorrect.

## Question 17

Answer C is correct. If the connection attempt does not match the conditions of the first policy in the list, the conditions of the next policy are evaluated. The permissions and profile settings of a policy are not evaluated until the connection attempt meets the conditions of a policy. Therefore, answers A, B, and D are incorrect.

## Question 18

Answer D is correct. Because the president needs remote access from various locations, you should select the Set by Caller option. To limit where network administrators can dial in from, select Always Callback To. In this way, the remote access server always calls them back at the configured phone numbers, ensuring that is where they are attempting remote access. Selecting No Callback disables this feature. Therefore, answers A, B, and C are incorrect.

## Question 19

Answer B is correct. If you delete the default remote access policy and no other policy exists, users will not be permitted remote access. Therefore, you must create a remote access policy to solve the problem. Answer A is incorrect because disabling and then enabling Routing and Remote Access re-creates the default policy, but it is not the easiest solution. You would have to reconfigure the remote access server afterward. Answer C is incorrect because dial-in permission can be granted through the properties of a user account, but a policy must still exist. Answer D is incorrect because you cannot configure profile settings until you create a policy.

## Question 20

Answer C is correct because the connection attempt matches the conditions of the first policy. The permissions and profile settings of this policy are evaluated. The profile settings restrict dial-in access after 5 p.m., so the connection attempt is denied. Therefore, answer A is incorrect. Answer B is incorrect because if a connection attempt does not meet the profile settings of the policy, no other policies in the list are evaluated and the connection attempt is denied. Answer D is incorrect because day and time restrictions are not configured through the user account properties.

## Question 21

Answers B and E are correct. The profile settings disconnect a session after 30 minutes of idle time, restrict the maximum session to 8 hours, allow users remote access during the hours of 6 a.m. and 6 p.m., and allow users to dial in to a specified number. Therefore, answers A, C, D, and F are incorrect.

## Question 22

Answer B is correct. When troubleshooting connectivity problems using the `ping` command, it is recommended that you use the following steps: ping the loopback address, ping the IP address of the local computer, ping the IP address of the default gateway, and then ping the IP address of a remote host. Therefore, answers A, C, and D are incorrect.

## Question 23

Answer C is correct. By configuring a display filter within Network Monitor, you can filter captured data to only display specific types of information. Answer A is incorrect because triggers enable actions to be performed based on a set of conditions that must first be met. Answer B is incorrect because capture filters specify the type of information that is captured. Answer D is incorrect because packet filters specify the type of inbound and outbound traffic a computer can accept.

## Question 24

Answer C is correct. By adding his user account to the Performance Monitor Users group, Joe can view performance counter data within System Monitor locally or across the network. Answer A is incorrect because adding Joe to the Performance Log Users group gives him permission to manage logs and alerts as well. Answers A and B are incorrect because it would give Joe administrative permissions to the server. Adding his user account to the Domain Admins group would give him too many permissions; therefore, answer D is incorrect.

## Question 25

Answer B is correct. If you configure a capture filter, Network Monitor only captures data that meets the criteria you specify. Answer A is incorrect because display filters filter data that has already been captured. Answer C is incorrect because triggers are configured to specify an action that should occur when certain criteria are met. Answer D is incorrect because IP packet filters are used to specify the type of traffic that is permitted to reach a computer.

## Question 26

Answer C is correct. By monitoring IP Datagrams/sec, you can monitor the total amount of IP datagrams sent and received by the computer each second. Answer A is incorrect because it is the number of outbound packets that could not be transmitted because of errors. Answer B is incorrect because this counter only monitors the number of TCP segments sent each second. Answer D is incorrect because this counter monitors the number of logon requests received each second by the computer.

## Question 27

Answer A is correct. You should open the Main Mode Security Associations on the server. The Main Mode Security Associations area displays the persistent security association for the computer that the MMC snap-in is focused on. Security associations are established between computers after the key exchange and mutual authentication. Answer C is incorrect because RSoP is used to determine the IPSec policies that are assigned to a computer. Answer B is incorrect because the security log only contains entries that relate to auditing. Answer D is incorrect because this command was available in Windows 2000 but has been replaced by the IP Security Monitor snap-in in Windows Server 2003.

## Question 28

Answer D is correct. You can use Device Manager to verify that a hardware device is functioning properly. Answer A is incorrect because System Monitor monitors performance. Answer B is incorrect because you use Network Monitor to capture and analyze network traffic. Answer C is incorrect because ping is a command-line utility used to verify network connectivity.

## Question 29

Answer B is correct. The Logon Total counter determines the number of logon requests the domain controller has received since the last time it was restarted. Answers A and C are incorrect because there are no such counters within System Monitor. Answer D is incorrect because this counter determines the number of logon requests received each second.

## Question 30

Answer B is correct. If the service does not start, use the Services console to verify that any services that DHCP depends on are also started. Therefore, answer A is incorrect. Answer C is incorrect because if the service fails to start, attempting to start it within the DHCP console makes no difference. Answer D is incorrect because it should be a last resort in terms of troubleshooting.

## Question 31

The correct answers are:

The computer can attempt to restart the service.

The computer can automatically reboot.

Service recovery actions do not include the ability to automatically restart the failed service's dependencies nor send an email to the network administrator.

## Question 32

Answer C is correct. You can use Network Monitor to capture and analyze network traffic. Answers A and D are incorrect because there are no such utilities included with Windows Server 2003. Answer B is incorrect because you use Network Diagnostics to gather information about the hardware, software, and services running on a local computer.

## Question 33

Answer B is correct. You should use the context menu of the Routing Interface Protocol (RIP) node to add at least one interface to RIP. When you add a routing protocol, the protocol is not configured by default to use an interface, so you must identify one or more interfaces, such as a Local Area Network (LAN) connection, that the protocol can use. Answer A is incorrect because the scenario does not indicate that there is a DHCP sever on the network. Answer C is incorrect because the routing tables will be built automatically. Answer D is incorrect because there is no need to remove all static routes from the routing table.

## Question 34

Answer C is correct. Before installing any new service packs, it is recommended that you test them first to determine any risks and vulnerabilities that they can introduce. Therefore, answers A, B, and D are incorrect.

## Question 35

Answer D is correct. The principle of least privilege is based on the idea that a user should log on with a user account that has minimum privileges. Therefore, Mary should create two accounts: one with restrictive permissions that she can use to perform day-to-day tasks and the other with additional privileges for performing administrative tasks. Answers A, B, and C are incorrect because they go against the principle of least privilege by providing administrative access.

## Question 36

Answer B is correct. When you see a red X beside a setting after running the Security Configuration and Analysis utility, the value for that computer setting does not match the value in the template. Therefore, answers A, C, and D are incorrect.

## Question 37

Answer C is correct. You should run the Microsoft Security Baseline Analyzer. This toll will identify any misconfigurations with the operating system and identify missing security updates. Answer A is incorrect because HFNetCHK.exe is only used to identify the security patches that need to be installed. Answer B is incorrect because the Security Configuration and Analysis tool is used to analyze security settings and compare them against a template. Answer D is incorrect because the Resultant Set of Policy tool is used to determine the impact of policy settings.

## Question 38

Answer D is correct. The security settings on a workstation or server are automatically refreshed every 90 minutes. Answers A, B, and C are incorrect because they do not represent the correct value.

## Question 39

Answer C is correct. When auditing is enabled, events are written to the Security log. Answer A is incorrect because events generated by applications are written to the Application log. Answer B is incorrect because there is no Audit log. Answer D is incorrect because the System log contains events generated by Windows components.

## Question 40

The minimum hardware requirements to install SUS include the following:

Pentium III 700MHz

512MB of RAM

6GB of storage space.

The remaining answers are incorrect because they do not represent the correct hardware requirements.

## Question 41

The IP address lease process occurs in the following order: DHCPDiscover, DHCPOffer, DHCPRequest, and DHCPAck.

## Question 42

Answer B is correct. You authorize a DHCP server using the DHCP console by right-clicking the server and choosing the Authorize option. Answers A, C, and D are incorrect because you cannot use these tools to authorize DHCP.

## Question 43

For a DHCP server to lease IP addresses to clients, you must perform the following actions:

Install DHCP.

Create a scope.

Activate a scope.

Authorize the server.

The remaining answers are incorrect. Configuring scope options is not required. Active Directory does not need to be installed on the local server and dynamic updates do not need to be enabled for DHCP to function.

## Question 44

Answer D is correct. When creating a multicast scope, you can use IP addresses in the range of 224.0.0.1–239.255.255.255. Answers A, B, and C are incorrect because they represent incorrect address ranges.

## Question 45

Answer C is correct. If clients are not configured with the IP address of the default gateway, they cannot access resources outside of their local subnet. Answer A is incorrect because the clients are already successfully leasing IP addresses from the server. Answer B would solve the problem, but it would not be the easiest solution; therefore, it is also incorrect. Answer D is incorrect because configuring the DNS server option allows clients to resolve hostnames but does not give them access outside of the local subnet.

## Question 46

Answer B is correct. The most efficient way to meet the requirements is to configure the Specify Intranet Microsoft Update Service Location option through a GPO. Answer A is incorrect because this would require more administrative effort. Answer C is incorrect because the UseWUServer option is not used to tell the client computer where to obtain updates from. It is used to enable the computer to use SUS. Answer D is incorrect. The Round Robin option in DNS is used to load balance requests across multiple web servers.

## Question 47

Answer C is correct. By creating a client reservation for each of the print servers, you ensure that they always lease the same IP address. Answer A is incorrect. You only need to exclude IP addresses that fall within the scope range that are statically assigned to computers. Answers B and D are incorrect. Both of these options will not resolve the problem.

## Question 48

Answer B is correct. The first elements in a remote access policy to be evaluated are the conditions. The first policy to match the conditions of the connection attempt is evaluated for permissions. If the permissions of that policy deny the user access, the connection attempt is denied. Therefore, answers A, C, and D are incorrect.

## Question 49

Answer C is correct. The refresh interval determines how often the secondary servers poll the primary server for updates to the zone database file. Answer A is incorrect because the retry interval determines how often a secondary server continues to contact the primary server if it does not respond. Answer B is incorrect because the serial number is used to determine when the zone data has been updated. Answer D is incorrect because Time to Live (TTL) specifies how long records from that zone should remain in the cache.

## Question 50

Answer C is correct. To eliminate any IP address conflicts, the IP addresses assigned to the print devices should be excluded from the scope. Answer B is incorrect because client reservations are configured for DHCP clients that must lease the same IP address each time. Answer A is incorrect because scopes are not defined for individual IP addresses. Answer D is incorrect because there is no option in DHCP called a client exclusion.

## Question 51

Answer B is correct. If you place a caching-only server in each branch office, no additional traffic is generated from zone transfers. Answers A and C are incorrect because each of these solutions result in zone transfer traffic on the WAN link or LAN. Answer D is incorrect because a primary DNS server already exists for the zone.

## Question 52

Answer B is correct. The authentication protocol must be enabled through the profile settings for the remote access policy. Therefore, answers A, C, and D are incorrect.

## Question 53

Answer D is correct. Because there is an existing 044 WINS/NBNS option configured at the scope level with the old IP address of the WINS server, it is overwriting the new one configured at the server level. DHCP options configured at the scope level override those configured at the server level. Therefore, answers A and B are incorrect. Answer C is incorrect because configuring this option defines how the client resolves NetBIOS names.

## Question 54

Answer B is correct. If you assign the Server (Request Security) policy, the server attempts secure communications with clients. If the client is not IPSec-aware, it is still able to authenticate. Answer A is incorrect because the server responds only to client requests for secure communications. Answer C is incorrect because the server requires secure communications and does not allow sessions for non–IPSec-aware clients. Answer D is incorrect because there is no such default policy.

## Question 55

Answer B is correct. To use the Windows Groups condition, you must first create the groups within Active Directory Users and Computers. You should create and configure two policies with the appropriate settings. Use the Windows Groups condition to specify the group of users to which the policy should apply. Therefore, answers A, C, and D are incorrect.

## Question 56

Answer C is correct. To clear the contents of the client resolver cache, use the `ipconfig` command with the `flushdns` parameter. Answers A and D are incorrect because there are no such parameters available with the `ipconfig` command. Answer B is incorrect because it displays the current TCP/IP parameters configured on the client.

## Question 57

Answers B and C are correct. SRV1 should be using the Server (Require Security) policy. This policy ensures that only secure communications are permitted. SRV2 should be using the Client (Respond Only) policy. This policy ensures that the server does not require secure communications but responds to any requests for it. Therefore, answers A, D, E, and F are incorrect.

## Question 58

Answer D is correct. RIPv2 is a routing protocol that you can use with nonpersistent connections and that supports password authentication between routers. Answer A is incorrect because implementing static routes means the routing tables must be manually updated. Answer B is incorrect because ICMP is not a routing protocol. Answer C is incorrect because OSPF is not supported by nonpersistent demand-dial connections.

## Question 59

Answer A is correct. A host (A) record must exist in the zone file to resolve the name to an IP address. Therefore, you must create a host record for Computer-12. Therefore, answer B is incorrect. Answers C and D are incorrect because PTR records are required to resolve an IP address to a host name.

## Question 60

Answer D is correct. You use the /p parameter to add a persistent route to the routing table. The route will not be removed from the routing table when the router is restarted. Therefore, answers A, B, and C are incorrect.

APPENDIX A

# Additional Resources

A lot of information is available about Microsoft certifications and the topics covered in Exam 70-291, "Implementing, Managing, and Maintaining a Windows Server 2003 Network Infrastructure." This appendix distills some of the best resources we've found on those topics.

## Web Resources

▶ Microsoft's Training and Certification home: http://www.microsoft.com/learning/default.mspx

▶ Windows Server 2003 home from Microsoft: http://www.microsoft.com/windowsserver2003/default.mspx

▶ Windows Server 2003 Deployment Kit online: www.microsoft.com/windowsserver2003/techinfo/reskit/deploykit.mspx

▶ Search TechNet on the Web: http://technet.microsoft.com/en-us/default.aspx

▶ Windows 2000 Deployment Guide: www.microsoft.com/windows2000/techinfo/reskit/dpg/default.asp

▶ CramSession's exam information and study guides: www.cramsession.com/

▶ Lockergnome's Windows Server 2003 and exam resources: www.lockergnome.com/

▶ MCMCSE certification resources: www.mcmcse.com/

▶ 2000 Trainer exam resources: www.2000trainers.com/default.aspx?tab=links

- ▶ TechTarget's Windows 2000 repository: http://searchwin2000. techtarget.com/

- ▶ Paul Thurrott's SuperSite for Windows: www.winsupersite.com/

- ▶ Active Network's PC and Windows resource: http://www.activewin.com/awin/default.asp

- ▶ Webopedia's online dictionary and search engine for computer and Internet technologies: www.pcwebopedia.com/

# Magazine Resources

- ▶ *Microsoft Certified Professional Magazine* is directly targeted at those certified by Microsoft: www.mcpmag.com

- ▶ *Certification Magazine* specializes in information for IT certified individuals: www.certmag.com

- ▶ *Windows IT Pro Magazine* focuses specifically on Microsoft technologies: http://www.windowsitpro.com/

- ▶ *Training Mag* is a resource for professional training and development: http://www.trainingmag.com/training/index.jsp

- ▶ *Computer* magazine is developed by the Institute of Electrical and Electronics Engineers (IEEE): http://www.computer.org/portal/site/computer/index.jsp

- ▶ *PC Magazine* is a staple for technology enthusiasts: www.pcmag.com

# Book Resources

- ▶ Abbate, Andrew; Kovach, Eric; Morimoto, Rand; Roberts, Ed. *Microsoft Windows Server 2003 Insider Solutions*. Sams, 2003. ISBN: 0-672-32609-4.

- ▶ Bixler, Dave; Schmied, Will; Tittel, Ed. *MCSA/MCSE 70-291 Training Guide: Implementing, Managing, and Maintaining a Windows Server 2003 Network Infrastructure*. Que, 2003. ISBN: 0-7897-2948-2.

- ▶ Habraken, Joe. *Sams Teach Yourself Microsoft Windows Server 2003 in 24 Hours*. Sams, 2003. ISBN: 0-672-32494-6.

- ▶ Jones, Don; Rouse, Mark. *Microsoft Windows Server 2003 Delta Guide 2nd Edition*. Sams, 2004. ISBN: 0-672-32663-9.

► Morimoto, Rand; Gardinier, Kenton; Noel, Michael; Droubi, Omar. *Microsoft Windows Server 2003 Unleashed (R2 Edition)*. Sams, 2006. ISBN: 0-672-32898-4.

► Poulton, Don; Tittel, Ed. *MCSE 70-294 Training Guide: Planning, Implementing, and Maintaining a Microsoft Windows Server 2003 Active Directory InfraStructure*. Que, 2003. ISBN: 0-7897-2949-0.

► Scales, Lee. *MCSA/MCSE Managing & Maintaining a Windows Server 2003 Environment Training Guide (Exam 70-290)*. Que, 2003. ISBN: 0-7897-2935-0.

► Schmied, Will; Shimonski, Robert. *MCSE 70-293 Training Guide: Planning and Maintaining a Windows Server 2003 Network Infrastructure*. Que, 2003. ISBN: 0-7897-3013-8.

APPENDIX B

# Accessing Your Free MeasureUp Practice Test—Including Networking Simulations!

This *Exam Cram* features exclusive access to MeasureUp's practice questions, including networking simulations! These simulations are yet another excellent study tool to help you assess your readiness for the 70-291 exam. MeasureUp is a Microsoft Certified Practice Test Provider, so these simulations validate your hands-on skills by modeling real-life networking scenarios—requiring you to perform tasks on simulated networking devices. MeasureUp's simulations also assess your capability to troubleshoot and solve realistic networking problems. If you are planning to take the certification exam for 70-290 or 70-291, you should expect to see performance-based simulations on the exam. MeasureUp's Microsoft simulations will ensure that you are prepared.

To access your free practice questions and simulations:

1. Retrieve your unique registration key number on the inside of the back cover of this book.

2. Go to www.measureup.com.

3. Create a free MeasureUp account or login to your existing account.

4. On the Learning Locker Toolbar, click Register Products.

5. Read and consent to the License Agreement by clicking the checkbox below the License Agreement.

**344**

Appendix B: Accessing Your Free MeasureUp Practice Test—Including Networking Simulations!

6. Type your registration key number in the Key box. Do not remove any dashes or substitute any numbers.

7. Click Register.

8. Click the Learning Locker Button to display your Personal Test Locker.

9. Click the Practice Test link and follow the instructions to start your test or the Learning Locker tab to return to your Learning Locker.

For more details about MeasureUp's product features, see Appendix C, "MeasureUp's Product Features."

APPENDIX C

# MeasureUp's Product Features

Since 1997, MeasureUp has helped more than 1 million IT professionals achieve certifications from the industry's leading vendors. Created by content developers certified in their areas and with real-world experience, MeasureUp practice tests feature comprehensive questions (some with performance-based simulations), detailed explanations and complete score reporting. As a Microsoft Certified Practice Test Provider, MeasureUp's practice tests are the closest you can get to the certification exams!

## Multiple Testing Modes

MeasureUp practice tests are available in Study, Certification, Custom, Missed Question, and Non-Duplicate question modes.

### Study Mode

Tests administered in Study Mode allow you to request the correct answer(s) and explanation for each question during the test. These tests are not timed. You can modify the testing environment *during* the test by clicking the Options button.

### Certification Mode

Tests administered in Certification Mode closely simulate the actual testing environment you will encounter when taking a certification exam. These tests do not allow you to request the answer(s) or explanation for each question until after the exam.

# Custom Mode

Custom Mode allows you to specify your preferred testing environment. Use this mode to specify the objectives you want to include in your test, the timer length, and other test properties. You can also modify the testing environment *during* the test by clicking the Options button.

# Missed Question Mode

Missed Question Mode allows you to take a test containing only the questions you missed previously.

# Non-Duplicate Mode

Non-Duplicate Mode allows you to take a test containing only questions not displayed previously.

# Question Types

The practice question types simulate the real exam experience, and include the following:

- ▶ Create a tree
- ▶ Select and place
- ▶ Drop and connect
- ▶ Build list
- ▶ Reorder list
- ▶ Build and reorder list
- ▶ Single hotspot
- ▶ Multiple hotspots
- ▶ Live screen
- ▶ Command line
- ▶ Hot area
- ▶ Fill in the blank

# Random Questions and Order of Answers

This feature helps you learn the material without memorizing questions and answers. Each time you take a practice test, the questions and answers appear in a different randomized order.

# Detailed Explanations of Correct and Incorrect Answers

You'll receive automatic feedback on all correct and incorrect answers. The detailed answer explanations are a superb learning tool in their own right.

# Attention to Exam Objectives

MeasureUp practice tests are designed to appropriately balance the questions over each technical area covered by a specific exam.

# Technical Support

If you encounter problems with the MeasureUp test engine, you can contact MeasureUp at 678-356-5050 or email support@measureup.com. Technical support hours are from 8 a.m. to 5 p.m. EST Monday through Friday. Additionally, you'll find Frequently Asked Questions (FAQs) at www.measureup.com.

If you'd like to purchase additional MeasureUp products, telephone 678-356-5050 or 800-649-1MUP (1687), or visit www.measureup.com.

# Glossary

## A

**authentication**   The process of confirming the identity of a user, typically by a username and password. Windows Server 2003 supports several authentication methods, including Kerberos v5, NTLM authentication, passport authentication, and digest authentication.

**authorization**   The process of granting or denying a user, group, or computer access to network resources through permissions and user rights.

**automatic updates services**   Enables operating system updates to be downloaded and installed automatically. This ensures that systems stay up-to-date with the latest updates.

## C

**caching-only server**   A form of a DNS server that is not responsible for maintaining or updating any zone information. It simply resolves name requests to IP addresses on behalf of DNS clients and caches the results.

**capture filter**   Filter configured within Network Monitor to specify the type of traffic that should be captured for analysis.

**Challenge Handshake Authentication Protocol (CHAP)**   An authentication protocol that uses the Message Digest 5 (MD5) hashing scheme to encrypt responses. With CHAP, the server sends a challenge to the client. The client then generates an MD5 hash result and returns it to the server.

## D

**delegation**   In Windows Server 2003, this is the ability of an administrator to distribute certain administrative tasks to other individuals or groups. In terms of DNS, a portion of a domain namespace can be delegated to another server that will then be responsible for resolving name-resolution requests.

**Device Manager**   A tool included with Windows Server 2003 that can be used to manage hardware as well as troubleshoot hardware problems.

**DHCP clients**   Clients configured to automatically obtain an IP address from a DHCP server. By default, Windows 2000, Windows XP, and Windows Server 2003 clients are configured as DHCP clients.

**DHCP database**   Database that stores information about client leases.

**display filter** Filter configured within Network Monitor after data has been captured to specify the type of traffic to display.

**domain** An Active Directory hierarchy component. Domains define the administrative and security boundaries within an Active Directory hierarchy. A domain can be created by installing Active Directory.

**domain controller** Computers that are used for storing directory data, user authentication, and directory searches. A computer can be configured as a domain controller by installing Active Directory.

**domain name system (DNS)** System used to translate host names into IP addresses. DNS is included as a service with Windows Server 2003.

**Dynamic Host Configuration Protocol (DHCP)** A protocol used to dynamically assign IP addresses to devices on a network. It can also be used to provide DHCP clients with optional parameters such as the IP address of the default gateway. DHCP in Windows Server 2003 can be integrated with DNS.

**dynamic update** Feature that enables a DNS client to automatically register and update its own host record with a DNS server. It can be used in conjunction with DHCP so that clients can update their resource records when IP addresses change.

# E–F–G

**Event Viewer** The tool used to view the contents of the Windows Server 2003 log files.

**forward lookup zone** A forward lookup zone maps hostnames to IP addresses. When a client needs the IP address of a hostname, the information is retrieved from the forward lookup zone.

**Group Policy** An administrative tool that can be used to administer various aspects of the client computing environment, from installing software to applying a standardized desktop.

# I

**Internet Authentication Server (IAS)** Microsoft's version of a RADIUS server. To ease the administrative overhead of managing multiple RAS servers, you can implement a RADIUS server to centralize the authentication of remote access clients and the storage of accounting information.

**IP routing** Routing is the process of sending a packet from the source address to the destination address. Because all IP packets have a source and destination IP address, it is possible to deliver them to the proper location.

**IP Security Monitor** Tool that can be used to validate that communications between hosts are indeed secure. It provides information such as which IPSec policy is active and whether a secure communication channel is being established between computers.

**IPSec**   A set of protocols used to support the secure exchange of data at the IP layer using encryption. In Transport mode, only the data portion or payload is encrypted. In Tunnel mode, both the header and the payload are encrypted.

**iterative query**   With an iterative query, the DNS server uses zone information and its cache to return the best possible answer to the client. If the DNS server does not have the requested information, it can refer the client to another DNS server.

# L

**lease**   DHCP clients can be assigned an IP address from a DHCP server. The lease duration determines the amount of time a client can use an IP address assigned from a DHCP server before it must be renewed. The default lease time in Windows Server 2003 is eight days.

**LMHOSTS**   A text file that can be used to resolve NetBIOS names to IP addresses. The file exists in the Windows directory and contains NetBIOS to IP address mappings.

# N

**Network Diagnostics**   A support utility that can be used to identify

and isolate connectivity and network problems.

**Network Monitor**   A tool included with Windows Server 2003 used to monitor and capture network traffic. It is useful for troubleshooting network problems.

# O

**Open Shortest Path First (OSPF)**   A routing protocol that uses the shortest path first or link-state routing algorithm. OSPF routers calculate the shortest path to each host and share that portion of the routing table.

# P

**persistent connections**   Windows Server 2003 implementation of WINS supports persistent connections, which means servers do not need to disconnect when replication is complete.

**Point-to-Point Protocol (PPP)**   A communication protocol used by dial-up remote access clients. PPP has become an industry-standard communications protocol because of its popularity; it provides support for multiple network protocols, including TCP/IP, IPX/SPX, and NetBEUI.

**primary zone**   Type of zone that maintains the master writable copy of the zone in a text file. An update to the zone must be performed from the primary zone.

# R

**recursive query**   With a recursive query, the DNS client requires the DNS server to respond with either the IP address of the request or an error message that the requested name does not exist.

**Remote Access Service (RAS)**
Service that enables remote clients to dial into a Windows Server 2003 server and access network resources as though they were physically attached to the network.

**resource records**   The data within a DNS zone file. Windows Server 2003 supports a number of different types of resource records.

**reverse lookup zone**   This type of zone allows for reverse queries, or the mapping of an IP address back to a hostname. Reverse queries are often used when troubleshooting with the NSLookup command.

**Routing Information Protocol (RIP)**
A protocol that allows routers to exchange routing information. It is designed for use with small- to medium-size networks. RIP routers periodically exchange entire routing tables.

# S

**scope**   Determines the pool of IP addresses from which a DHCP server can assign IP addresses.

Every DHCP server must be configured with at least one scope.

**secondary zones**   Zone type that stores a copy of an existing zone in a read-only text file. To create a secondary zone, the primary zone must already exist, and you must specify a master name server. This is the server from which the zone information is copied.

**secure baseline**   Establishes a set of rules or recommendations that outline the minimum acceptable security configuration for new installations.

**Security Configuration and Analysis**
Windows Server 2003 includes a tool known as the Security Configuration and Analysis tool. Using this tool, you can analyze the current security state of a server or workstation by comparing the existing settings against an existing template.

**security templates**   Holds a number of security settings that Microsoft considers to be appropriate for a server, domain controller, or workstation. Windows Server 2003 includes several default templates with preconfigured security settings based on various computer roles. Custom templates can also be defined.

**Shutdown Event Tracker**   This tool enables an administrator to monitor why users shut down or restart their computers. When Shutdown Event

Tracker is enabled, users are prompted to provide a reason as to why they are shutting down or restarting a computer. The information is then recorded in the system log.

### Software Updates Services (SUS)
One of the options now available for distributing updates. SUS consists of two components: the server and the client. The server (which can be running Windows 2000 or Windows Server 2003) downloads updates from Microsoft and stores them locally for clients to download without having to retrieve updates themselves from Windows Update servers on the Internet.

**stub zones**   This type of zone is new in Windows Server 2003. A stub zone maintains only a list of authoritative name servers for a particular zone. The purpose of a stub zone is to ensure that DNS servers hosting a parent zone are aware of authoritative DNS servers for its child zones.

**System Information**   This tool provides configuration information about the local computer or a remote computer.

**System Monitor**   A tool included with Windows Server 2003 that can be used to monitor the real-time performance of system components as well as services and applications. System Monitor can be used to collect and view real-time performance data, view data saved in a counter

log, and present captured data using various views.

# T

**Task Manager**   This tool can be used to view a variety of information about the local computer. Task Manager displays the applications and processes currently running, provides performance and network statistics, and shows any users currently connected to the computer.

**tombstoning**   Records in the WINS database that are tombstoned are marked as being extinct, which means they are immediately released from active user by the WINS server.

### Transmission Control Protocol/ Internet Protocol (TCP/IP)   An
industry-standard suite of protocols that enables two hosts to establish a connection and exchange data.

# W

### Windows Internet Name Service (WINS)   Microsoft's version of the
NBNS is called a Windows Internet Naming Service (WINS). A WINS server maintains a dynamic database used to resolve NetBIOS names to IP addresses.

**WINS Proxy**   A computer that allows non-WINS clients to participate in a WINS environment by listening for name request broadcasts and forwarding them to a WINS server.

# Z

**zone**  A database file that contains the resource records for a single domain or a set of domains. There are three types of zones in DNS: a forward lookup zone for mapping names to IP addresses, a reverse lookup zone for mapping IP addresses to domain names, and a stub zone for determining which DNS servers are authoritative for a zone.

# Index